DOMBROWER'S
ART
OF INTERACTIVE
ENTERTAINMENT
DESIGN

Dombrower's
Art
of Interactive
Entertainment
Design

Eddie Dombrower

McGraw-Hill
New York   San Francisco   Washington, D.C.   Auckland   Bogotá
Caracas   Lisbon   London   Madrid   Mexico City   Milan
Montreal   New Delhi   San Juan   Singapore
Sydney   Tokyo   Toronto

Library of Congress Cataloging-in-Publication Data

Dombrower, Eddie
    Dombrower's art of interactive entertainment design / Eddie
Dombrower.   p.   cm.
    Includes index.
    ISBN 0-07-017497-0
    1. Interactive multimedia.   2. Computer games—Programming.
I. Title.
QA76.76.159D67   1998
006.7'76—dc21   97-23962
                                             CIP

McGraw-Hill

A Division of The **McGraw·Hill** Companies

1 2 3 4 5 6 7 8 9 0 DOC/DOC 9 0 2 1 0 9 8 7

P/N 0-07-017489-X

PART OF

ISBN 0-07-017497-0

*The sponsoring editor for this book was Scott Grillo, the editing supervisor was
Frank Kotowski, Jr., and the production supervisor was Tina Cameron. It was set in
Vendome by Renee Lipton of McGraw-Hill's Professional Book Group composition unit.*

Printed and bound by R. R. Donnelley & Sons Company.

McGraw-Hill books are available at special quantity discounts to use as premi-
ums and sales promotions, or for use in corporate training programs. For more
information, please write to the Director of Special Sales, McGraw-Hill, Inc.,
11 West 19th Street, New York, NY 10011. Or contact your local bookstore.

*This book is printed on recycled, acid-free paper containing a minimum of
50% recycled de-inked fiber.*

To the unsung creative heroes of the interactive entertainment business: the programmers.

CONTENTS

PREFACE

Designing interactive entertainment is both a craft and an art. This book was written to provide a resource for those interested in the tools and techniques, or the craft, of game design. I also provide my personal set of philosophies and principles intended for designers that strive to improve the state of their art.

And, if you're simply skimming this book to check out my rules of design, I have placed this icon ⏩ in the margin indicating that a rule is listed in the corresponding paragraph.

This book covers many of the basic elements and processes of designing an interactive product, selling a design concept to publishers, and communicating your design vision to a production team. Throughout the book, I try to provide some perspective on how designs actually come to life by telling stories about the production of many products from the past 20 years.

First and foremost, I start with the basics: there is a certain amount of history and technology every designer should know. In the first two chapters I discuss the history of the industry, product genres, game platforms, and breakthrough products. In Chap. 3 there is a quick overview of computers and video game systems. Later in the book, in Chap. 13, I give a more detailed explanation of computers and computer programming.

In Chaps. 4 through 6, I describe the contents of all of the work that a designer does: the preliminary design document and all the elements of the game design document itself. I start with an overview of each document and subdocument and then go into great detail on what each element must include to be truly complete. While doing this, I provide many of my personal philosophies as to what to consider, think about, and do in regard to each design element.

My principles of game design are detailed in Chaps. 7 through 9. I spend two entire chapters on design principles meant to make a product feel more realistic or, in the current vernacular, more immersive. In the final chapter of this section, I provide a list of smaller, but no less important, principles that have very specific applications.

Chapter 14 talks about one document that the designer should take an active role in creating: the technical design document.

Finally, Part 7 concludes the book with my thoughts on the future of interactive entertainment and the challenge of successfully achieving these goals.

My original goal in writing this book was to provide a game design resource for those in the interactive entertainment business and for those wanting to learn about it. My hope now is that in providing the philosophies, principles, and rules that I use, it will help others in creating breakthrough interactive products.

—EDDIE DOMBROWER

ACKNOWLEDGMENTS

Without people such as Peter Plantec, this kind of book would never get written. Peter, who writes books on interactive media himself, generously helped me find an outlet for this book. But first he helped me discover that I even wanted to write a book on it in the first place.

I would also like to thank the people who helped put me on, and move me along my professional path. Starting with Eric Level who first thought there might be something I could do to combine my love of dance and my aptitude with computers. Continuing on with my gratitude to Ellen Porter, Roger Banks, Don Daglow, David Grady, Richard Hilleman, Bob and Gail McDowell, Peter Doctorow, and Cheryl Weiner, each of whom, in their own way, helped me discover new paths to travel in the computer entertainment business.

Finally, without my wife Laura's love and support and her willingness to give up many evenings and weekends with me, I could never, ever have completed this book.

PART **1**

If You're Interested in Computer Games...

The Art of Interactive Design

Game design is about creating an interactive entertainment experience. Regardless of what platform you're talking about—video games, computer games, network games, or the Internet—I believe there are certain fundamental elements required for a high-quality interactive experience. Of the elements that make for great game play, high levels of interactivity, great rhythm, naturalness, entertaining characters, and intriguing stories all play a large part. Weaving these and the other key design elements into a game is the art of interactive design. It is my hope that my thoughts on the subject enable you to more fully appreciate what has been accomplished and what great potential lies ahead.

My goal in writing this book is to provide a somewhat comprehensive resource about design for *anyone* interested in interactive entertainment (what we used to call computer games, in the old days). If you're interested in improving your skills as a designer, becoming a designer, breaking into the business, learning more about the games industry; if you play games or simply know someone who plays games; then this book will give you a lot of information suited to your needs.

For Whom This Book Is Told

This book is a resource about computer game design for

- Designers
- Game players
- Producers
- Friends and family of devoted game players
- Interactive executives
- "Wanna-be" interactive professionals
- Skimmers

For Skimmers

If you want to just skim the book for cool tidbits of information about game design, I've included a way for you to do this. Wherever I state a rule, principle, or strong opinion about game design, the role of the designer, or the games industry, you will find this icon in the margin: ➠. Look for the corresponding ⇒ in the text.

For Game Players (and Their Friends and Relatives)

Throughout this book there is much information about the history of games (including "must play" games) and what goes into making them. I hope that this will help you, as a consumer, to become more knowledge-able and therefore more sophisticated about your choice of product. After all, it is the games you are willing to pay for that ultimately tell us what is really good. If you are not a game player but instead are someone whose loved ones are playing games for who-knows-what reason, read on. Perhaps by looking at what the computer entertainment industry does to attract and keep your loved ones' attention, you may gain some insight into the often bizarre behavior that game players exhibit. (Perhaps it will motivate you to even try playing a game with a whole new outlook.)

If You're Looking to Break into the Business

If you are interested in a job in the interactive entertainment business, there is no better way to decide if that's a good idea than to look at the fundamental *creative* element of interactive entertainment: the game design. ⇒ I've come to the belief that the next wave of great interactive designers will probably come from the ranks of professional writers. However, many disciplines foster the types of talents needed to be a good, or even great, game designer. Even if you don't fancy yourself a potential game designer, at some point in your new career in this business, you'll need to understand the elements of design. The information found in this book can help you to acquire in-depth knowledge of game design, as well as the history, philosophy, issues, and production methods of the game business. Once aware of these things, you might be better able to figure out where you could fit into this industry that's filled with misfits.

For Recent Newcomers

For the newcomers and relative newcomers to the interactive entertain-ment business (and by that I mean you have less than 5 years of actual work experience), I hope to provide some perspective. Although the new-ness of this industry is often mentioned, there are enough years and products to provide some context for moving forward at a greater rate than we are currently. There is nothing more frustrating for me than seeing, yet again, an idea for a game or product that is similar to an older, often classic product and finding out the person presenting the idea has no idea of this fact. I'm not a big fan of recreating the wheel, and anything I can do to prevent it I will. So, for you newcomers, I hope this book is a way for you to skip a step or two in your development in whatever part of the business you work.

Are You Experienced?

If you are, then here's an opportunity to weigh your hard-earned opinions and philosophies against someone else's. I hope to create a written resource for you to use to bounce your ideas off. I don't care much if you agree or disagree. I am simply providing a set of ideas for you to start with.

For Simply Learning the Business of Creating Games

Finally, this book will provide you with some basic knowledge and understanding of what it takes to design a great interactive experience and why there are so many people trying to do this. Of course, money is part of the equation, but I believe there is something much bigger.

⇒ I've personally been drawn to this business because I believe that there is a unique and important value from interactive entertainment. By writing this book, I hope that I can help in the development of the breakthroughs that will help this growing industry reach its potential.

Theory, History, Technology, and a Few Good Stories

In addition to the practical information in this book about my theories and the principles of game design, the game design process, and the design documents themselves, I've included a smattering of other information to provide some perspective.

Before we jump into the description of the design document itself, there is a section about the history of computer games and short digressions into technological issues that influence designs of the past, present, and future. I strongly recommend taking the time to work through the technical discussions. Doing so can give you a better basis for understanding the issues that face the most experienced game designers.

Also, as I've been in the business for a while, I have many stories to tell. You may have heard of some of the people in these stories. Most of these people you probably will not have heard of, due to the unfortunate nature of the games business.

Elements of an Interactive Design

In Part 4 of this book, I go into great detail about how to write an interactive design. This design document is like a script for a movie in that it's the blueprint for the production. Unlike a script, there are typically about 20 elements that the game designer needs to create.

Elements Typically Found in a Complete Game Design

- High concept
- Genre
- Target platform (i.e., which computer or game system)
- Target audience
- Story
- Characters
- World(s) and maps
- Interactivity
- Interface
- View-by-view descriptions
- Flowcharts, algorithms, and/or game logic
- Scoring, winning, losing, saving, loading, starting, stopping, and playing again
- Art and production design

- Storyboards and sample art
- Transition design
- Audio and music design
- List of physical production elements
- Competitive products
- Marketing ideas
- Follow-up products

A typical game design includes a section on each of the items listed above. I'll be discussing each of these throughout the course of this book.

Principles and Other Good Things to Know

After you learn about the elements of a game design, several sections will help you improve the quality of your design. Part 4 is on the Principles of Game Design, Part 5 is on Production Information for the Interactive Designer, Part 6 is on Technical Issues for Designers. Finally, Part 7 discusses what I believe is the future of interactive entertainment—interactive storytelling.

I believe that, using these principles and other information about production and technology found in this book, someone could create an interactive storytelling experience that will replace my favorite game.

My Favorite Game

⇒ As I mentioned before, interactive entertainment is simply another name for computer games. It's more glamorous to use the newer expression, but it's important not to lose sight of the fact that the moment you include the audience in the entertainment experience (i.e., interacting), there are elements of game play afoot. So, I will use the two expressions interchangeably so as to not lose focus on the more mainstream direction we're pursuing in this business and at the same time remember that these products are, after all, games.

I've often been asked what my favorite game is. I have to admit, that since I started in the business as a programmer, my favorite computer game is programming the computer. Designing a program and then executing it are first, an exercise in "beating" the computer and, second, a challenge to win against every person who actually uses your program. Beating the computer is simply a test to see if you can get the computer to do exactly what you want when you want. While the test is simple, the task is often not. Imagine trying to figure out how to get a computer to recognize a chair in a digitized picture or, more to the point, as in some of the first computer games, to try to get the computer to understand any sentence that you might decide to type in English.

My other favorite games (in no particular order): Monkey Island, King's Quest 5, Shark Shark (for Intellivision), Tempest, Pole Position, Monty Python's Complete Waste of Time, Rebel Assault, Carmen Sandiego, Oregon Trail, Virtua Fighter, Lemmings, Shanghai, and, of course, Zork.

Beating the computer is one thing; "winning" against every person who uses your program is quite another. No matter what a person using your program does, you must ensure that the program responds without mistake. If you do, you win (of course, so does the user). For a computer game, this can be as many as hundreds of thousands of people who are trying every conceivable thing they can to succeed at your game. For me, this is like a giant multidimensional game of chess where I have to anticipate every logical action as well as every silly thing someone wants to try.

So you see why designing and programming computer games are my favorite games of all (it does make me seem a bit of a masochist I suppose). However, even if this "game" doesn't appeal to you as a potential favorite, keep in mind that game designers are always playing this game; how they win at this gets to the heart of this book.

My Story

Like many people who have been in the business a while, I came to be involved in computer games in a very roundabout way. Although I did grow up playing board games, I mostly played sports (which will become more apparent as you read my analogies) and the cello. However, the first real step toward getting me into this business occurred when I decided to take up ballet in high school. I continued to pursue a career in ballet and dance throughout my college years, where I began as a chemistry major.

Obviously, these two courses of study didn't coexist well, so I quit college. After a year off dancing, I returned as a math major, a *much* better choice for an aspiring premiere danseur.

For my first course back, my new adviser suggested I take a math class being taught by a visiting Fellow from IBM. This class was experimental and used computer programming to teach linear algebra. So I learned to program in APL. This probably doesn't mean much to many people, but this language is literally in Greek on a teletype terminal. For some unknown reason, I showed quite an aptitude for programming and understanding three-dimensional mathematics using the computer.

Over the next few years, I took a few more formal programming classes, continued my math studies, and earned a scholarship at the Joffrey Ballet. It was a weird enough combination of things that it caught the attention of one of my resident advisers in college. He suggested that I apply for a postgraduate grant that would involve math and dance. So I came up with the idea of studying computers and their use in choreographic notation. Again, it was unusual enough to catch someone's attention, so I received a Thomas Watson Fellowship to study in England.

Thomas Watson was the founder of IBM, and although the grant program had nothing specifically to do with computers, the coincidence of the IBM connection was not lost on me, my friends, and my advisers. The program was actually set up to send students abroad to study independent of academic institutions.

While on my fellowship, I met my first Apple computer. I had arranged to work under the supervision of Roger Banks of Custom Electronics in Biggleswade, England. Fortunately for me, he had one of the very first Apple II's to be sold in the United Kingdom, and I got to program on it. I designed and programmed a computerized system for notating any kind of movement by animating a 3D wire-frame dancer moving at 5 to 6 frames per second on the Apple II.

Roger taught me one of the most valuable lessons any software designer can learn: ⇒ Design the product to do your idea right; the technology will eventually catch up. It took 15 years for the technology to make movement notation possible in the way I envisioned it. However, I've applied Roger's lesson time and again, and often the wait was nowhere close to 15 years.

When I came back to the United States, I alternated my time between computer programming jobs and dancing in various productions. I also continued work on the movement notation system, and in 1982 various science and computer magazines featured my work.

One day I was visiting my alma mater, Pomona College, and my friend Dave Warhol, who was helping run the academic computer system. While we were talking, I saw a note from career planning and placement on his desk. It said that Don Daglow, class of 1974, was looking to hire programmers at Mattel Electronics for Intellivision programming. I asked Dave if he minded if I also applied for the job. He said, "No problem," and we both started working for Don on the same day in July of that year.

Dave Warhol now runs Realtime Associates which has created so many games, I can't possibly list them here.

Don Daglow is president of Stormfront Studios whose most famous series of products are the Tony LaRussa Baseball games.

At Mattel, I designed and programmed World Series Baseball—the first sports game, as far as I know, that used statistical modeling combined with a physics simulation, a TV-style split screen, a variety of TV-style camera angles, and a digitized audio play-by-play announcer. In other words, it was a multimedia baseball simulation in 1982. Don was instrumental in helping me to conceptualize the product and guiding my design, which, in my opinion, is really the granddaddy of sport simulations as we know them.

Thinking about this game brings a sad story to my mind. One of the features in World Series Baseball was the database of players that kept track of all their playing and personal stats including skin color. As we couldn't afford to license real major league ballplayer names, we used approximate yet recognizable stats of famous players and then assigned them to names of people on the Intellivision staff who were fondly referred to as the Blue Sky Rangers. Since many of these players are African-Americans and, unfortunate as it may be, almost everyone working at Intellivision was not, we had to assign some staff names to black players. While I didn't think this was a problem, we decided it was best to check. So we circulated a memo and identified everyone whose name we were going to use and what skin color assignment we were going to make. Someone (whose name I fortunately have forgotten) actually objected. However, we didn't honor that request to remain assigned to a white ball player; we simply used another staffer instead.

The Blue Sky Rangers was the nickname of the Intellivision Programming staff. The name became a part of the video game folklore when TV Guide *ran an article about some of the Rangers in 1983.*

The Blue Sky Rangers have such a following to this day that they still receive fan mail at their Web site.

I left Mattel to join the Los Angeles office of Atari. This group was hired to translate popular Atari games to run on the Intellivision. I worked on Pole Position (one of the great driving games of all time). I spent hours playing the arcade version of Pole Position for free as well as programming it. Before I could finish, Atari's strategy changed, and two teams were assigned to work on Sesame Street products with Children's Television Workshop. Before we could finish and release those games, Atari's strategy changed again, and this time it decided to do away with almost all the software staff.

> *After the Trameils bought Atari, there was a major downsizing. We kept working but without really any guidance. Eventually, we called them and asked them what we should do. They said "What office in LA?" and within the week we received pink slips.*
>
> *Rumor has it that a similar office in New York was much more clever and stayed on the payroll for quite some time.*

After leaving Atari, I started my own company, Mirage Graphics. I did odd jobs, including programming an interactive robot for the 1984 Olympic Arts Festival at the Los Angeles Museum of Science and Industry. Then Dr. J vs. Larry Bird came out, and everything changed.

Don Daglow had become a producer at Electronic Arts (EA), and on the heels of the success of Dr. J vs. Larry Bird, EA decided to create other celebrity-based sports games. When it came to baseball, Don suggested that I might be a good choice; and after a few phone conversations, I signed on to create what was to become Earl Weaver Baseball.

For the next 8 years, my company and I created many versions of Earl Weaver Baseball (EWB) along with a few other products. Baseball software became my life; I burned out. But as I did, my team and I designed and produced the sequel to EWB—Earl Weaver Baseball II (EBW II).

> *The Mirage Graphics team included Bill Rommerdahl and Bob Dietz (both of whom went on to Davidson), Mark Wittlesey and Mike Burton (who went on to Interplay), Ken Dullea (who went on to Activision and Sega), and freelancers Ann Westfall (from Freefall Associates), Teri Mason (who was the sound designer for EWB and the musical director of Return to Zork), and Nathan Wang (the composer for many TV shows as well as several game titles including Return to Zork).*

For many people, this product was a disappointment. In terms of what it portended for the future of the sports games industry, it hit the design nail on the head. While the original EWB used a split screen, a simple overview of the field, an announcer, and some TV-style effects all in the tradition of World Series Baseball, EWB II was designed so the "camera" could be placed anywhere and look at anything at any time. The underlying simulation was the same as in EWB 1, but the graphics were designed to show a 3D world moving in real time. Unfortunately, we were targeting IBM 286 computers running at 16 megahertz (MHz) that couldn't redraw the scenes fast enough. Our compromise was to create a "director," which was a computer program that selected shots. These shots displayed the action from one of hundreds of angles that would only change every 3—5 seconds or so.

On a 16-MHz IBM 286 computer, the program was underpowered but, based on the standard for sports games today, the game design was not. Once again, my friend Roger was proved to be right. This time it only took 5 years.

Due to a bizarre set of circumstances, my next and final work for Electronic Arts never really saw the light of day. The EWB line was to be extended with what was internally called Baseball '93, which I designed and for which I provided the code for the underlying engine for EA's programmers. I went on to other things, and EA didn't publish another baseball game for 4 years.

I was offered a job at Activision to produce the graphic adventure sequel to the Zork series of text adventure games from Infocom. I jumped at the chance, and I went to work with some great industry veterans, including Bill Volk, Peter Doctorow, and Tom Sloper. We had a working design from Doug Barnet, an incredible franchise to follow on, and a mandate to use some form of video footage combined with computer-generated backgrounds. For the next year and one-half, my team worked with Doug's design to create Return to Zork (RTZ).

The first game I ever played was the Zork text adventure. I was staying with a friend and her fiance in New York while I was training with the Joffrey. She brought her computer home at night and hooked up to her company's computer via a 300-baud acoustic modem. After she was done working, she introduced me to The Great Underground Adventure.

RTZ attempted to break new ground in lots of areas from interface design to its visual style, created by art director JP Asperin. Zork, being one of the best-known worlds in the computer game world, presented some huge challenges in moving from text to graphics. The lessons learned were invaluable. One of them was that ⇒ the quality of the source material should be created for the highest possible resolution so that we could take advantage of any unforeseen improvements in technology. And RTZ was one of the very first MPEG games to be created due to the quality of the source material and the technology used to display it. This time the technology caught up with the design idea just after the product was released. The Macintosh version of this game uses the high-resolution imagery, but, unfortunately, a high-resolution PC-compatible version was never made.

While completing Return To Zork, I began creating the strategy for Activision's next adventure games. My group planned and began producing Planetfall with Steve Meretzky, Spycraft with William Colby, and Zork: Nemesis.

Although Planetfall was never completed, Cecilia Barajas and Andrew Goldman did a great job of producing Zork: Nemesis and Spycraft, respectively.

When I joined Activision, it had just downsized and moved to LA to be near the Hollywood creative community. I was one of the first two dozen employees in the LA office. Within a year of the release of Return to Zork, Activision employed well over 100 people and was a much bigger and much different company than the one I joined. Also, an unbelievable opportunity presented itself.

Jim Henson Productions (JHP) was looking for someone to help them start up their interactive division. For many reasons, both personal and professional, this seemed the chance of a lifetime. So, for the first time in my career, I joined a company whose first priority was not computer software of any kind. I've learned many things during my time at JHP. ⇒ As the products we've coproduced demonstrate, there is much to be gained from the talent of film, TV, and theater professionals working closely with talent from the computer games industry. The Muppet CD ROM: Muppets Inside, The Muppet Calendar, the Brighter Child Software, the Sega Pico games, the Muppet Treasure Island Web Site, and The Muppet Treasure Island CD ROM have all contributed valuable lessons to me in how to successfully coproduce interactive products.

John Cutter, who started his career at Cinemaware in the early 1980s, designed and produced The Muppet CD ROM. His design sense and producing experience really showed in the way in which he incorporated the wild musing of the Henson creative staff into a truly great game.

The Vocabulary of Choice

⇒ I often consider the interactive entertainment or game business the business of designing choice. After all, choosing is one of the fundamental elements of interacting.

In the early 1980s an attempt was made to create standard nomenclature for the things that we do and the people who do them. For better or for worse, many terms from the television and film business were adopted or adapted for the interactive business. Unfortunately, they don't always have the exact same meanings. Throughout the book I use several words that have different meanings in different industries. Table 1-1 is a list of some of the more commonly shared terms.

TABLE 1-1

Term	Interactive Entertainment Meaning*	TV, Film, Theater Meaning*
Development	The process of building a product. People who do this are called *developers*. Often developers are a small group of people working in a house, garage, or small office. Sometimes they are employees of a software company.	The process of coming up with a product idea and bringing it to the point where it's ready to produce. The people who do this are called *development* or *creative executives*.
Production	(1) The physical manufacturing of the product; (2) the making of the part of the product that involves standard TV or film techniques (see right); (3) if working with someone from the TV or film industry, the same as *development* (see above).	The process of making a TV show or film or play. This is usually preceded by a bunch of preparation work called *preproduction* and followed by even more work, called *postproduction*. So the *production* phase is, more accurately, the period in which the performers are in front of a camera and/or microphone.
Publisher	The company responsible for marketing, manufacturing, sales, and distribution of software products. Sometimes the publisher creates products with its own in-house development staff, and at other times it hires companies or individuals to create products for it to distribute.	A company responsible for marketing, manufacturing, sales, and distribution of books, magazines, or newspapers. Sometimes the publisher creates its own content from its own staff, and at other times it hires individuals to create products.
	When small publishers don't have the financial or personnel wherewithal to market, manufacture, sell, and/or distribute their own products, they make an *affiliated-label* arrangement for a larger publisher to market, manufacture, and/or distribute the small publisher's products. Depending on how many of these services the large publisher provides, the chunk of income that it gets increases (thereby greatly reducing both the risk and financial reward to the smaller publisher).	

TABLE 1-1 *(Continued)*

Term	Interactive Entertainment Meaning*	TV, Film, Theater Meaning*
Multimedia	A recently coined term for the integration of audio, video, text, pictures, animation, and/or music with computer programming to create software products. Notice that the word *interactivity* is not included in the definition of multimedia. ⇒ A game, in my definition, requires *interactivity* in addition to multimedia. I would label games *interactive multimedia* as a distinct category of products from multimedia products. Also, if you look at a strict definition of multimedia, it is not a new phase of computer products, but actually is something that has been part of the industry from the first video game consoles and personal computers. (For that matter, the first main-frame computer program that used a video monitor technically qualifies as multimedia software.)	A term from the performance art and theater world meaning the integration of live performance with video, audio, slides, music, and/or other previously recorded media to create a theatrical piece or experience. In a sense, either opera is a multimedia experience, or, if you don't quite buy that, it laid the groundwork for what would become multimedia. Another venue for multimedia production is the corporate or academic presentation that includes a speaker (a human being speaking, not a woofer and tweeter in a box), handouts, slides, videotape, and other prerecorded media.
Producer	The person who (1) is in charge of both the creative direction and management of a product; (2) has to convince upper management and marketing that the product will sell and that it will be done in time for the holidays; (3) convinces the developers that the idea is possible with current technology and that they have to be done by August so that they really will be done by September so that they can release for the holidays; (4) hires the TV or film producer to produce the taped, filmed, or recorded elements of a product; and (5) often has to do programming, art, writing, composing, sound effects, and/or any other development that the developers can't get done in time. Although this is changing somewhat (especially in the last category of responsibilities), it explains why successful producers have to be a computer jack-of-all-trades. In addition, as a product is prepared to go on the shelves, very often the producer fills the role of product manager (a consumer products industry term) and shepherds the licensing, marketing, sales, and public relations efforts along for the life of the product.	The person who budgets, schedules, and otherwise manages preproduction, production, and postproduction. This includes hiring of all staff and talent. Sometimes, the producer has creative input, but the amount depends on the director (and on which medium, as this can be different in the TV and film worlds).

(Continued)

TABLE 1-1 *(Continued)*

Term	Interactive Entertainment Meaning*	TV, Film, Theater Meaning*
Director	Until recently, few products have a director listed as part of the team. However, more and more we see a director listed in an attempt to (1) free up the producer to focus more on management, (2) remove the creative responsibility from the producer, and (3) make it seem more like Hollywood. Kidding aside, in the new paradigm, the director is responsible for the decision making in regard to the look and feel of the product, which include the game play. This means that the director is an important factor in the creation and evolution of the game design as the product is being developed. Sometimes, the director directs the film, video, or audio productions as well (see right). An additional meaning of the word *director* is in reference to the software tool called Director (from Macromedia) that allows the scripting (see below) of multimedia (see above).	Person responsible for the creative leadership of a film or show including script approval, casting, providing direction for the performers, and direction for the sets, scenes, and shots. Usually the director is also involved in the editing during postproduction.
Script	Depending on the phase of development (and whom you're talking to) a script is either (1) the part of a very high-level computer program that is so simplified that all levels of programmers (including producers) can quickly and easily create multimedia and, we hope, interactive portions of a product or (2) the actual dialogue and stage directions that the performers will use in the recorded production portion of a product (see right).	The dialogue and stage or set directions from which the entire production is created. Changes are made to the script during preproduction, days before shooting or even right on the set. Occasionally, the director (or even the producer) realizes that changes need to be made in postproduction, so new lines are "looped" (i.e., new dialogue is lip-synched over old dialogue) to improve either the quality or the content of a scene.

TABLE 1-1 *(Continued)*

Term	Interactive Entertainment Meaning*	TV, Film, Theater Meaning*
Programmer	The person (and often a creative person) who writes the computer instructions that take all the elements the producer and director can create and integrates them with the game design to create a product. In the early days of the industry, the programmer was the producer and director, too (as well as the artist, animator, musician, sound effects creator, writer, and box designer). Programmers are among the lower-profile members of the interactive community. However, they are the true talent without which there would be no industry. Programmers can be classified at many levels of talent and expertise. Often referred to as *coders,* they range from low-level coders (working down at the bare metal of the computer in assembly language) to scripters (writing only scripts). The programmers on a development team are a key element in the game design process. Unless they are working on a truly simple product, there will be holes in the design that the programmer is going to fill either by necessity (see Chap. 12: The 3 A.M. Green Syndrome) or by design.	The executive in charge of which shows go on the air on a television network. These are among the highest-profile and highest-paid executives in the TV business. The only computer programmers I know of in the film business are on the technical teams working on special effects (see left).
Art director	The person who comes up with the look of a product and often creates art and supervises other artists in the creation of art during development. Good art directors know how to create art in a multitude of ways (both traditional and using the computer) as well as have a great technical understanding of what it takes to "engineer" art to work with a computer program.	The person who manages the artists, set decorators, etc., who are executing the designs of the production designer. The production designer is the person who comes up with the look of a film or TV show.
Designer	The person who creates and documents the idea for a product including all the interactivity. Depending on how thorough the designer is, the designer may or may not abdicate large portions of the design to the producer, director, or, most likely, the programmers.	Not a term often associated with TV or film production. Sometimes it is used to refer to the production designer (see above).

(Continued)

TABLE 1-1 *(Continued)*

Term	Interactive Entertainment Meaning*	TV, Film, Theater Meaning*
Design or game design	The set of documents that define an entire product. This includes but is not limited to (yes, some of my best friends *are* lawyers) descriptions of each interactive element, view or scene (the game play); the story; the world (including maps and descriptions); the characters (along with costume designs if there is to be film or video); the dialogue script; any on-screen text; the art design; storyboards of all scenes; any charts, tables, or algorithms that describe exact interactive outcomes; the interface elements; user navigation design, sound designs, and lists of sound effects; and a music design (unfortunately often left out). On top of all of that, the designer or producer usually has to come up with a few documents for the marketing folks such as the high concept and what I call the dust jacket description of the product.	Again, not a term used except to refer to the production design.

*All meanings are approximate!

As you can see, some of the meanings are the same, others are similar, and still others are substantially different. Throughout the book, I use the standard game industry terms and expressions.

Getting Ready to Create a Game Design

1

A Brief History of Interactive Entertainment

Among the first things you need to know, if you want to create an interactive entertainment design, is some history of what has come before. While the industry is relatively new and is constantly developing, there is still a rich history of successful interactive products that until recently were simply called computer games.

If you are new to the business and are trying to break in as a designer, I think that knowledge of these games is essential. Telling a potential publisher that your idea is a cross between M.U.L.E., Lemmings, and Joust says volumes about your knowledge of game design. Compare this to, for example, your saying your most innovative design idea is an interactive role-playing adventure like Quake. Of course, the executive's or producer's knowledge, or lack of knowledge, of these things can also speak volumes to you about what they know about the business. So it serves you to know these things, as they can provide you with a great jumping-off place for creating and selling the next big design breakthrough.

For those who are already familiar with computer games, I hope to provide some insights as to why certain games and designs are good to know.

⇒ For all designers, it is important to know what has succeeded and failed in the past 20 years so that they can borrow from the best and avoid repeating the simple, obvious ideas that clearly did not work in the past.

The following history is a simple overview and focuses on what I personally consider the major breakthroughs and trends in the interactive entertainment business. I provide only brief descriptions of what the games were like; if you don't know them, try to find and experience them.

1960s and 1970s: The Mainframe Game

The first computer games, in the 1960s and 1970s, were on-line, multiplayer games. This is important to realize, given the current idea that the Internet multiplayer game is the next great thing. While it may very well be the next great thing, it is by no means new. This is where it all started, and it makes sense that this is where part of it should end up.

Unlike today's on-line games, these games were played on teletype and text-only monitors with text-based descriptions of the scenes and actions with interactivity through a computer keyboard. These games were created on college and military computers and included several important game designs that have stayed with us through the years:

Adventure: While this may not have actually been the first text adventure-style game, it certainly is the most famous of its kind. With text descriptions of the world you are in and simple text commands to move from place to place and interact with objects, this game set the standard for the classic puzzle-based adventure game. Other games from this era include The Great Underground Cave and, of course, Zork.

Star Trek: Unlike Adventure, where you play by yourself in the world created by the computer, Star Trek allows you to play in a world where other players play. If one player does something in your sector of space, it impacts your game.

Flight Simulators: Even though most of us never go to see them, many talented interactive designers and programmers were working on military flight and battle simulators. The work on these paved the way for some of the most commercially successful games of all time.

Life: This is every programmer's first gaming assignment in school. In this simple game, you pick a starting point and watch a symbolic life-form live, create offspring in an adjoining space, or die.

In the 1970s computer games continued on mainframes but began appearing on specially equipped televisions, the first personal computers, and in pinball arcades. Pong was, to my knowledge, the first commercially successful action game with graphics. When I discuss rhythm in game design, my guess is that you will see why this was such a big success.

Zork was split into three parts by a company called Infocom and sold millions of copies and introduced the text adventure to the general computer-owning public, not just college students with access to mainframes.

The Oregon Trail, one of the enduring educational games of all time, combined the strategy of allocating resources with the fun of hunting for your dinner.

The First Video Game Dynasty

As the 1970s ended and the 1980s began, the Atari and Intellivision home video game systems, the personal computer, and the video arcades launched a lot of new games featuring graphics, sound, text, and animation—what in current terms would be called multimedia. Of course, there was limited video footage, but it was multimedia nonetheless.

The first big design and commercial successes were video games and arcade games (quarter-eaters, as we call them). Some of the key games from this period are Pacman, Tempest, Joust, Donkey Kong (where Mario was first spotted), Star Wars, Defender, Hitchhiker's Guild to the Galaxy, Space Invaders, and Pole Position, as well as the first flight simulators and many simple sports games.

The Revenge of the Computer: Floppy Disks

As the 1980s began, Electronics Arts (EA) made a decision to focus on personal computers because it could deliver products on floppy disks and not the cartridges required for Atari and Intellivision systems. EA, along with several other publishers launched an entirely new breed of game that not only used graphics, sound, and text but also took advantage of the things a computer has: a keyboard (back again from the mainframe days), more memory, a rewritable storage device (e.g., a floppy disk), and usually a printer. Important computer games were born, such as Archon, Pinball Construction Set, Carmen Sandiego, M.U.L.E., Sky Fox, King's Quest, Dungeons and Dragons, Dr. J and Larry Bird Go One on One, and Ultima as well as many new flight simulators and sports games.

So the next great success story was the floppy disk game created for personal computers.

The Second Video Game Dynasty

Then, establishing the pattern for the games business for years to come, in the mid-1980s the video game system began to make a comeback. Nintendo and Sega introduced new systems and new games that could outdo computer games. Of all the stars born here, none shone as bright as Mario from Nintendo. These Nintendo and Sega systems became known as 8-bit video game systems.

The PC Strikes Back: 640K RAM, Sound Cards, and 3.5-Inch Floppy Disks Required

In the middle to late 1980s, personal computers became powerful enough to outperform the 8-bit video game systems. Many new types of games came out that took advantage of the increasing computing power, better peripherals, larger hard drives, and multimedia: New King's Quest games, Monkey Island, many great flight simulators, SimCity, Lemmings, The Manhole (the first entertainment CD-ROM ever published), The Bard's Tale, and the first sports simulators for computers.

During this phase, it became necessary for consumers to carefully read the packaging. Not only were there all kinds of special minimum configurations, but also the IBM PC compatible (PC) was quickly replacing the Apple computers as the computer game machine of choice. (In my opinion, this was due to Apple's misunderstanding of the game development community and the lack of support offered to this group of tremendously creative technical talent. Apple required Macintosh programs to adhere to a few too many rules, and as great as the operating system was, game programmers generally like to "own" the machine, which means working around the operating system; Apple, to my knowledge, wasn't then and isn't now too keen on this style of programming for its equipment.)

The Third Video Game Dynasty

As the 1990s approached, video game systems came back: This time it was the 16-bit Sega and Nintendo. Led by great sports titles (for Sega) and Mario again (for Nintendo), they could outperform the PCs in action games.

However, on the educational front, many breakthroughs were occurring on personal computers, e.g., Living Books' Just Grandma and Me, Reader Rabbit, and Math Blaster. Also, some products remained in the domain of the computer: Adventures and RPGs such as Indiana Jones, Monkey Island II, Colonel's Bequest, more Ultima, and the new breed of strategy games such as Populus, Civilization, and A Train began to appear.

Return of the PC: Multimedia, CD-ROMs, and the Pentium

In the early and mid-1990s, the multimedia craze really set in, production values went way up, and, fortunately, we still saw some design breakthroughs: The 7th Guest, yet another King's Quest, Myst, Return to Zork, Under a Killing Moon, and Full Throttle all made attempts at redefining the adventure game as the graphic adventure game, Ultima and The Elder Scrolls redefined the presentation and depth of RPGs, sports games all seemed to adopt the physics, stats, and "VR"-style gameplay, while racing games and flight simulators moved more toward more visual realism. Strategy games have greatly improved with games such as X-com and Command and Conquer and the hybrid space shooter/storytelling products such as Wing Commander and Rebel Assault have repeatedly topped the charts.

And, of course, Doom reinvented the trough game and created an action game rage on personal computers; Monty Python's Complete Waste of Time was the first game to truly capitalize on repurposed* material from another medium and still be interactive as well as entertaining; and You Don't Know Jack proved that multimedia doesn't always mean great pictures.

The (Sixty) Fourth-Bit Dynasty: Video Games Rise Again

Finally, as the emergence of the next generation of video games is currently upon us, once again Mario has appeared in a truly innovative product. The new Nintendo and the Sony Playstation and Sega Saturn are all bringing out ever-better racing, flying, shooting, and sports action games that outdo PC games.

Many, many other great games have been created over the years. I mention some of these throughout the book even if they did not appear here. I tried to provide a sense of what games were important to me in the evolution of interactive game design. Some of the great games of all time may not be on this list. I simply chose a list of games that influenced me as a game designer. Many of the great, older games are being re-released, and it's worthwhile to find them and play them.

What's Next? Probably Another PC Comeback

If you've observed the trend that I inundated you with, there's definitely a pattern here. Video games tend to lead the way with better graphics, faster game play, and innovative designs that cannot be accomplished on current computers. Then the computer technology catches up, and not only can the programmers create the same kinds of games

---

*A term used to describe a reuse of existing materials for another medium, i.e., a new or repurpose for the original film, video, or recorded content.

on personal computers, but also the additional peripheral equipment available on the PCs (more RAM, faster processors, hard drives, printers, keyboards, modems, etc.) allows designers to come up with things that can't possibly be done on a video game console. Then the entire process repeats itself.

So, following this pattern, the future probably holds some sort of PC comeback. In addition to faster processors, more memory, larger hard drives, and the ever-increasing size of the delivery medium (for example, CD-ROM moving up to DVD), either the next generation of computers will be hooked up to the Internet with a reasonable speed connection through ever-faster modems, or, just as likely, these computers will be integrated with the TV and some sort of special Internet connections (such as a cable modem) to add multiplayer capabilities to games.

The work going on now in the on-line world seems to be laying the ground for the PC's comeback. As the delivery of information over the Internet and private networks increases, many of the game design features from the most innovative games of the past will appear. However, the new on-line world does have certain limitations and unique attributes that I hope will spawn some new forms of interactive entertainment.

While some of this is going on now, considering that we're just entering the 64-bit video game phase, we have yet to see what the PC's comeback will really look like when it once again takes over.

And Then, Another Video Game Dynasty!

It's even more fun to consider what will happen after the PC's next comeback! Just imagine what video game systems will have to be like to compete with a fully Internet-connected PC/TV with a 2-Gbyte hard drive, 200+ MHz processor, and a true 24-bit (or more) graphics display. Honestly, I cannot wait.

Many newcomers to the world of game design seem to focus on computer games as opposed to video games. If you observed the important trend in the industry I just described with alternating periods of domination between video games and computer games, then you probably realize that you need to be able to design for either type of equipment.

Looking ahead to the next game platform is crucial to your design and your career.

The Myth of the Mass Audience

Throughout the history of the interactive entertainment industry, there has always been an underlying dissatisfaction with the fact that products generally don't appeal to a mass audience. Although an argument can be made that video games have not suffered from lack of mass appeal, for many years many key demographic groups don't seem to have any interest in video games or computer games. Computer games have a much lower overall appeal than video games. In particular, the older population, very young children, women, and girls are all groups that don't purchase or play computer and video games as much as boys and men between the ages of 10 and 45.

I think that the idea that people will purchase computer games as they purchase music recordings is a myth. At best, it is a reality that is many, many years off. It has been my feeling that this is more a function of product design than any inherent quality of interactive entertainment. However, we still have a relatively large and growing audience. And the better we do at expanding our audience, the better the chances we have of making this myth into a reality. The only way to reach the mass audience is through truly innovative game design.

By looking at the successful designs of the past and by studying the principles of interactive design, I hope to provide some inspiration for breakthrough game designs. With luck, the next generation of interactive game designs will begin to bridge both the generation and gender gaps.

2

Where to Start: Genres, Platforms, Audience, and Where Hollywood Missed the Mark

It often surprises people how many genres of game play there are and how specific and evolved they've become. Fans of certain styles of games often buy only the games that adhere to the conventions they are used to. At the same time, fans also expect some innovation within the constraints of those designs.

Know Your Genres

⇒ It is best to know your genres, the rules you have to adhere to, and where you can make attempts at improvement.

Without going into too much detail, Table 2-1 shows how I subdivide the types of products in the interactive entertainment business. I've grouped them in such a way as to draw distinctions between often mislabeled genres. Note that the action and the "edutainment" genres are very general supercategories and, as such, won't be listed.

Hybrids

More and more often we're faced with successful games that are hybrids (for example, adventure-trough, sports-simulation) and attempts to integrate two or more seemingly incompatible genres (e.g., war games—living book), but the games often take us into new territory. Unfortunately, the nature of the business often makes the hybrid a difficult product to sell.

Here are a few examples of hybrids that work:

- Adventure—role playing
- Adventure—flying
- Adventure—fighting
- Sports—simulation
- War game—simulation

Platforms

In the interactive world, the word *platform* has a special meaning. It is used to describe the hardware and software system for which a product is created. For example, the Nintendo Ultra 64 is one *video game platform*, the Macintosh with System 7.5 or higher is an example of a *computer game platform*, the Internet via subscription is an *on-line game platform*, and so forth.

When thinking about your design, you must consider not only the genre, but also the platform for which it is to be *first* developed. Many famous products become successful because of either shrewd or lucky planning as to the platform on which they were introduced. ⇒ The right

TABLE 2-1

Adventure	This is a game of exploration and puzzle solving. The player's character is often seen from a third-person point of view. In other games, the user sees a first-person point of view. These games are often slower-paced and attempt to tell or reveal stories as the player uncovers clues and solves puzzles. Adventure, Zork, Hitchhiker's Guide to the Galaxy, Monkey Island, King's Quest, The 7th Guest, Myst, and The Neverhood are all adventure games.
Role-playing game (RPG)	In RPGs, the player assumes a persona that changes over time. Often the player's persona is part of a team. All the characters in the world, including the player's persona, are assigned a range of physical and other attributes that change over time. These attributes also change as a result of the user's actions. The typical RPG is constructed after the *Lord of the Rings* fantasy story. A group of unlike souls sets out to save the world. The player is often the Frodo character—the leader with no especially interesting talents. The rest of the group, however, is full of talented folks, each with a specialty. It is the job of the leader to assign tasks to members of this team. Based on the skills and attributes of the assigned members, the team may or may not have luck in solving whatever problem is placed in front of them. The consequences of this may be death or simply an inefficient solution which results in a lessening of individual attributes (such as health or skill in fighting). The art of playing RPGs lies in mastering the complex relationships between the attributes and skills of each of the team members at any given time. Example RPGs include Ultima, Bard's Tale, and The Elder Scrolls.
Fighting	Two or more characters duke it out with fists, feet, and other hand-to-hand combat weapons in fighting games. The player(s) is (are) usually playing from a third-person point of view. Mortal Kombat and Virtua Fighter demonstrate the genre.
Shooter	In this game you or a weapon under your control (such as an aimable cannon) are shooting bullets, missiles, etc., at moving objects. These games can be third-person point of view (which gives a 2D style of aiming and shooting) or a first-person point of view where you shoot directly into your line of sight. Defender and Virtua Cop (at most video arcades) are an early and recent example, respectively.
Flying/driving	In this game the player is seated in a cockpit or behind the wheel of a vehicle. Controlling the steering device(s) and all other navigational tools keeps the user from crashing. Most of these games strive for absolute accuracy in terms of the controls in the selected vehicles. Some of these games use third-person point of view. Some incorporate shooter elements to increase the interactivity.
Platform or side scrolling	This is a third-person point-of-view game in which you make your character run, jump, punch, kick, roll, shoot, and do other action things while you navigate a 2D maze. Usually your character is moving from left to right with up and down detours. You avoid the bad guys and pitfalls (one of the best side scrollers of all time is called PitFall from Activision) and try to find and capture power-ups. Your goal is to "clear" each level by avoiding or dispensing of all the bad guys and defeating or otherwise getting around the Boss Monster for the level. You die a lot in these games, but you're often granted (or can earn) additional lives on each level. Mario 64 uses the side-scrolling design and moves into 3D. It's well worth seeing!

(Continued)

TABLE 2-1   *(Continued)*

Trough	Based on the final action scene in Star Wars, you are moving down a trough, shooting straight ahead at bad guys. Usually you can ricochet left or right off the walls of the trough and move a little up and down to avoid bridges and things that are sticking up. Bad guys are either coming at you (which you need to dodge) or shooting at you (which you need to dodge), all while you are trying to clear the level by shooting at targets determined by the story you're in. Trough games are really 3D shooters in a limited environment. While Star Wars used to be the best explanation of a trough game, Doom has eclipsed it due to its recent popularity. (However, most people refer to games like Doom as Doom-style games as opposed to trough games.)
Simulators	A game that physically models the world and allows you to control characters and objects in that world in order to see the resultant behaviors. Flight simulators are the most obvious example. Most computer sports games use this model now, and some other real-time battle games use the techniques from the simulator modeling games. Microsoft Flight Simulator, Links, EWB, and EarthSeige are all examples.
Sims	Like a simulator but a specific style based on the SimCity game. In these games, the world being modeled is a functioning, living ecosystem, economic system, and/or political system. You set up the conditions of the world (land, water, crops, number of people, houses, schools, etc.), and the Sim shows you what happens as time goes by. You are evaluated with regard to your ability to create a balance among the many elements that you can deploy in the world. These are highly addictive games that can teach you a lot about the way the world seems to work.
Strategy	Based on the model from popular board games such as Risk, you take turns devising and deploying strategies either against a computerized opponent or against another player. In the computer version of a strategy game, the computer "acts out" or performs the results of your "moves" or strategies.
War games	War games are named more for their theme than for their design. Most often, war games are strategy games or sims. Sometimes, however, they include action elements from other game types such as fighting, simulators, or shooters.
Sports	As with war games, this broad category has to do more with the subject matter than with the game design. Recently, the trend has been toward simulators with strategy elements thrown in.
Living books	This genre of game was invented by Broderbund with a title *Just Grandma and Me*, for young children. In this design, each page of a real book is displayed on the computer screen. When the page first appears, the words are read out loud (over the speaker), and the words are often highlighted as they are being spoken. The child can click on almost any part of the page which will trigger animations (if the child clicks on an interesting part of the artwork) or rereading of the text (if the child clicks on the text).
Board games, puzzle games, activity games	There are a lot of other types of designs that don't fit neatly into the list above. Most fit into one of these categories. Tetris, Shanghai, Solitaire, Monopoly, and Timon and Pumba's Activity Center games are all popular examples of games of this genre.
Productivity	These are products that you can make things with, such as greeting cards, calendars, banners, computer artwork, and music. The entertainment versions of these include branded elements (such as Hallmark Greeting Cards or the *Sports Illustrated* Swimsuit Calendar) or "kid" versions of real software tools (such as Kid Pix for making art and Creative Writer for word processing).

product on the wrong platform may never get a chance to be seen in its best light.

⇒ In selecting the platform for your game, be sure to study the life cycles of the video game and computer platforms. It takes from 6 to 18 months to create a product, so you have to anticipate what will be the popular platform in that time frame.

Identify Your Target Audience

Now that you've picked a genre and an appropriate platform, be sure you understand who is your target audience. Very often, the audience is just like you; designers usually like to design products they themselves would like to play. If this is the case, be sure to accurately identify the group *you* belong to.

Most important, though, is to be realistic. The "gamers" out there will buy games written just for them. They are not a huge crowd, but are they loyal! If you provide a fresh new game aimed at this market and it hits, you will have a substantial number of sales on your hands. You will also have the opportunity to create a series of sequels. However, it is important to respect and respond to loyal fans and followers. ⇒ Personally, I believe it is *not* a great idea to attempt to use a popular sequel to broaden the interactive gaming audience. If that's your goal, create a new game; make the sequel for your fans. Your dedicated followers will never forgive you for simplifying or otherwise overhauling the experience they've come to enjoy.

⇒ If you are making a game for a new platform, make a game for games. People who invest in new game hardware, either computers or video games, are often referred to as *early adopters*. In the first months of a new platform's availability, the entire market of potential purchasers of your product comprises these early adopters who are, undoubtedly, gamers.

Once a platform is more mature (say, 6 months to 2 years), your options open up for market groups other than gamers. From a practical point of view, go after relatives of the person who bought the equipment in the first place. In the video game world, that is sisters and younger siblings. In the computer world, that is wives, daughters, fathers, and young children.

This isn't to say that women and girls don't purchase these things; but for now the predominant buyers of games for themselves are boys and men (depending on the equipment).

⇒ Once a platform has peaked and is beginning its descent, the target audience often shifts to young children. So if you carefully study the ebbs and flows of the video game console and computer game markets and combine this with knowledge of typical audience demographics, you can see that there is almost always an audience for any type of game design in any genre for any demographic group. Notice that the only thing that isn't completely open is the platform. You have to choose the platform that makes your product work in the marketplace.

⇒ If the choice of platform is important to you, then be sure to pick your genre and audience very, very carefully.

Know Who Buys Software

It is one thing to design a great product and have it produced. It is quite another to have people purchase it. One important consideration in creating your product is knowledge of exactly who will be the primary influences in getting your game from the shelf into the consumer's home.

This business is like no other in this regard. There is very little opportunity to experience a product to know if it is worth the purchase. There is little name recognition for most products. There is only a tenuous chain of information passed on from the publisher to the distributor to the retailer to the consumer. And often the purchaser is not even the actual user of the software.

So, in order to guide you in the positioning of your product, I've assembled some of the common wisdom as it has been passed on to me about who buys and influences the purchases of software.

Common Wisdom about Game Purchases

1. Almost all software purchases occur within 6 months of the purchase of the computer.

2. Game players buy the latest equipment and keep their equipment upgraded regularly (now see item 1).

3. The primary purchasers of software for children are mothers.

4. The primary users of software for children are fathers with their children.

5. The primary decision makers for software purchased for kids aged 12—18 are kids aged 12—18.

6. The primary seller of software is a retail salesperson having little experience with computers or software for other than his or her own specific tastes and purposes. The salespeople are rarely old enough to have children and rarely play kids' games themselves.

7. There are three types of customers who enter a store to purchase software:

   ■ The *knowing buyers* need no help other than to find the exact title they came in to buy.

   ■ The *browsers* scan the shelves, hoping that something will pop out at them. The box (with a familiar name on it), a special display of top sellers, or the salesperson assists browsers in overcoming the visual noise presented by shelves and shelves of packages.

   ■ The *bewildered buyers* rarely, if ever, purchase software.

To sell a product to the knowing buyer, you need to create great word of mouth; to the browser, you need great name recognition (e.g., a licensed property such as Star Wars), unbelievably great packaging, or, more likely, a great sales force that can position the product both in the store and in the mind of the retail salespeople; to the bewildered buyer, you can only reach through retail salespeople, which requires gigantic efforts on the part of the distributor's sales force.

I used to call around to all the software stores in town to check up on my baseball products. I would tell the salesperson that I wanted to buy a baseball game for my brother and wanted to know what she or he would recommend. I would say that 90 percent of the time the answer was something like "Oh, buy game X because it just came out and it's the hottest new game." Even if it were my game, I would then ask, "So you've played it and it's really great?" To which they would often reply, "No, but it's the newest baseball game."

In other words, in addition to creating a great product with great word of mouth, you need to be sure that the retail salesperson is somehow convinced (e.g., with incentives to actually play your product) that your product is worth mentioning to curious shoppers.

Hollywood Tries It Out

Now that you know what genre of game you're designing, the platform on which it will first appear, and the game's audience, you may have realized that interactive entertainment is a reasonably well-defined entertainment medium. What many newcomers to the industry fail to realize is that it is not a good idea to get stuck on the idea of making interactive products as defined by the delivery medium. One of the best and most recent examples is how the Hollywood entertainment community embraced CD-ROM as the next big entertainment business to be in. Now, at first glance, this makes sense. However, if you examine the chronology and the stated logic of the companies involved, it's pretty easy to see where they went astray and why they had trouble making successful "interactive CD-ROM" businesses.

History Repeats Itself: There's a Business Out There

In the mid-1980s, during one of the upswings of the computer games business (i.e., just after the peak of a video game period), there was a lot of financial and business news about the huge financial success of certain companies and products in the computer games business. In the 1980s it was Atari and Intellivision and floppy disk computer games (from companies such as Electronic Arts and Broderbund) that prompted many book publishing companies to conclude that they could profit by making computer products out of their catalogue of book titles. In the 1990s a specific phenomenon caught the attention of the movie businesses: Mortal Monday.

Mortal Kombat started off as a "coin-op" (quarter-eating) video game found only in video arcades. After a giant promotional effort, Acclaim released Mortal Kombat for both the Super NES (Nintendo 16-bit video game console) and the Sega Genesis (Sega's 16-bit video game console) on the same day, "Mortal Monday," in late 1992. According to some reports, the combined gross sales of both of these products exceeded $200 million in the first weeks alone! That's enough money to catch any movie company executive's attention.

A few months later, a report appeared in a major financial journal that the combined gross sales of the interactive games business were in the billions of dollars per year. These figures certainly caught some people's attention. What wasn't so clear was that most of these sales were from video games, not computer games.

The Promised Land: Multimedia CD-ROM

At about the same time, the news reports were full of stories saying that the next big innovations coming for the computer games world were multimedia as content and CD-ROM as the device that would allow distribution of multimedia to all computers. One of the many things that CD-ROM adds to computer games is the ability to include all kinds of multimedia including full-motion video (FMV). Well, that's one thing that film and TV companies understand—producing film and video content.

Since the next big thing in computer games was multimedia and CD-ROM (and therefore video as content on the computer) and since the interactive business was so big, it was time for all the entertainment companies to start their interactive divisions! So many of them, if not most, started CD-ROM divisions.

History Repeats Itself: It's a Bust

The result, as in the mid-1980s, was a near catastrophe. Using all their available licenses, lots of money, and multimedia CD-ROMs as their target product, most entertainment companies missed the true market.

First, the key ingredient to the successful products driving this (apparently) newly successful industry was interactivity—or, more plainly put, great game play. This has nothing to do with CD-ROM or multimedia. ⇒ The success of the industry reflects great game design—in other words, the integration of interactivity with the current state-of-the-art production capabilities of the current platform.

Second, it takes time and experienced personnel to gear up to create products and a business. Business planning has to take into account the nature of the games business: You have to create and design products appropriate for each platform's success cycle when your product hits the shelves.

⇒ Finally, it is important to build products using tools that allow truly interactive use of the technology. In the 1990s many tools and multimedia products made it easy to script multimedia products very quickly. However, many of these products weren't terribly interactive (i.e., there wasn't much, if any, game play) although they had great content. So store shelves were crammed full of multimedia products with a few interactive products sprinkled in the mix. Consumers, however, couldn't easily tell one from another, and when they purchased one of these not-very-interactive multimedia titles, they often became disillusioned about the entire interactive entertainment genre.

Delivery Media versus Interactive Medium

Since many of these business plans were built around CD-ROM as the product type and multimedia as the key ingredient, you can see why they missed the market. In my opinion, confusing the delivery media (CD-ROM) with the interactive medium (computer games) is the main reason why there was so much money lost on interactive divisions. There lacked a focus on creating great interactivity and on the platforms coming on the horizon.

Business Plans That Need to Move

I believe that in order to succeed, you have to build your business plan around

- Interactive products (e.g., games even if you call them interactive multimedia)
- Platforms that will be coming into their own when your products hit the shelves (e.g., the Nintendo Ultra 64 or Sony Playstation if you started up when the CD-ROM market was just before its peak)
- The ability to turn on a dime when new developments occur in the games industry (e.g., the trend in the mid-1990s toward trough games, war games, and strategy games, and, of course, great video games)
- A willingness to make video games, as they seem to always come back in vogue
- The true desire to be in this business to create great games and to stick it out until your company finds its niche; in other words, a willingness to constantly change and adjust your plan.

This is an unusual way to create a business plan as one of the fundamental ingredients is the willingness to rewrite the plan every few months. It means that a company's staff has to have a great understanding of the business, the company has to be willing to make constant adjustments to its strategy without demoralizing its personnel, and the decision makers have to agree to make video games and the company have the burning desire to stick it out.

A simpler way to put it is this: If you want to be in the interactive entertainment business, design interactive games to have great game play and not for today's platform. The game is where the entertainment is.

3

What Every Designer Should Know about Computers

You've got the game genre in mind, you've picked next year's platform of choice, you know your target audience, and you know how to design your game so the kid at the local software store will rave about your game to everyone and anyone who will listen. So you are prepared to tackle the task of designing your game—almost.

We've looked at all the external things that will determine what type of product you will design. Now it's time to look inside to understand how the product needs to be designed and where the true opportunities to innovate are: in the bits and pieces that make up a computer system.

Computer Systems

I lay out some of the basics of computer systems below in order to focus generally on what designers should know. Throughout the book I elaborate on specific topics as they relate to game design issues. If you feel you want to know more about computer systems, there is certainly much room for further study. While there are many books and classes that cover the details of how computer systems work, nothing beats getting your hands dirty.

Open the Box (but Back Up Your Hard Drive First!)

My recommendation for those interested in learning more about computers than what is in this book is to learn how to disassemble the major parts of a computer system and to program some simple software. Those are seemingly big undertakings, but your subsequent level of understanding will surpass anything you could possibly get from a book. Just be sure to back up your hard drive first.

Students of mine have balked at the thought and have tried to draw analogies to other industries, saying things such as "A screen writer, producer, or director doesn't need to know how a camera works or how film is processed in order to do her or his job, so why should a game designer?" First, I don't think it is necessary for a designer to know amazing levels of detail about how a computer actually works. But I don't think their analogy quite works.

Why Learn So Much Technology? It's Not Necessary in Other Mediums

When designing a computer game, you as designer have to communicate a significant level of detail to programmers and possibly electronics engineers (e.g., you are working on a special or new piece of equipment). They have to know exactly what you want to happen and when you want it to occur.

⇒ If you can't accurately communicate this information to the technical team (which often requires a significant amount of knowledge about how computer systems work), you abdicate a significant part of your role as designer and leave yourself open to the 3 A.M. Green Syndrome (see below). You also leave yourself open to the remark, "Sorry, that can't be done" and you won't know whether it's true.

Finally, since the technology changes extraordinarily fast, you have to be able to envision what the new technology can contribute to the interactivity in your design on equipment that doesn't yet exist. Unless you have some understanding of computer systems, it is pretty hard to anticipate the ramifications of the new technology on your design.

Except in extraordinary circumstances, a writer, producer, or director never has to tell the camera operator or the film lab how to work the equipment. Even more rarely do these jobs require the ability to adjust to new camera technology or new film development processes.

Basic Computer Components

The five basic computer components are

1. Input devices

2. Processing devices

3. Memory and storage devices

4. Software and data

5. Output devices

With few exceptions, everything you find in a computer system falls into only one of these categories. If you're into exercises, before you turn the page, see how many components you can think of and in which category each belongs. Also, find out which elements of a computer system can fall into more than one category. Then compare what you've thought of with my list in Table 2-2.

TABLE 2-2

Component	Examples
Input devices	Keyboard, mouse, joystick, microphone, stylus, paper cards, touch screen, buttons, dials, modem
Processing devices	CPU (e.g., Intel Pentium, Motorola PowerPC), math coprocessors, graphics coprocessors, audio processors, synthesizers, video display cards
Memory and storage devices	Random access memory (RAM), read-only memory (ROM), hard drives, CD-ROM, tape drives, paper tape or cards, digital versital disc (DVD)
Software and data	System software, programs or applications, firmware. Data usually exist as files created by or for programs or applications.
Output devices	Screens, speakers, printers, modems, joysticks

The Basic Computer

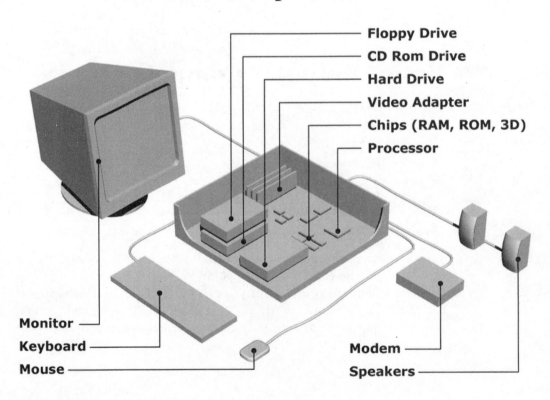

Floppy Drive
CD Rom Drive
Hard Drive
Video Adapter
Chips (RAM, ROM, 3D)
Processor

Monitor
Keyboard
Mouse

Modem
Speakers

Nowadays, the basic computer consists of

Input:	Keyboard, mouse, often a modem, and possibly a joystick and/or microphone
Processor(s):	Intel Pentium or Motorola PowerPC, a video adapter, and possibly a 3D assist chip
Memory and storage:	RAM, ROM, flash memory, a hard drive, a floppy drive, and often a CD-ROM drive
Software and data:	An operating system (Windows, Mac OS, etc.), utility software (word processors, spreadsheets, databases, etc.), and data for your programs
Output:	Screen, speakers, printer, modem

Components of Typical Video Game Console System

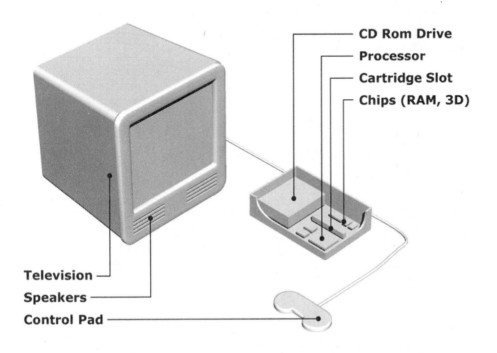

CD Rom Drive

Processor

Cartridge Slot

Chips (RAM, 3D)

Television

Speakers

Control Pad

Input:	Game pad (a specially made device with a direction indicator and buttons)
Processor(s):	RISC Processor (CPU), video chip, sprite (i.e., animation) chip, sound chip, and usually now a 3D chip
Memory and storage:	RAM, ROM, a CD-ROM drive, or a ROM cartridge slot
Software and data:	Usually only the software that is on the currently installed CD-ROM or ROM cartridge. In the old days, there was often an operating system found on a ROM in every system.
Output:	Screen and speakers

Before we continue, look through Table 2-3 where the strengths and weaknesses of each type of system in terms of interactive design are described.

The Way Things Work

I have devoted the chapters in Part 6 to a technical discussion of the way computers work. If you aren't fairly familiar with the underpinnings of computer technology already, I strongly suggest that you read through these chapters. Otherwise, carry on.

What Can Computers Do that Designers Need to Know?

So you know your way around computers, you've read Part 6, or you're just skipping to the good parts. In any case, we're now getting to the heart of the matter: As a designer, you need to keep in mind all the things a computer can actually do. When I'm working with designers, we often go through this exercise of listing everything we can think of in order to inspire our tired minds into taking advantage of the medium.

TABLE 2-3

System	Strength	Weakness
Computer	More RAM and expandable RAM; faster processors available every few months; equal graphics capabilities of video game system from a few years before; printers; hard drive storage; wider variety of resolutions; can use for other purposes than just games; removable storage; a keyboard, a printer, a mouse, and peripheral connectors that allow you to add input, output, and storage devices (such as modems); freeware and shareware available to download onto hard drives or into RAM for low-cost or free software; the ability to "patch" or update/upgrade software that exists on the hard drive	Not as fast as state-of-the-art video game systems; doesn't have specialized graphics or sound processors at the same quality or capability level as on video consoles; lacks standard configuration (so installation and reliability are often problematic); does not typically include a game input device (such as a joystick or game pad) so it either needs to be bought separately or played without one or designed around it; doesn't hook up to TV (at least not easily) so must be played in, typically, an office space. Also, it is relatively easy to create and make available software, so there are usually a large number of low-quality titles that high-quality products have to rise above.
Video game consoles	State-of-the-art graphics and sound coprocessors for displaying sprites (animation), 3D images, video, audio, and music; specially designed input device (game pad) hooks up to TV for den or living room entertainment experience; standard configuration so you simply plug in and play, no operating system to wait to boot up; high-speed dedicated processor for high-speed response; no association with educational benefit (i.e., it's a toy plain and simple so it's not off-putting to kids); can only be programmed by low-level programmers at somewhat great expense, which eliminates much competition for the first years of a platform's life cycle	No ability to plug in peripherals such as printers, keyboard, mouse, high-resolution monitor, or (usually) a modem. A fixed amount of RAM in the machine is typically inadequate for second-generation games for any particular machine (which can be made up for by higher-priced game cartridges that have RAM on them); no way to save significant amounts of data (i.e., no hard drive or floppy-disk-style storage); too costly and not technically feasible to create patches or upgrades

⇒Here's my simple list of what computers can actually do:

- Count
- Do arithmetic
- Remember what's been done
- Store data
- Look up data
- Manipulate data
- Make sound come out of a speaker
- Make graphics on a monitor
- Print on paper
- Choose random numbers
- Do logical comparisons
- Read a mouse or joystick
- Read a keyboard
- Send and receive data from a modem or over a network
- Look at its clock and tell the time and date
- Remember what it was doing and return to it after being interrupted to do something else

⇒Keep this list handy, and use it as a reminder of all the things you want to consider as you design your product. I've found this really helps to make a well-rounded design; and although they can't exactly identify how, most users will notice the higher level of interactive quality.

For a more detailed discussion of each of these elements, read Chap. 9.

The Design Proposal and Preliminary Design

As you prepare to design your game, keep in mind your role throughout the product's life. There are many phases in preparing the design, selling it to a publisher, completing the details of the design, and producing the product. Before the heavy-duty design work begins, you'll need to work on two documents: the design proposal and the preliminary design.

Design Documents for the Life of a Product

Each phase of a product's life cycle has one or more design documents associated with it. Table 2-4 is a list of these phases and their associated documents.

Who Are These For Anyway?

It's a good idea to understand for whom these documents are written before you start. I find that in each case, before I start writing a document, I have the key person involved in reviewing that document supply me with an example that he or she likes. Then I follow the format as closely as possible. I also look for the style of presentation that he or she prefers. Of course, you can go even further by asking this person what she or he would have liked better about the example documents.

Some of these documents can get rather lengthy, so it's often wise to get a sense of the reading style of the key person. Does she or he like bullets and charts or lots of well-written prose? People are more likely to actually read a document if it's in a style they like. Table 2-5 lists each design document, its purpose, and for whom it's really intended.

TABLE 2-4	Phase	Design Document(s)
	Idea or pitch	Design proposal
	Pre-green light or preliminary design phase	Preliminary design and treatment
	Preproduction or predesign phase	Game (or product) design
	Production	Design revisions and sequel design specifications
	Postproduction	Localization specifications

TABLE 2-5

Design Documents	Purpose	Target Audience	Things to Consider
Design proposal	Sell the overall idea of the design	Acquisitions executive, executive producer, other funding resource executive	These people see a lot of proposals, and if you're lucky, they are into games. It's key to focus on both the "cool" interactivity and any compelling characters and stories.
Preliminary design	Sell the product to the publisher	The heads of marketing, production, and technology	They should be able to use this document to determine if they can build it, sell it, and fit it into the company's overall publishing strategy. If it's possible to create a working prototype or demo, I highly recommend it.
Treatment	Tell the story	Creative executives who consult for the above executives or the executives themselves	Often these consultants are not from the games business, but are from the traditional entertainment businesses. They are looking to see if the story, characters, and world are valuable. Also, if you want to be the writer as well as the designer, this is the person whom you have to impress.
Game or product design documents, technical design, and production plan	Specify exactly how to build every aspect of the product from technical programming to physical production	Producers, programmers, writers, artists, sound engineers, composers, audio and video producers, manual writers, product managers	These are documents that determine the interactivity as well as the content-related production elements. There are always things that change from the "approved" design, but the thing to watch out for is the missing elements that others will have to improvise in your absence. Try to have the technical director create small proof-of-concept demos of key interactive elements.
Design revisions and sequel design specifications	These are like change orders to a contractor	Producers, programmers, writers, artists, sound engineers, composers, audio and video producers, manual writers, product managers	One of the most difficult tasks for any producer is to keep everyone in the loop on design changes. Creating a method for writing and circulating these changes can be crucial to the timeliness of a production schedule.

(Continued)

TABLE 2-5   *(Continued)*

Design Documents	Purpose	Target Audience	Things to Consider
Sequel design specifications	Usually in the form of an extended preliminary design document, this provides information on how a sequel or other follow-on product fits into the scheme of things	Executives of marketing and production as well as technology and the current production's producers and programmers	Not only does this extend the designer's job and plan for the future life of the product, but also this gives the current technology team a chance to build elements in the current product that can, in some way, pave the way for the sequel.
Localization specifications	A specification of what things need to be localized and with what production techniques, budgets, and schedules	Product manager, producer, programmers, artists, audio and video teams, and marketing executives	This document is often put together by an associate or assistant producer and, if done early enough, can help to anticipate tough localization problems (i.e., translation to other languages taking into account their cultural idiosyncrasies and current idiomatic expressions).

Designer Documents

For the purposes of this book, I focus on the three main design documents that a game designer must create in order to pitch, prepare, and specify a game for production:

- Design proposal
- Preliminary design document
- Game design

Design Proposal

The design proposal is typically included in a set of three documents whose central element is your outline of the design. If you are an independent designer and want to submit a product idea to a publisher, you need to include a cover letter and resume along with the design proposal. If you do not, you only have to create the design proposal outline. In addition to providing information about the design proposal itself, in Table 2-6 I list some pointers about the cover letter and resume. The dressing of a

TABLE 2-6

Great Cover Letter	If you're submitting as an independent, please make the letter great but short!
What you want	Start right off with what you'd like to have happen: "I have an idea for a product that your company might be interested in for development. I've enclosed a brief proposal for your consideration."
Who you are	It helps to let them know who you are: "I've been writing TV sitcoms for the past few years but am a serious computer game player and have learned a little about programming in my spare time. I would really like to work on games, as they are my passion."
	It's always easier to hire contractors for a short-term job first and then consider them and their own projects. And it's easier to consider people for a project if they know and like computer games. Of course, some familiarity with computers themselves is a plus!
Why you picked the reader's company	It's amazing how many people leave this out. If you don't let me know why my company would be the best home for this product, then I get the feeling that this is a form letter that you're sending to everyone in the business. Even though I know you are doing this, the consideration of personalizing it makes a huge impact. You can always go one step further and identify someone by name. Aside from the obvious flattery, it can show an awareness of the business that most unsolicited designers do not seem to have. "I've played (your or) your company's games for years and have always wanted to do a product with the same attention to quality and great game play as (name a game or two that you especially like)."
When that's enough!	Stop here in your letter. Sign off and let them get on to reading your proposal. Keep this cover letter to less than one page, use a relatively large type size, and be sure that all your contact information is easy to find (including your e-mail address).
Your Resume	**If you are submitting this design proposal as an independent designer (or producer for that matter), attach a separate resume. I strongly suggest not including it with the proposal.**
Design Proposal	**This is a six- to eight-page document that provides an overview of your complete idea. Put a nice cover page on this, and if you can, bind it nicely. Be sure that the title, your name, and the date are instantly noticeable and legible. (I've gotten cover pages with very clever but unreadable logos.)**
One-page executive overview	**An overview to catch the reader's attention**
High concept	One very short paragraph (one sentence is best) that describes the product. Make this either a bullet point or simply use the high-concept sentence(s) as a subtitle to the product's name on the first page.
Genre	A single bullet point that says what type of game this is. Even if it's a hybrid, say it. Just be sure you use the interactive industry's terms!

(Continued)

TABLE 2-6   *(Continued)*

Platform	A list of bullet points:
First or main platform	The target platform for its first appearance
Other platforms	List in the order that you think they should be done
Target audience	A list of bulleted points:
Primary audience	For whom it really is designed. Marketing needs to know and agree.
Other possible audiences	If there are secondary audiences, list them here.
Unique features and selling points	A list of bulleted points that identify why this product is different, better, or newer and/or will last longer (e.g., as a series of sequels). This can be a good place to demonstrate your understanding of design by mentioning an "engine" or algorithm-related design elements that will allow for add-on products and low(er)-cost sequel productions.
Interactivity	**Two to three pages of short paragraphs and diagrams for the people who know games. If nothing else, this lets them know that you understand the difference between interactive and linear entertainment.**
Goal	When the user plays, what's the goal—win, score points, kill all the bad guys, save the world, learn about geology?
Interface	There are many paradigms for interfaces. Again, you can score a lot of points if you are aware of these and refer to yours in comparison or contrast. It's a great frustration to me when someone proposes a "new" concept for a user interface that's been around for 10 years. If you do have a new twist or idea about your interface, then pictures and even simple drawings can be of great use. Don't go into too much detail, though; focus on the main thrust of the interface.
User experience	Now that the reader knows what the goal is and what the computer's interface is, talk briefly about what the user actually does. Does the user manipulate objects, collect things, fight, create strategies, converse, build, read? How about saving and loading information? Keep it brief but tie it into the goal and the interface so it flows nicely into the next section.
Flow of game (with flowchart)	If you can create a simple flowchart of the game, do it here. Don't fill more than one page with this and leave yourself some room for a title, a one-paragraph explanation at the bottom, and clearly labeled flowchart elements. Color is always good here. ⇒ I find that it is often helpful to use color in flowcharts to distinguish what the user does from what the computer does.
Interactive rhythm of game play	Now, give the reader a sense of timing in a few short paragraphs. Does each step in the flowchart take 1 minute or 10? How long does a typical session last? How long does the entire experience last? What keeps the user coming back for more? Think about how you would describe the major components of Lemmings, Doom, Tetris, any Mario action game, Myst, an Internet Soap Opera (a "Webisodic"), or Wing Commander as examples.

TABLE 2-6   *(Continued)*

How the user marks progress (scoring, winning, losing)	Finish this section with a brief summary of how the user tracks progress toward the ultimate goal, as stated at the beginning of this section.
Use of algorithms, randomness, and logic trees (i.e., branching)	**In a separate section devote one or two pages to equations, tables, and explanations of algorithms or logic that you think are the key underpinnings of how the computer creates the experience. This will speak volumes about the product and about your understanding of design for interactivity.**
Physical production	**On one separate page, discuss all the following:**
Style of art and animation	What it will look like and what type of production technology it might take [e.g., full-motion video, Claymation, still art with animations, animated GIFs (animated art formatted for Internet and other software)]. Sometimes it is helpful to include example art here.
Style of audio effects	Keep audio separate from music. This can usually be quite brief unless it is a truly key element of your design (as in "You Don't Know Jack").
Style of music	Think about music now. It sets a tone when you see a production, and most people can understand the intended tone of your production as easily through example music as they can through descriptions of art style. If you say you want to do a role-playing game and all the while country and western music is playing, that's a much different tone from when you have sitar music from India. (It can also let them know if you should be involved in the music design.)
Wrap-up	**One-page conclusion**
Competitive products	In a single bullet point, list all the competitive products you can think of. Not only does this help the reader understand the marketing task, but also it helps identify you as someone who understands the business.
How this product stacks up	In a few short paragraphs, review the list of unique features and selling points from the executive overview page, and drive home how your product will compete and win against the above list.
What role do you want to play?	Finally, in one or two sentences, make a clear statement about what role you want in this production. While this issue may be addressed in your cover letter (if you wrote one), that letter often gets separated from the design proposal document.

great cover letter and resume is very important as it sets the tone and mood for the executive who will review your submission.

What to Do with a Design Proposal

Once you've written your proposal, you've got to find the companies and people to send it to. First, identify appropriate companies ⇒ (and, of course, play their games so that you can write a truthful cover letter!).
⇒ Pick companies that

- Make games in the genre of the one you want produced
- Purchase and use designs from nonemployees
- Make games on a variety of platforms

Another type of company to consider is a company looking to expand into genres for which it has previously not created products. This means it doesn't necessarily have an infrastructure for designing and developing games already and is more likely to look for outside help.

After picking a list of companies and playing their products, you need to find out to whom you should send it. This can vary from company to company. Sometimes it's a specially assigned acquisitions executive, sometimes the individual producers are left to handle incoming submissions. Your best bet is to log on to their home pages and do some homework. They may have a submissions contact listed on the home page. At least they'll provide a way to contact them which you can use to ask where to send an unsolicited idea.

An alternative tack would be to identify key production personnel in the company and contact them directly (usually by sending a letter or E-mail to the company to this person's attention). Be aware that this isn't necessarily the most popular thing you could do; but if you've played some of that person's games and described what an honor it would be to have him or her consider your idea, you just might overcome her or his impatience.

Most likely, you will hear from someone's assistant or a "reader" who will want you to sign an unsolicited submission form or a nondisclosure form before she or he can even look at your idea. Expect this, and do not be insulted or put off. ⇒ Read the unsolicited submission or nondisclosure forms carefully, realize that they are completely in the favor of the publisher, and weigh your options. If you don't sign, the publisher won't read your proposal. The publisher will rarely take the time (and money) required to make changes in these forms just for you.

The best possible next step is for the publishing staff to like your idea so much that they set up a meeting. What's the purpose of this meeting? They want to see if they can afford to move onto the next phase. If they really like your idea and want to move forward, they might

- Pay you a fee for your idea and hope you go away
- Pay you a fee for your idea and hire you to work on the coming effort
- Pay nothing to you for your idea, but contract with you (for money) to work with their producers to create the next element of the design, the preliminary design documents.

Preliminary Design Documents

The preliminary design documents are drafted by a team, and when they are complete, they allow the publishing executives to decide whether to press ahead with or "green-light" actual production. In the old days, one person created the preliminary design documents. Today, there is a greater appreciation for the idea of spending a little more money in this stage. This new attitude allows the hiring of experts in various creative areas to create a document from which you can actually produce a product. This includes hiring the game designer.

⇒ While you may find that some people wear more than one hat on the team preparing the preliminary design, there are usually at least three or four people doing five or six jobs.

Preliminary Design Team

The jobs that the preliminary design team performs include

- Game designer
- Writer
- Production designer or art director
- Producer
- Technical director or lead programmer
- Sometimes, a game director

In any such group, someone has to have the final say in order to maintain some sense of vision for a product. This role is usually determined on a project-by-project basis and varies from company to company. In most companies, if a game director is assigned to a project, then this role falls to this person. However, if there is no game director, there can be quite a struggle for control. In my opinion, the two best candidates are the game designer and the producer.

If the game designer is able to stay actively involved throughout the life cycle of a product, then this person is usually the best person to have the final word. However, if the producer either is more experienced or will be the only one there during the entire course of making the product, then the producer is the better choice.

What Needs to Be Done

The subdocuments that make up a preliminary design include

- The design proposal
- The treatment: story, worlds, and character backgrounds
- Production design with example storyboards
- Interactive breakdown with flowcharts
- Technical issues document
- Physical production estimate(s)
- Approximate schedule
- Approximate budget
- If possible, a prototype, demo, or proof-of-concept

Who Does What?

To help you understand the subdocuments in the preliminary design documents and who works on them, look at Table 2-7.

The preliminary design documents are a lot of work and usually need to be done in 3 to 8 weeks. The timing of this work depends on the size of the project and the commitment by the publisher to have a thoughtful product approval phase. Some companies skip this phase or minimize this step, but most will require a significant amount of work to complete the preliminary design. This phase of predesign is a good time to establish a working team relationship between the principal players of a production so as to have a common vision for a product as well as a clearly defined leader.

TABLE 2-7

Document	Who Works on It	What It Is
Design proposal	Designer and producer	A revised version of the original six- to eight-page document described above
The treatment: story, worlds, and character backgrounds	Writer with assistance from designer and production designer	A three- to ten-page document featuring ■ The high concept ■ The dust jacket version of the story (i.e., what would appear on the back of the package). This is useful throughout the life of the product. ■ The short story—the story in enough detail to understand its full impact on the design ■ Descriptions of all the locations where the game takes place. Backstories (background) for the locations are sometimes helpful. ■ Descriptions of each character and, if appropriate, their backstories ■ Sample dialogue of some of the key characters
Production design	Production designer with assistance from writer and game designer	It is as many pages as necessary and includes example storyboards and "color boards" (i.e., a table of colors for each scene so you can see the color plan) for the following: ■ Each major world in the product ■ The opening and closing sequences ■ Transitions ■ Major character designs ■ Costume designs for major characters, if appropriate ■ Interface elements (often forgotten about until the production designer is gone) ■ Sound and music suggestions (while this doesn't normally go here in other phases of the design, it is the best place to include it for this phase) ⟹ Also include at least one completely rendered scene or animation, because many people cannot envision a scene simply from storyboards and color tables.

(Continued)

TABLE 2-7 *(Continued)*

Document	Who Works on It	What It Is
Interactive breakdown	Designer with producer and technical director	In addition to a flowchart of the sequence of events in the product, this document lays out all the interactive elements of the product. It should include

■ Style of navigation (movement from place to place in the game)

■ Starting up and quitting—what do the user and computer do?

■ Saving and loading—what information gets saved and/or loaded?

■ A list of modes of play if there are multiple modes (e.g., bringing up an Options screen is a separate mode from a game play mode)

■ Input commands for mouse, joystick, and/or keyboard for each mode

■ A list of how the computer responds to each type of input in each mode

■ When and how the computer thinks for itself (i. e., AI!)

■ If a puzzle-based game, a list of puzzles or at least an example puzzle with a count of how many others there will be

■ If there are opponents, a chart of opponents

■ A scoring or progress-tracking description

■ A list of special algorithms, tables, or other elements that will determine the outcome of events (note this is only a list, not the actual algorithms or tables themselves)

■ How the product deals with errors and messages

⇒ In addition, it is a good idea to include a sample interactive scene to demonstrate how the product will work. Sometimes this is referred to as a *walk-through,* which step by step shows a typical user's interactions and experience.

TABLE 2-7 *(Continued)*

Document	Who Works on It	What It Is
Technical issues	Technical director with game designer and producer	This document is really just two lists: ■ Technical issues that have to be addressed to determine whether it is possible to produce the product at all and, if so, to produce it in a reasonable time at a reasonable cost and so that it is robust technologically ■ Preliminary data structures list. This list lays out all the important data tables and structures so that in the process of creating the actual design document, everyone can appreciate the ramifications of adding features. Adding features without understanding the ramifications is often referred to as *feature creep.*
Physical production estimate(s)	Producer with game designer, production designer, and technical director	A series of lists that roughly capture the types of physical production necessary to create all the "content" elements of the product. These lists might include the number of ■ Screens of background art ■ Frames of partial screen animations ■ Minutes of voice-over (VO) ■ Minutes of full-motion video (FMV) ■ Lines and pages of dialogue ■ Actors for voice-over and FMV ■ Sets and costumes for FMV ■ Sound effects ■ Musical compositions (MIDI and digitized) ■ Other art elements (e.g., interface art, partial animations) ■ Pages of written text ■ Bytes of code ■ Bytes of save data per game and maximum number of saved games ■ Bytes of entire final product

(Continued)

TABLE 2-7 *(Continued)*

Document	Who Works on It	What It Is

Approximate schedule	Producer and technical director	Using the above list, estimate the personnel needed and periods of time for
		
		  ■ Creation of final design
		
		  ■ Preproduction
		
		  ■ Development to "alpha" stage
		
		  ■ Alpha to beta stage*
		
		  ■ Beta to final stage (includes testing)
		
		  ■ Creation of any add-ons
		
		  ■ Localization (i.e., translation to other languages)
		
		  ■ "Porting" to other platforms (i.e., converting for other systems)

Approximate budget	Producer and technical director	Using the physical production elements list and the approximate schedule, list an approximate budget. Don't forget to include overhead items such as software, rental equipment, licensed software engines, outside testing services, and, of course, lots of pizza, chips, and coffee.
Demos	Technical director	If possible, create a few small programs that actually demonstrate the viability of your innovations, the type of interactivity, the look and feel, or anything else that's better seen than read about.

*Alpha is a term that loosely means the point in the project when the product is entirely functional but still has some bugs, missing features, and placeholder art and audio. The beta stage is when the developer believes the product is finished and ready for testing. At this stage the only changes left to be made are small bug fixes and minor editorial changes to art and audio.

Once the preliminary design is complete, it's time for the publisher to decide whether to fund the project. This will require the repeated presentation of this material for such executives as the heads of production, marketing, licensing, quality assurance (or, in simpler terms, testing), customer service, sales, and distribution. Some companies even require a pitch to be made to the president and CEO and other executive officers of the company. In smallish companies this is often not a problem as these folks either are from the business itself or usually understand the business.

In larger companies, especially those whose primary business is not games, presenting the preliminary design documents (or "pitching") can be a frustrating experience. Often these executives don't understand the fickle nature of the business and how important it is to be flexible with design goals. In other words, they often have trouble with the language you are really speaking, the creative new uses for the interactive entertainment, the costs involved, the typically low profit margins, and who the customer is. If they are committed for the long haul and have interactive executives that they trust, your job will be a lot easier. If not, you may spend as much time teaching as you do pitching your idea. However, in the long run, it can be a valuable experience for all parties involved.

If your preliminary design is approved, this usually means that the project is funded and it's time to move on to the real task at hand—creating the design.

Game Design Document

The game design document is one of three documents that should be created before an interactive project goes into production:

- Game design—the designer's blueprint for the game
- Technical design—the technical director's plan for creating it
- Production plan—the producer's plan, schedule, and budget

Typically, the game designer is responsible for the game design document with the assistance of a writer, production designer, sound designer, and music designer. This is the focus of Part 3.

Later in the book, I touch briefly on the technical design, which is the domain of the technical director and the producer, and the production plan, which is most often the responsibility of the producer and director. However, it is in the best interest of the game designer to understand these other two documents and even participate in their creation.

PART

3

The Game
Design
Document

CHAPTER 5

The List of Elements and the Tools to Create Them

While the game design is the responsibility of the game designer, in a large project, many of these elements might be assigned to specialists. For example, if the game designer is a writer, then artists need to be hired to create the storyboards and character designs.

⇒As you look through the list of elements, you'll probably conclude that no one tool can handle all the various types of subdocuments within the game design. I think that's right. However, there are off-the-shelf tools that will work very well.

Elements of the Game Design Document

Here is the table of contents of a typical game design:

- High concept
- Genre
- Target platform (i.e., which computer or game system)
- Target audience(s)
- Story
- Characters
- World(s) and maps
- Interactivity
- Interface
- View-by-view descriptions
- Flowcharts, game logic, algorithms, and rules
- Scoring, winning, losing, saving, loading, starting, stopping, playing again
- Art and production design
- Storyboards and sample art
- Transition design
- Audio and music design
- Physical production elements list
- Competitive products
- Marketing ideas
- Follow-up products

See Table 3-1.

Tools for Building an Interactive Design

As there has yet to be a single tool created for designing an interactive game, it's best to plan on the use of a suite of tools. These tools are all easy

TABLE 3-1

Summary of the Game Design Document

Warning: Use of this summary alone may prove hazardous to your career. Cocktail party discussions of the design elements below of more than a few phrases may indicate a knowledge of buzzwords only. Please consult the details section before attempting to talk about game designs at any length. The following is intended for reference only.*

High concept	One-line description of the product
Genre	Category of game type
Target platform(s)	For which computer or game systems the game will be produced and in what order
Target audience(s)	Who will buy this game and why
Story	Dust jacket, short story, and complete story if game has one
Characters	Descriptions, visualizations, and scripts for all characters
World(s) and maps	Descriptions, visualizations, and maps for each world or level
Interactivity	An in-depth discussion of all elements of interactivity
Interface	A complete description of how the interface works in all modes
View-by-view descriptions	The heart and soul of the design. A database of each view (or scene) listing interactivity, multimedia assets, navigation, and transitions
Flowcharts, game logic, algorithms, and rules	The brains of the design. The underlying logic and algorithms that create the experience for the player
Scoring, winning, losing, saving, loading, starting, stopping, playing again	A reference section for the programming team for these key elements
Art and production design	The description of how the product will look and how this look will be created
Storyboards and sample art	A complete set of storyboards of views, removable objects, characters, and the interface. Some completed demonstration art is found here, too.
Transition design	Your instructions for the transitions in the game and a philosophical discussion of the importance of their implementation to the success of the product
Audio and music design	The description of how the product will sound and what the sound track will sound like. Also, a discussion of the techniques that need to be used
Physical production elements list	An exhaustive list of each and every multimedia element required to create the product and their associated filenames. Remember, include the code!
Competitive products	Know your competition…and list it here.

*Should you experience dizziness or nausea because others speak only in game design buzzwords, please immediately perform the "Dombrower maneuver." Apply the next sections directly to their eyes.

(Continued)

TABLE 3-1

Summary of the Game Design Document   *(Continued)*

Marketing ideas	Put down everything you can think of to market your product. It may be your only chance to communicate these ideas.
Follow-up products ⮞	⇒ The long-term value of a product is often gained through sequels and add-ons, both of which are very important to discuss here. Put down all your thoughts about what the products might be and how to create your game with the production of these secondary products in mind.

to use, but they usually offer little specific help with the task at hand. The typical tool suite consists of

- A word processor
- A database program
- A spreadsheet program
- A flowcharting program
- A prototyping program

There have been attempts to make tools that borrow features from some or all of the above programs in order to create a system for inputting all the game design elements. However, one of the great things about the games business is that it thrives on innovation. I'm not sure if it is possible to create a program for describing game designs without presupposing a set of limitations on the interactivity you're attempting to invent.

⇒ So until there is a universally accepted program specifically for designing interactive programs, it's better to use the above suite of tools with all their features than a single tool that has some features of each.

Word Processors

⇒ Choose a word processor either that is used by everyone you will deal with or, better, that saves files in universally understood formats.

The notion of a word processor format is foreign to many people. But if you are going to design games and you understand the principle of sharing data files between programs, then you can understand that each word processor saves data in its own specific format.

Many of the documents in your game design can be written on a word processor. One of the great advantages of using a word processor (or any of the other tools in the above suite) is that you can supply *files* to people instead of reams of paper.

⇒ However, when you are about to send a file to someone, find out the word processor and computer on which it will be used. If you are working on a Macintosh and plan to send someone a file to read on a PC, send a PC-formatted disk! PCs don't do a good job of reading Mac disks, but Macintoshes almost all read and write PC-formatted disks. And if you don't know the word processor in which people will read your documents, either save each file in several formats or save them all in Rich Text Format (RTF) that is almost universally understood by all word processors. To save a file in a specific format, look for the File Type section on the dialog after you choose Save As.

Database Programs

The database program you use should be the workhorse of the design tools suite. I believe the view-by-view description should be written in a database program since most of the production team will be using this database. Also, project management and assets tracking are often aided by database programs.

Use a simple database program, unless you are a very sophisticated database user. These are the most important issues in choosing a database program:

- The data should be *exportable* to other database programs.
- The data should be exportable to word processing programs.
- You should be able to easily search for records based on combinations of criteria for several fields.
- You should be able to reference and view images, sounds, and possibly other media.
- You should be able to have fields of variable length and repeats.
- The program should be able to automatically number and date records.
- The program should be able to prevent the entering of duplicate names or IDs (i.e., creating unique IDs).

Most of the stand-alone database programs support these features. It may be harder to find all these features in software suites that have a "lite" version of a database program.

If you are going to design a game and you don't know how to use a database, don't worry. Database programs are easy to use, and once you get the hang of using one, you'll find all sorts of other fun and practical uses for this new tool.

A Spreadsheet Program

Spreadsheets are great for making lists and keeping track of numbers (as in budgets). Many of the functions performed by a spreadsheet can be found in database programs. However, spreadsheet programs are optimized for speed in dealing with numbers and equations (like those found in budgets) and are generally easier to use when you want to create equations and do other manipulations on your lists and numbers (especially for budgets).

A Flowcharting Program

This type of program is useful for describing the basic flow of your product's interactivity. In quickly creating "maps" of your game's world, flowcharting programs can be of great help.

The real purpose of using a flowcharting program is to map out, in some detail, the flow of the game program and the individual algorithms. Flowcharting programs are especially good at diagramming the logic of an algorithm (as opposed to the arithmetic in the algorithm). Be careful, though. If you've taken my advice and are creating algorithms that are more arithmetically based and include lots of random and statistical behaviors, it will be difficult to describe such algorithms with a flowchart alone. The flowchart will notate the "flow" of the algorithm by listing the equations and the sources of information, but it will probably not include much more than the basic logic. Another way to look at it is that the less logic there is in your algorithm, the more boring the flowchart!

Typically, the technical team will create flowcharts by hand (on paper!) and won't look to the designer too often for help here. But if you *can* diagram some of the key design algorithms and the flow of the game using flowcharts, then do so. And if a flowcharting program helps you create these flowcharts, then buy one!

A Prototyping Program

A prototyping tool is a computer program that allows you to quickly mock up the general behavior of a real program. If it is created with a prototyping program, the performance of the prototype will be much slower, the rhythm will be less controllable, and many of the interactive elements will not be possible to see. What you will see, though, is a sense of the look and feel of your design. Prototyping tools can be great, but there's good news and bad news.

First, the good news. Prototyping programs allow you to include all the multimedia and basic logic you could ever want. They're very easy to use to prototype a product quickly, and they're easy to use by nonprogrammers and nontechnical people.

Now, the bad news. Many people have the mistaken idea that prototyping tools are good enough to create commercial games. Prototyping tools are often adequate for commercial multimedia products that don't include games (what I refer to as coffee table CD-ROMs). In fact, they can be great at nongame multimedia titles. But in terms of interactivity, great rhythm, naturalness, and other key game design principles, these prototyping tools are rarely good enough for true interactive entertainment. I say that prototyping tools lack the ability to build products because you could not have built more than one or two of the important breakthrough games in the history of the games business with a prototyping tool. To me, this means that these tools are not up to the task. Prototyping tools create a box of interactivity from which you can work. To create an innovative interactive experience, you need to get past this box.

⇒ In any case, I highly recommend using a prototyping tool to quickly test your basic design ideas. Be forewarned: You will probably not be able to create a prototype of the type of randomness, statistical behaviors, great transitions, and overall rhythm of the experience that you actually want in the final product. With improvements in prototyping tools, this may change; but I think it will be a while.

Testing Your Design

⇒ The first test for your design will likely be a *proof of concept* built with a prototyping tool. The second test should be a paper test. In a paper test, you play out your game on paper. Cut out images to represent objects and characters in the world, and create a map of the world you want to navigate. I find that it's best to put the storyboards up on a wall for this test.

⇒ Once you have all the paper tools, set aside a few hours and, with a few colleagues, talk and play your way through the game. Be sure to take notes; you'll discover all sorts of things you've missed.

Trust Yourself

After you've played through the prototype and the paper test of your design, lots of people (including you) will have lots of feedback and criticism. This is great, and you'll need to coordinate the adjustments to your design.

⇒ You will have to balance the feedback from executives who barely know the industry, first-time game testers who are overly enthusiastic, the production team who probably think everything is just great, the marketing staff who want to know how it will stack up against the competition, and others who simply want to get their two cents in.

⇒ Listen to it all. Consider it all. Some of the best suggestions I've ever received I've gotten from people with a specific agenda, a lack of experience, or simply too much enthusiasm. However, you also have to discard an enormous amount of feedback if you want to stay true to your vision.

⇒ Keep in mind that most people cannot look at a work-in-progress and see the promise of the complete product. Usually only the design and production team can really imagine what will be from what's being demonstrated.

My best advice is to do your homework and to trust yourself. If you've been playing and studying which games are successful and which aren't, you have a great frame of reference for evaluating the feedback and the game itself. Ultimately, the person responsible for the design must maintain a certain clarity of vision about what the product is intended to be.

6

The Game Design Document: Details

In the following chapter, I discuss the elements and issues involved in creating each portion of a game design. Just as a forewarning, typically the largest, most difficult, and most time-consuming sections of a design are the view-by-view descriptions, the physical production elements list, the flowcharts and algorithms, and the storyboards. It's good to keep in mind the scope of these sections when you schedule the time and effort needed to create the entire design.

The Game Design Document: High Concept

As discussed earlier, this is a very short statement of what the game or product is. The goal is to achieve this in one short sentence. If it's a truly innovative product, it may take as many as two or three sentences. But make it no longer.

Let this evolve. Quickly create two or three versions, and let them percolate on the front page of your design while you're writing the rest. You'll pick a favorite soon enough. Also try your high-concept ideas out on friends and colleagues. You'll also find that some ideas actually *sound* much better than others. Since this is part of the purpose of the high concept, don't ignore the impact of a great-sounding version.

⇒The high concept is used in many places and, if you write it well, can almost become a subtitle for your product. It will be used by marketing people to quickly position the product and by company executives when answering questions about product lines. Also, a good high concept gets used for press releases, print ads, and very likely on the packaging.

Examples

For Return to Zork (RTZ), we tossed around a few ideas along the following lines:

> "Evil waits...underground."
> "Return to the Great Underground Empire."
> "Zork. With Pictures."

We wanted to communicate many things. We knew that the name *Zork* in the title was already working for us, as Zork has had a huge following since the late 1970s. So we felt we didn't need to repeat the name in the high concept. We wanted to be clear that this was a graphic adventure, but we were pretty sure that people would figure that out. It was important to emphasize the size and scope of this game. Some other adventure products of the time weren't very large. Others, such as The 7th Guest and Myst, created such large multimedia worlds as to be considered the beginning of the next generation of graphic adventures. Even though *evil* was part of the story of RTZ, it wasn't necessarily how we wanted to position this title, because it also has a pretty offbeat sense of humor. Finally, to attempt to intrigue those who hadn't heard of Zork, we wanted to give something of the unusual nature of the world of Zork, which is that it mainly consists of the Great Underground Empire. So we came up with

> "An epic adventure in the Great Underground Empire."

This worked so well that it was used in all the press releases, advertisements, and packaging.

A Home Run Concept

With Earl Weaver Baseball (EWB), the product managers and marketing folks at Electronic Arts (EA) worked the high concept for the product. As with RTZ, baseball fans know who Earl Weaver is (at the time, as the manager of the Baltimore Orioles, Earl Weaver, was the most winning manager in modern baseball) and the sort of things he is known for: great strategy, a great personality, and arguing with umpires. So we didn't need to include him in the high concept line. While Weaver is known for his many great one-line philosophies about the game (e.g., "Praised be the three-run homer"), he never created comical sayings as did Yogi Berra (who said, among other things, "It ain't over 'til it's over"). So they wanted the high concept to sound as if Weaver said it himself. Finally, they wanted to give the impression that this was the be-all and end-all of computer baseball designs.

They finally adopted and used

> "Computer baseball like it oughta be."

Again, it ended up in the ads, press releases, and packaging.

Mis-Conceptions

The Muppet CD-ROM: Muppets Inside took a long time to come up with a high concept that everyone was happy with. It took so long, in fact, that it wasn't completely evolved until the packaging was ready for manufacturing. For this product, we wanted to emphasize that the product was a game, that the game was somewhat like an adventure, that it was for adults as well as children, and that it was full of typical Muppet humor. To make a long story short, this is what we ended up with:

> "A misadventure game for ages 99 and under."

⇒I strongly feel that the high concept, short as it may be, is a very important decision for the designer to be involved in. In all the above examples, it took many months to come up with the final version, and in each case it was worth it. It helps sell not only the product to the publisher and to the marketing and sales team, but also the game to the press and to consumers. And no one knows the entire product as well as the game designer, and this is why, if at all possible, the designer should be the driving force behind the evolution of the final high concept.

Genre

Unlike the high concept, this step won't take long to write or require too much thought. My only issue with the description of the game genre is accuracy. Remember that many people with a variety of backgrounds will be reading this part of the document (as it's the short overview part). Some of these people will really know the business and will expect you to use the correct jargon here. However, some people may only have a marginal background in games and will rely on their knowledge of other media such as film or theater in order to interpret what you're saying.

⇒I prefer to use the correct jargon and, if possible, provide a few very quick examples of other products of the same genre.

The action-adventure genre

One of the more common miscommunications between people in the games business and people who don't know it inside out is the action adventure genre. This genre is well defined for film, TV, even books. However, adventure games as a specific genre have a long tradition (going back to the mainframe days of games like Adventure and Zork). Action games also have a long tradition, dating back to the first stand-up arcade games and home video game systems. These are very different types of game genres, each with its own specific set of rules, interfaces, paradigms, and audiences.

⇒In my mind, there is no pure actual action adventure genre in the games business; it is a hybrid genre!

Another of these mix-ups arises with *adventure role playing*. To me, these are two different genres. Role-playing games (RPGs or FRPs if you like to include fantasy as an element) often include some of the puzzlelike gaming elements of adventure games but usually have many more elements as well. Adventure games rarely, if ever, include the more fundamental RPG design elements such as creating characters and character attributes, rolling dice, and so on. The RPG audience is a loyal audience and will often play adventure games. For whatever reason, the opposite is not true. The adventure game is a more accessible computer game format, and many people who play few other types of games play one adventure game after another.

So the point is, get the genres right. The sales and marketing people, producers, technical directors, programmers, and anyone else who's a dyed-in-the-wool gamer will notice and appreciate this. For the others, as I said, provide examples:

A graphic adventure with some sim elements:
"It's like The Neverhood with a little of SimCity 2000 thrown in."

A football sports sim with a flight simulator and shooter:
"It's like Madden Football crossed with Rebel Assault."

These may seem like absurd examples, but they can help everyone understand exactly what genre the product will be in the minds of the consumers.

Target Platform

By the time your product gets the green light, everyone should know what platform you're designing for. However, it is good to provide as much detail here as possible for the primary, secondary, and any other follow-up platforms. If nothing else, should the product be more than a year in the making, it's great to have an official record of the platform everyone agreed on. This is just in case someone starts to wonder why certain features are not possible, or why you may have to go over the budget and schedule to put in a new feature to deal with a technology that wasn't planned for in the original design. Believe me, this happens. Another benefit of providing details here is that it serves as a reference and reminder to the technical design team of the minimum configuration platform you intend to support. Finally, give a rough estimate of when the secondary and follow-up platform versions of the product will be completed.

Provide the following details here for each platform:
For video games:

- Base system name (e.g., Sony Playstation)

- Delivery medium (for example, 1 CD-ROM, 64K* cartridge or "cart")

- Any special minimum system requirements (e.g., extra flash RAM on the cartridge, special controllers)

- Any special optional equipment the product will support (e.g., multi-player controllers, on-line connections)

For computer games:

- Type of computer (e.g., PC-compatible, Macintosh)

- Delivery media (e.g., number of CD-ROMs, floppy disks, size of download from on-line service)

- Minimum system(s) supported (for example, 486 16-color Multimedia, Performa)

- Minimum graphics required (for example, 8-bit graphics—usually not an issue on Macs)

- Minimum system speed (for example, 66 MHz)

- Minimum system memory required (for example, 16 MB*)

- Minimum hard drive space required (e.g., none, 100K*, 45 MB*)

- Other minimum system requirements (e.g., math co-processor, mouse, joystick, modem)

- Optional equipment supported (e.g., modem, printer, joystick, 17-inch monitors, second monitors)

- Recommended system—minimum system requirements that provide optimal game performance

---

* ⇒ Note that when you specify data sizes with either KB or MB, it is a good idea to state somewhere whether you are measuring data in *bits* or *bytes*. For some reason, since the days of the 8-bit Nintendo, video game systems have specified cartridge size in kilobits (Kbits or KB) which is 8 times larger than the number of bytes (probably because it looks more impressive). This can mean that in the video game world, MB stands for megabits, or 1,000,000 bits. Almost always in the computer world, KB and MB refer to byte counts. And often in the discussion of baud rates for modem data transfers, data transfer is measured in bits per second instead of bytes per second!

Target Audience(s)

As with platforms, it is a good idea to write a clear explanation of the target audience both for publisher's executives and for your production team's reference. There isn't too much need for detail here, but I recommend making a thoughtful list of secondary audiences (including foreign markets) as a reference for the product managers and marketing and sales and distribution staff.

Story

⇒If you are creating a relatively large and complex project that involves a story of any sort, I recommend writing three sections within the story portion of the design document:

- Dust jacket story
- Short story
- Complete story

Each of these three versions will be useful to have around throughout the course of design, production, marketing, public relations, packaging, and sales.

If you are creating a smaller product or one with little or no story, use your best judgment as to how to simplify, shorten, combine elements, or even eliminate this section. Also, if you are not a professional writer, have one create all three subdocuments for you.

The *dust jacket story* is a version of the story, in only a few paragraphs, that sums up the tone, style, and scope without giving away any of the good twists or the ending. This is just like the text you'd find on the back or inside flaps of a book cover (hence the name *dust jacket*), on the back of a videotape, or, I hope, on the back of your product's package once it's on the shelves.

⇒It's worthwhile to create this version of the story early in the process, as it is second only to the high concept in use for public relations, marketing, sales, distribution, and advertising. If you don't have this written as part of the design, someone from each of the aforementioned groups will write his or her own (and may not share!). I always try to get the dust jacket story done early in the process and distributed so everyone is literally on the same page. It helps with focus for the production and marketing of the product, and if the product will take a while to produce, it can be a great "teaser" to provide at trade shows.

The *short story* is in many ways the least used of the three story versions. However, I've found it useful in some companies to have a short story written that's about three to eight pages long for the creative executives who won't be able to spend a lot of time familiarizing themselves with the entire product. It's also good for other members of the design and production team, and when you're ready for the press to preview the game, it can come in quite handy.

The *complete story* is, for many products, the key ingredient to complete the design (assuming that your product intends to tell or follow a story). If not, the short story or even the dust jacket story may be enough.

The production designer, technical director, director, producer, audio designer, composer, and audio and video producers all need to know the story in as much detail as possible. Of course, so does the game designer (in case the writer and designer aren't the same person). In working out the details of the complete story, the game designer and writer have to integrate the interactivity with the story. If not, you'll end up with either a great story with bits of interactivity irrelevantly sprinkled on top or a great game with only telltale signs of a story.

Characters

First, let me say this: If you aren't a writer and you can get one on your design team, have the writer create this section.

And second: If you aren't a visual designer and you can get one on your team, let her or him create the look of your characters. Many interactive products have characters in them, and the quality and presentation of these characters are important to the quality and presentation of the products. In other words, the better the characters, the better the products. This is especially true if you want the user to interact extensively with these characters.

A well-written character description with a well-designed visual image can go a long way in helping to inspire dialogue, casting performers, directing performers, creating costumes, and/or drawing and rendering these characters. And, most importantly for interactivity, if the character is well written, complex, and interesting, it can improve the quality of the character's behaviors in the game.

Given all that, Table 3-2 lists what goes into this section of the design document for each character in the world.

TABLE 3-2

Name or ID	Even if this character is never referred to by name by the players or the nonplayer characters (NPCs), the design and production teams, in particular the programmers, need to be able to identify each character. In some games, such as large RPGs where they either create NPCs on the fly or have a vast number of NPCs in the world, sometimes just an ID number is required.
One-sentence description	Just as with the high concept, this is a useful tool for quickly identifying the gist of a character. Include sex, age, role in the game or story, and a few major identifying attributes (physical behavior, etc.).
	With large numbers of characters in a world, this may be broken down into a table entry for each minor character and may be all that is ever described about the character.
Brief (one to two paragraphs) description	For characters that are seen a lot, either through the interactivity or through the storytelling elements of the product, write a good extended description.
	I find that the information provided up to here is usually enough to get the visual character designer started.
Visual design	A drawing or series of annotated drawings that define the look of a character and the character's costumes.
	While it is best to have at least some of these in color, it is sometimes more efficient to get black-and-white sketches accompanied by example pictures from magazines, comic books, or other similar resources.
⇒	⇒Be sure the sketches show a number of different poses (so you can see how the character moves) as well as a variety of different points of view of the character.
⇒	⇒Also, it is important that all the character's images be drawn to the same scale. In this way, you are also creating the first resources for a style guide should you need one for subsequent products and support materials.
Backstory (if your product requires it)	If a character is going to be extensively involved in the story and/or the interactivity, there will no doubt be some sort of dialogue to write for the character to be performed as VO (voice-over), FMV (full-motion video), or on-screen text (OST). Also, it is probably desirable for this character to have a range of appropriate and realistic behaviors in response to the player, the NPCs, the interactivity, and the story.
	It will help everyone in creating the dialogue and the behaviors if there is a back story to this character. Any competent writer will know about this and will probably do this without being specifically asked. If, for some reason, a writer cannot be part of the team, there are any number of books in which to look for help.

(Continued)

TABLE 3-2 *(Continued)*

Attributes (if required)	Some products require that each character be endowed with a set of attributes and, possibly, a rating for each attribute.
	This is a tried-and-true method for creating NPCs very quickly and efficiently (e.g., in real time or for sending down a modem line) and for allowing algorithmic behaviors to be programmed for all NPCs at once, as opposed to creating behaviors for each and every NPC.
	Of course, some special characters will have unique or specific behaviors and responses, but in highly populated worlds, this isn't practical for the majority of the characters. I think this is one of the most important design features that can be used in creating future interactive storytelling games.
	Until now, most games that use attributes focus on physical (or metaphysical) attributes for tracking the abilities and general well-being of a character, e.g., health, strength, wisdom, magical ability, dexterity, courage, friendliness, battle experience.
	I've always imagined extending this design metaphor to things such as command of language, education, mood, feelings about other characters (and the user), style of speaking, etc. Some designers have been working with these ideas over the years, but these games haven't quite broken into the mainstream consciousness of publishers, designers, and game players yet.
Behaviors (if required)	Similar to attributes, this is a list of behaviors that each character might exhibit and when. You can think of this as a bunch of triggerable behaviors. In more sophisticated designs, the behaviors are tied directly to the attributes. For example, an NPC who has accumulated great strength and courage might begin to exhibit behaviors that put her or him in great physical danger on a regular basis. This same character, before attaining this level of these two attributes, wouldn't exhibit this behavior.
	As you can see, this can be, for the more sophisticated designer, more of an algorithmic description than a logical one.
	Unlike attributes, where every NPC shares the same attributes which are "rated" at different levels (including 0 or none!), behaviors can come and go from a character. This is a subtle distinction but can be a powerful feature in the future of game design.
	You could add behaviors to your world as you would add characters. When it comes time for each character to respond to something, that program could look at the list of behaviors and, by examining the algorithm for the cause of the behavior (a combination of attribute ratings for the character and actions going on in the world), choose a behavior.
Dialogue (VO, FMV, OST)	Depending on the overall design of your product, this dialogue could go in this section, in the view-by-view section, or, as is often the case, in a separate section.
‖▶	⇒Unfortunately, sometimes due to a lack of foresight, parts of the dialogue show up in more than one section in a design document! Try to avoid this if at all possible.

TABLE 3-2   *(Continued)*

Dialogue (VO, FMV, OST) (Cont.)	When you are preparing to write this dialogue (or preparing the writer to do so), keep in mind a few things:

If it's performed, it will undoubtedly change from the exact text during recording; and if it's written, you will probably make last-minute changes and additions to "tweak" the game in the final stages. This means that there will be changes from the dialogue as it appears in the design documents. Keep your design documents up to date with each dialogue change, as you will need this information to accurately and efficiently localize the product for different languages.

⇒Get some dialogue written for each and every character to be performed (either in VO or FMV) before you finish all the dialogue. Creating these "sides" will help you start on the casting before the entire, generally huge script is written.

Be sure the writer is aware of certain interactive elements that can affect details of what is written. For example, if the game is from a first-person point of view, it's generally a good idea to address the user in a gender-neutral way. This specific example requires a surprising amount of vigilance. As another example, be sure that hints are given only on purpose *and* only within the normal behavior of the character.

Be sure the writer is aware that the user will do the same thing over and over and that variations in behavior and responses create a more natural and less annoying experience. Having a character say, "Oh, it's you again" after the third visit is a lot better than having him or her say, "Hello stranger, welcome to my inn" each time the player enters (hopefully the inn).

Try to have the writer include some context for the actors. Often actors are required to read the same or similar dialogue over again for interactivity's sake.

⇒Finally, try to keep everything as short as possible. Remember, this is an interactive product you're designing, and the user wants to interact, not watch.

Vocabulary of motion	For actors and animated characters alike, include a list of moves that each character will perform. This is a surprising exercise and will often force you to change your design or the technical design to accommodate the many things you want each character to do.

For example, assume you want each of 10 characters to have 10 moves of 10 seconds each, and you're planning to animate them at one-quarter screen at 30 frames per second. This means you'll require 30,000 frames of animation of one-quarter screen each. In the simplest terms, one-quarter screen of a standard high-resolution 8-bit PC game requires a maximum of 76,800 bytes (1 byte per pixel). The total number of bytes for this relatively small amount of animation is 2.3 gigabytes of data! (This is why the technology director is so crucial to the design process.)

Experienced designers can really achieve a lot of variety with very small vocabularies of motion. This can also be one of your most cost-effective uses of actors in front of a camera.

World(s) and Maps

⇒Before you start to write this section, review the first two rules of writing the characters section. They apply here, too:

1. If you aren't a writer and you can get one on your design team, have the writer create this section.

2. ⇒If you aren't a visual designer and you can get one on your team, let her or him create the look of your worlds.

Worlds is a term that is used in the interactive design community to designate all the environments in which the game and its story take place. The user may never see every part of this world, but that doesn't mean that you don't have to describe every part. As with characters, the more background, depth, and completeness with which you describe the worlds of your game, the higher-quality the experience for the user and the better odds you have of having the worlds created by the production team to your satisfaction.

It's often useful to divide the worlds in a game almost as if they were characters. Each environment can be designated a world so that, from both the visual and the technical design points of view, it can be created as a unique experience from all the other worlds. The simplest examples come from platform games (and many other types of action games) where the user moves through the game in levels. Each level is often a different world with special rules, different landscapes, different obstacles, different creatures, different attributes, and different behaviors.

This should lead you to the following conclusion: Describing a world is remarkably similar to describing a character (see above). Table 3-3 lists all the elements to describe for each world.

One unique element of the worlds subdocument is the need to draw maps. The maps should be drawn by the game designer while the world descriptions are being created. Maps serve the following purposes:

■ A reference for the writer and production designer (or art director) so that there is continuity between the game designer's map of a world and the way in which the world looks and behaves

■ A reference for the technical designer and programmers for building the navigation through the worlds

■ A tool for indicating general interactivity (e.g., you could indicate where certain people, obstacles, helping items, or objects are located)

- A tool for testing the navigation of the worlds once the game is in any way playable
- A tool for charting the progress of the production of the product
- Often a tool for users that appears either in the documentation of the product, in an on-line Help area, or in the product itself

Producers, including myself, seem to have an obsession with posting maps of the worlds of a game on a wall somewhere while the product is being designed and produced. We use these to get a bird's-eye view of the interactivity, to be able to "walk through" the entire product, and to tick off parts of each world as they go through various stages of production.

TABLE 3-3

Name or ID	As with characters, even if the player never sees the name of this world, the production team needs to have a name for it. While it may seem like a good solution to call it something like "world 12a," it's not a very descriptive name. "The Ice World" is something everyone could remember. And, surprisingly enough, these "working names" often end up being used by players when they discuss your product in news groups on the Internet.
One-sentence description	List the role of the world and a few major attributes—in other words, the high concept of this world. This could also be a table or list of attributes and behaviors that each world possesses, if these aren't story-based worlds.
Brief (one to two paragraphs) description	For story-based games, provide more details for the visual designer.
Visual design	A drawing or series of annotated drawings that define the look of the world. Again, try to provide some sense of the colors found in this world.
Backstory (if your product requires)	If there is a history for this world, put it here. This is very useful for the writer when laying out the story and creating the dialogue for the characters.
Rules	List any rules specific to this world. For example, is gravity different, does your character only have three lives in this level, what are the maximum points, how is time calculated, how long does it take to grow a plant, or how many outs are in an inning?

Often the rules and attributes (see below) can be listed together. |
| Attributes (if required) | Depending on the type of game you're designing, you may or may not have to create this section. If each world in your game has specific attributes, especially if they are quantifiable, list them here, e.g., how hot or cold, how many opponents, how many "power-ups," how many minutes you have to traverse it.

There is a lot to be done in terms of using this design feature to further the sophistication in the game designs of the future. Assigning attributes to worlds has, so far, been mostly relegated to simulators and RPGs. Folding these concepts into other kinds of games brings a level of design and computing power to the experience that we have yet to see. |

(*Continued*)

TABLE 3-3　*(Continued)*

Behaviors (if required)	A list of behaviors of the world. Another way to look at this is as a list of responses of the world. For example, if you do the right rain dance, does it rain? If you light something on fire, does it burn down? And does it cause other things to burn, too?
	There are more subtle behaviors that a world can have, too. For example, perhaps the longer you stay in a world, the more erosion affects the stability of the surfaces you're walking and climbing on. Or if you behave in an aggressive fashion, the world creates new enemies that are particularly well suited to combat your style. In this way, the world can "protect" itself. But it requires the ability to create characters in real time with certain attributes and behaviors (see these sections in the character descriptions above).
Environmental aspects	List the types of animations, sound effects, transitions, and random events that bring this world to life.
	Note that the specific list of individual elements is often located elsewhere. However, this gives the audio and visual designers a sense of what has to be created and the technical designer a sense of how these creations are to be used.
Map	Each world needs a map.

Interactivity

Although interactivity is one of the most important parts of the design document to write, it is also one of the most difficult to explain. Your goals in writing this section are to

- Explain in general terms what the user does
- List all the modes of interaction
- List all the game "states"
- List all commands and options the user has in each state in each mode and the computer's responses

The technique for listing this information succinctly varies widely between designers and types of products. In any case, communicate what the user does and the rhythm of the game play. For example, in an adventure game, users are typically navigating (or exploring) the world at their own pace, collecting objects and information. Users consider the information and objects they've collected in order to solve puzzles which unlock the story and achieve their goal. In a trough game, users are navigating through tunnels at high speeds while fighting, choosing weapons, and using these weapons on adversaries.

In a sim, users lay out the physical components of a world, set the goals and parameters for the world, tinker with the elements (including population) of the world, and then sit back and watch the fruits of their labors. Then the users continue by alternating phases of building and tinkering with watching and waiting.

Mode-ality

The word *mode* in software refers to the current scope of the interface. When you are in one mode of interactivity, the interface can support only a limited set of actions. To perform other actions, you must switch modes. For example, in a navigation mode, all you can do with the keyboard and joystick is to move from place to place and to indicate that you want to switch to another mode. When you switch to conversation mode, the interface only lets you talk and listen.

If you use a computer at all, you've experienced *dialog* boxes (e.g., "Save this file as...") that won't let you past unless you click on OK or Cancel. These are *modal* dialogs because the entire interface is restricted to dealing with the dialog box.

⇒My rule of thumb for games is this: Create as few modes as possible.

⇒Try to list all the possible modes of operation of your game. Even the most elegant designs usually have more than one mode (even if they subtly hide the changes between modes). Be sure to indicate here how the user knows which mode the game is currently in. There's nothing worse than changing modes and not making this obvious to the user. In this way, the user at least has a fighting chance of understanding that the interface has changed.

A word of caution: If you are designing a computer game, don't forget that launching the product from the operating system is, more or less, a mode.

Table 3-4 is a complete list of modes you can use as a starting place.

The State of the Game

Partially related to the different modes of interactivity are the various states of your game. If the designer lists these early in the process, absolutely everyone benefits.

One of the principal ideas behind the implementation of most game designs is the computer's ability to remember and keep track of the program's game states. There is even the programming notion of a *state engine*

TABLE 3-4

Example Mode	What Can Be Done in this Mode
Launch	Start the game from the operating system.
Opening sequence	If you haven't considered giving the user the chance to interact here, do so!
First-time-only menu	Some products do this once and then never again. This is a good idea.
Starting or main menu	Some products need this, but many don't. Try to avoid this.
Options menu	This is for system settings, game play preferences, etc.
Navigation	This is for moving from place to place within or between worlds. Often distinct from all other actions found in other game play modes.
User's player character actions	Sometimes this is a distinct mode from navigation (e.g., in third-person point-of-view games). This includes things like running, jumping, turning, fighting, kicking, throwing, talking, and other moves and behaviors.
Selecting objects	The user often wants to point at or otherwise select an object. Some games allow several options within this seemingly simple task, such as asking about, identifying, picking up, moving, changing the state of (such as in a dial), or otherwise using a selected object. Remember, not all games are of the point-and-click type; you may have to do this through verbal or typed commands!
Using objects	This is for looking at, choosing, and using objects in the world or in the user's or an NPC's possession. This includes manipulating controls in the computer world such as instrument panels, doorknobs, combination locks, and baseball bats.
Interacting with other characters	Talking, exchanging objects, looking at, and fighting are typical character-to-character interaction modes.
Manipulating parameter lists	Many games allow users to change the settings and parameters of their on-screen personas, the world, or their team. Changing your lineup, adjusting the percentage of taxes spent on schools, and setting your aviator to look like a cyclops are all examples of what you might do in this mode.
Strategy	Some games have a strategy mode to think about and set up performance and strategic parameters.
Observation	This is for games that allow you to observe the results of your strategic planning. Often there isn't a lot, if any, interaction in this mode.
View selection	This allows the user to change points of view and sometimes adjust virtual cameras. Also, this mode gives the user a choice of styles of view.
Replay	Some games have a replay mode that gives the user the chance to watch a sequence of events again and again. Freeze-frame advance, variable speed, changes of view, and skipping the ending are often features of this mode.
Saving and loading	Specify a saved game and load in a saved game.
⫸ Quitting, pausing, continuing, and	⇒In these modes you are typically asking users, "Are you sure?" when they probably are! Make these as painless as possible.

which gives you some idea of the amount of thought that computer scientists put into the use of states.

Put another way, a game state is the set of conditions that at each moment in time dictates the behavior of the computer program. The state *can dictate* the mode of play, the level of difficulty, the next sequence of events, the artificial intelligence of the game, the behavior of a character, interface options available to the user, and so on.

The conditions that define a game state are often quite complex and can be set by any combination of the user's actions, the user's choice of settings and preferences, the history of what the player has done so far, the rules of the world, the rules of the game, random acts (not only of kindness, but also of the environment, NPCs, etc.), the actions of other users (in multiplayer games), the score, etc. One specially named state is *initial conditions*. This state is a set of conditions at the beginning of a play, a level, or even an entire game. Keeping track of the initial conditions allows you to put the user back to a known state over and over to try and try again.

A complete list of states can be quite lengthy. Usually, the technical designer will create an exhaustive list for your product. If not, this is left to the programmers to figure out during production. It's up to you and the technical designer to decide which states you want to specify and which to leave up to the programming team.

Table 3-5 might give you some idea of the kinds of states to include and some that you might not immediately consider.

List of All Commands and Options in Each Mode

This is a crucial list for the programmers, manual writers, and testers as well. I find this is best done in tabular format. For each mode, include every command, the input for that command, modifiers for the input (if any), and shortcut keys.

⇒When you design the keystrokes, button presses, mouse movements, and other input commands, try to develop a logical relationship between the commands and the input device. If you don't have to conform to a genre's standard input conventions, do everything you can to minimize button and key presses, pull-down menus, and excessive hand-and-eye movement.

One last word of advice before you make your list: Always list the commands in order of frequency of use by the user. Even though this may

TABLE 3-5

Example State	What It Means
Not installed	The user must install the game before doing anything else.
Game start-up for first-time player	The user has never played or, quite possibly, not yet set up the game (though this should usually be done during installation). Often this state indicates that the user should be forced to watch some introduction or some such thing. Be careful of forcing the user to do anything! It's usually not too popular.
⟱▶ Start-up for repeat player	⇒An often-ignored state. If users have played already, there should be some way to acknowledge this and to allow them to very quickly get back to where they were in the game. Remember, this is the state most players (including reviewers) play in.
Quitting in midgame	You'll probably recognize this state's typical behavior as "Are you sure?" or "Do you want to save your game first?"
Quitting the game at a logical ending place	This should be a distinct state from quitting midgame.
Game over	The user loses. Don't further penalize the user by forcing him or her back into the start-up for repeat player state. Figure out a way to get users back to playing as quickly as possible (I just played a game that, after I failed to finish a level, forced me to wait while it loaded in a title screen. The reloading of the title screen forced the game *to reload the same level* before I could continue. This took an additional 2 to 3 minutes between rounds! Needless to say, I played fewer rounds than I otherwise would have.)
The user has seen this FMV clip	This is a state well worth keeping track of. If the user needs to see a clip at least once all the way through for some important piece of information, figure out a way to remember that. Whenever the game calls for the clip again, allow the user to skip it subsequent times, skip it for the user, or substitute another multimedia element. There's nothing worse than being forced to watch a 3- to 10-second clip every time you simply want to get to the top of the stairs.
The user is down to the last life, out, minute, etc.	This is an example state where you can modify the behavior of the NPCs, the world, or even the rules to accommodate a user who's very close to the end of something important (such as game over).
The user is trying the same thing for the umpteenth time	This is another example state where you can modify the game or provide hints to help the user along. Some purists don't like this, and frankly, this is only practical in certain types of games. However, it can be a great way to get the user over a difficult hump and to keep her or him from getting overly frustrated.
Game not saved	This is also good to know if the user is about to embark on a disastrous course of action. You can take advantage of this state by prompting the user to save the game before doing this silly thing, saving the game for the user (into a "revert to last game" file), or providing an undo function.
Game saved	It's saved—allow the user to proceed with impunity.

TABLE 3-5 *(Continued)*

Example State	What It Means
Object X in user's possession	This is good to know for the state of the user's inventory. Also, it can help identify the state of the graphical scene where the object was once a part of the on-screen imagery.
Information Y imparted to user	This is often used to inform the game that the user can say or do something new based on this information. It can also affect the behavior of the NPCs and the world.
The various attribute "ratings" of NPC's, player character, and world	As each attribute for each character and the world adjusts (e.g., the President's health has sunk to a 2 on a scale of 0 to 10 with 10 being perfect health and 0 being dead), the state of the game changes. While this can be among the most complex elements of figuring out the current game state, it is among the most powerful ways to implement a game state.
The user chose the joystick as input device	The user's choice of input device (and other preferences) should impact the interface.
It's user's birthday	Start the game with some celebratory mention (don't sing "Happy Birthday to You" without permission—it's copyrighted!). This idea is really here to inspire you to think of other states that might be unique to your product.
The user unlocked this door	Many, if not all, puzzles are ultimately about unlocking some sort of door (even if it's a metaphorical door). Some games make you unlock the door each time you come to it. Others remember both the state of the puzzle (i.e., that you can unlock the door) and the state of the door, so you don't have to unlock it again.
The disk is full and other error messages	Surprisingly enough, many game designers and producers either don't think this is their responsibility or they don't think about this at all. This means that errors go unreported, the operating system has to interrupt your game to alert the user (and sometimes shut down your game), or the programmers have to improvise a solution. In my opinion, none of these is acceptable. The designer should consider how to deal with errors in the game (as there will be), and the technical director should consult with the game designer to create a system for dealing with errors that works within the context of the product.

not seem logical at first, it is the best way I know (before actually testing a product) to ensure that the fewest keystrokes are required for the most frequent activities. It always surprises me when something I do all the time requires more than one keystroke or the use of a Shift or Alt key while other commands which I hardly ever use are assigned to single keystrokes. Take your best guess as to which commands real users will use most, then be flexible enough (including warning the production team and executives that you're going to do this) to change things based on actual testing experience.

Table 3-6 is an example of what a partial input command table might look like.

Although this isn't exactly how the pitching worked on EWB, it does give you an idea about how to lay out a command table. As you can see,

TABLE 3-6

Mode	Command	User Input	Modifier	State	Result
Only list each mode once	List each command for the current mode. If there are multiple inputs to generate this command, don't repeat the command.	List each input that will trigger the command.	If an input is modified by, e.g., the Shift or Alt key or by holding down a second button. List each on a separate line.	If the state of the game can alter the result, be sure to list each state on a separate line.	List the result for the combination of all the elements to the left.
For example:					
Pitcher's ready to pitch.	Select type of pitch: fastball	Numeric keypad—5; press and release left mouse button without moving the mouse.	None	No runners on base	Pitch a fastball.
				Runners on base	Come to set position, then pitch fastball.
			Shift	No runners	Pitch fastball but just out of strike zone.
				Runners on base	Pitchout.
	Select type of pitch: knuckleball	Numeric keypad—8; click and drag mouse straight up, and then release button.	None	No runners on base	Pitch a knuckleball.

this can be a very large table. Again, if you don't do this for each command in each mode, you give up the chance for a consistent, easy-to-understand program interface. Not making a complete list can also create conditions for the 3 A.M. Green Syndrome.

⇒Be sure to include operating system commands for starting up the game. For example, in both the Windows and Macintosh worlds, it is possible to assign information to a saved game so that the saved-game file itself can be double-clicked or dragged onto the program icon. ⇒If the user does double-click on the saved-file icon, your program should go directly to where the user left off in the saved game. There is no reason to force the user to go through the normal start-up of the game in this case. Yet, most games do this.

Even in the DOS days this was possible. With some games, if you typed in the name of a saved game on the DOS command line after the name of the product, the game would resume wherever you left off.

⇒And remember to include commands for switching between modes and interrupting current activities. If you do forget, due to circumstances that will be out of your control, you're likely to force the user to wait. Sometimes users will be waiting for some unknown reason before they have an opportunity to skip ahead to do the thing they want to do. There is rarely a reason to force a user to wait for the completion of a computer task. It is very easy to program the computer to read the keyboard and mouse and to look for the "interrupt this task" input from the user.

Interface

Even though you have described each and every command in the inter-activity section, there are still a few items worth discussing in the interface section. Sometimes this section is integrated into the interactivity section, but I prefer them to be separate. In this section, a general philosophy about the interface should be stated, a graphic and audio design for the interface should be presented, interface rules should be listed, and any technological issues should be discussed.

⇒Many designers forget to consult with their production designers or art directors about interface design, and that's a big mistake. All today's game machines and computers can alter their on-screen appearance at every conceivable level including cursors, wait graphics, and dialog.

⇒So, after you state your philosophy underlying your choice of command interfaces, show drawings of all the interface elements in as much color as you can (or cross-reference to the art and production design section). Be sure to consult with your technical director so the artist understands the size and color restrictions. This includes visual design for

- Cursors
- Wait cursor or icon (for a brief wait while the computer thinks or acts)
- Disk access cursors or icons (for when a disk, hard drive, or CD-ROM is being accessed)
- Download cursors (to indicate that an on-line download/upload is in progress; not typical for unknown reasons)
- Alerts and dialogs (for error messages)
- Progress dialogs and bars
- Any menus
- Pop-up control panels
- Game status display (e.g., fuel level, position in the world, wisdom attribute of an NPC)
- User status display (e.g., score, lives left, timers, system preferences)
- Desktop icon for the game
- Desktop icons for saved games and other game file types

Creating a visual design for your interface elements is one of those details that often is overlooked but should not be as it helps keep the user immersed in the experience. Certainly The 7th Guest did a great job with the animated skeleton hand leading the user through the house. I'm proud to say that, thanks to a suggestion by Bing Gordon at EA, as early as 1985 we put an image of Earl Weaver on the screen for the wait cursor whenever Earl's artificial intelligence engine was making the user wait (as when Earl selected lineups for the user or when the user asked Earl for advice).

⇒Remember, sound is often part of the interface. Short, distinct, and not-too-loud sounds are best. Create a list of interface sound effects that work in your product. Don't rely on the operating system's sounds!

The list of interface rules is important for the programming team. If they know the rules in advance, they can create a lot of reusable code. Here are some types of questions to keep in mind:

- When, if ever, does the cursor change shape (e.g., when "passing over" or "rolling over" items or after clicking)?
- Which cursor or icon is used at what time?

- At what exact point does a wait icon appear and disappear?
- Is there ever a time when there is no cursor or interface icon on the screen?
- If there is a pop-up interface, when and where does it pop up?
- What, if anything, does the interface remember from the user (e.g., the user's place in a list)?
- What sounds are played with the interface?
- What happens first, the sound or a change in the cursor or icon?
- How close is close (i.e., is there a programmable margin of error for clicking in the neighborhood of an on-screen object)?
- Where is the hot spot on the cursor?
- How do you alert the user about the progress of a lengthy task (e.g., progress bars, counters, sound effects)?

⇒ Here are two rules of thumb about these questions:

1. Always provide instant response to an input request from a user (even if it's a "not available now" sound).

2. Always indicate progress of tasks and count in such a way that the user can discern when the task is completed.

For example, if you start counting the number of NPCs you need to create before moving onto the next level and you begin at 1 and count upward, then the user has no idea when you'll complete the task. So, count backward toward 1 or 0. The user shouldn't expect negative (or imaginary!) numbers and will have an idea of when the program will be ready to resume.

I saw a program (which shall remain nameless) that put up a progress bar for each file that it processed for me. However, when I asked it to process a bunch of files at once, it didn't count off the files remaining to process. So unless I counted the files beforehand and ticked them off in my head as they went, I had no idea how long I'd have to wait. Tracking progress is so simple, yet many designers and programmers miss it.

The final part of this section in the design is a technological discussion. This is where the technical director can specify information for the actual pixel size of icons and cursors, file formats, color limitations, sound file formats, and other technical issues that the creators of these assets and the programmers need to know. Be sure you, as the designer, remain involved in the technological discussion.

⇒For example, elements of the interface should always be kept in memory, and the technical staff needs to be told this in no uncertain terms.

Imagine the program having to stop to load the "loading from disk" icon from the disk before it needs to be displayed during a data file load! I've seen it happen. As another example, if there are any timing issues, they should be discussed here. In real-time simulators, the accuracy of the input information is crucial. If the technical director feels that input only has to be accurate to 0.01 second, that should be stated here.

View-by-View Descriptions

For me, as a designer, producer, or executive producer, this is the heart and soul of the design document. By reading through this usually enormous document, I can get a sense of the story, interactivity, look, and rhythm of a product.

My preference is to have the view-by-view description created in a database program so it can include images, sounds, and text. Because of the amount of data (which are often redundant) required to be entered in each view, database programs can be an added efficiency as they can automate much of the process. A database program can allow you to use pull-down menus, use precreated lists of text, and automatically date records and create unique IDs. If you're working on a local-area network (or even a wide-area network), most database programs will allow several people to access the same exact database at once. This ensures that everyone is working from the most up-to-date data.

Also, a database program will give you the option of printing out selected sections of the design based on any number of criteria. In addition, if you are disciplined in using a naming convention for every element of the production, a database program can directly look up and show you any uniquely identified piece of art, audio file, text file, or video clip. Regardless of how the view-by-view description is created, for me this is the glue of the production process.

Over the years, I have become used to this way of looking at game designs. I used to call this subdocument the *scene-by-scene* descriptions. Unfortunately the word *scene* connotes many things to many people in many disciplines. Over the years I've been involved in many meetings about nomenclature for design documents. In an attempt to come up with a standardized set of expressions for design elements, scene-by-scene descriptions came to be called view-by-view descriptions.

For each view, the view-by-view description includes

- A unique ID for the view (see the discussion of naming conventions)
- A plain-English name for the view (try to make it unique)
- State of the game
- Modes of interactivity
- A visual description of the view with a picture, if possible
- Filename of view's art
- A list of "removable" graphic elements that are visible in this state
- A list of navigation "hot spots" and commands cross-referenced to the new views
- A list of all nonnavigation hot spots and commands with a description of the interactivity that can be triggered by the user
- A list of any characters that appear in the view
- A list of sound effects, music, VOs, FMV, and/or animations that are triggered by the environment or world's behavior
- Creation and modification dates
- The production status of this view

If you are using a database, each of these elements will become the *field* for data entry when you create a new "record" for each view.

Because the view-by-view description is so full of information, the designer should keep this to as few views as possible. Some views with key states that behave uniquely should be listed separately in the view-by-view description. Whenever possible, several states should be folded into one view. Now for some details:

A Unique ID for the View

When you start, this may seem unimportant. But once you are in the middle of the production, you'll find that keeping track of a seemingly endless list of views can be a nightmare. If they all have unique IDs, you, the producers, and the programmers will be able to quickly and accurately discuss a specific view.

Try to create view IDs that have some relationship to the view's plain name (for example, Lhe2 for lighthouse exterior 2, DOVls3 for visitors' dugout long shot 3).

A Plain-English Name for the View

Be brief but unique and accurate. Also, I recommend starting the plain name with the most common part of the name. In this way, you can sort all the views by name, which will cause these views to be grouped together. For example, if all the lighthouse views start with lighthouse followed by exterior or interior and then a specific description, using the database program, you could sort by the plain-English name and come up with a portion of the list that looks like this:

View record 345—lighthouse exterior close to door with view of road

View record 346—lighthouse exterior extreme closeup of door

View record 347—lighthouse exterior from far away

View record 348—lighthouse interior first view of downstairs area

View record 349—lighthouse interior looking up the stairs

View record 350—lighthouse top inside looking at door to outside

View record 351—lighthouse top looking down the stairs

View record 352—lighthouse top outside looking over valley

State of the Game

This is only necessary if the interactivity of this view is greatly changed by a specific state of the game. List the specific state or states that make this version of the view different from other views with the same art. For example, if the player has acquired some new tool for interacting with the environment, perhaps there are new and different hot spots or the old hot spots have new interactivity. Try to use this sparingly, and put as much of the specific state information as possible in the conditions associated with the hot spots and commands.

Mode of Interactivity of User in This View

As with the state, you need to do this only if there are multiple modes possible within the same view. As a change in mode usually implies a change in interactivity, it is often difficult to clearly describe all the interactivity in one view if you are constantly having to say, "If you click on this hot spot in this mode, then do this, in mode 2, do that, and in mode 3 do this other thing."

It's also often true that when the mode is different, the hot spots change or possibly go away. Think carefully before you omit this "field" of the view-by-view description, but don't put it in unless it's absolutely necessary.

A Visual Description of the View

Often, this description along with a picture, if possible, a cross-reference to the storyboard image of the view, the list of hot spots below, and the production designer's visual design documents is all that the storyboard artists have to go on. So be specific and thorough. If an exit has to be on the right side of the screen for some reason, be sure that's clear.

Once the storyboard artist has created an approved storyboard, insert the actual image into this document and/or provide a cross-reference to the storyboard's unique ID.

Filename of View Art

It's also a good idea to provide the actual filename or image ID of the piece of art that will be used as the foundation or backdrop of this view in the product. This puts the responsibility of coming up with this filename in the hands of the game designer. This reduces the chance that a crucial piece of art, such as the background art for a view, will be mis-named or named something that's not terribly useful. (These naming problems often arise when the artists are creating art on Macintoshes and the production team is working on PCs, where there isn't as much flexibility in filenames.)

A List of Removable Graphic Elements Visible in This State

Often a view is composed of a backdrop piece of art (see above) with many smaller graphical elements "pasted" on top. This is usually done when these elements are removable from the view, as this saves enormous amounts of space on disc, in memory, or coming down line. For example, if there's a book that the user can click on to remove from a desk in the view, then the book is best done as a removable graphical element. Redrawing that portion of the view without the book is a minor effort at best, and you've only had to have the book as a separate and probably small art file.

Be sure to cross-reference any drawings of the removable elements and provide the actual filename for the final art for the artists.

Here's a hint. ⇒When you create these removable graphical elements, have the art engineers or artists place the art in the scene with anti-aliasing (don't worry, they'll know what that means) to make the removable graphic look as if it fits more naturally in the scene. Then cut out the image from the view with the anti-aliased information attached. Thus when you paste it in during game play, it will look as if it were composed in the scene.

A List of Navigation Hot Spots and Commands Cross-Referenced to New View

These hot spots and commands are what allow the user to move from view to view. List each navigation hot spot and command and the associated view ID to which the program switches. I try to add at least one more element to this list—the *transition* that occurs during navigation. After consulting with your production designer and technical director, you can usually work from a list of TV or film-style transitions such as

- Jump-cut
- Cross-fade
- Fade to black, then fade up
- Play new music, a sound effect, or VO and then jump-cut
- While playing new music, a sound effect, or VO, cross-fade
- Cut to black, play music (with music file ID), then fade up
- Scroll to new view
- Horizontal wipe
- Play an FMV clip of the salesperson at the first view, then cut to black while playing VO of the salesperson to cover the load of the new view, then fade up on the new view

Depending on your willingness to include separate views for each state, you may need to include one last element in this list. You might want to list the *conditions* in which the user is or is not allowed to navigate from this view. For example, you might want to allow navigation to a special new view as a reward for solving some puzzle. Or you might want to pro-hibit navigation out of a location until the user has accomplished some specific task under certain conditions.

A List of All Nonnavigation Hot Spots and Commands

This is a list of all the types of interactivity the user can do other than nav-igation. Remember, not interacting is an interactive choice that the user makes. It's generally not a user's mistake, so don't punish the user as if it were! Be sure to include in your list items such as "If the user does nothing, after a random period of time between 15 and 27 seconds, do this thing."

For each hot spot in your list include all VOs, FMVs, animations, sound effects, music, or changes in the view (as opposed to switches to a new view) that are triggered by interactivity. Always refer to each by the ID or filename as this will save the programmers and engineers an enormous amount of time. Also, use of the IDs or filenames will reduce the headaches of the producer in ensuring the correct asset is being used as you envisioned.

Include any states changed by the user's interactivity. For example, if the user clicks on a character, this may trigger the FMV of the character's welcome speech *and* cause the game's state to reflect that the user has now been greeted by this character. Since the game's state has changed, clicking on this character again will trigger a different FMV clip saying, "I already said hello. What do you want?"

⇒If the interactivity triggered by the user causes a new view to appear, then this hot spot or command belongs in the navigation list.

If you include state information that affects the commands, add appro-priate responses based on the individual. For example, if they try to start a car that's out of gas, you may need to list a response that includes both the sound effect of the car's not starting and another character's making a wisecrack about trying to start a car with an empty gas tank.

A List of Characters in the View

Using a database offers many ways to list the characters. The point of doing this is mostly to help to produce the dialogue, the VO, and FMV scripts for live performers or animation lists for animated characters.

⟶I think it is great to list characters, performer names, costumes, complete dialogue for the view, and vocabulary of motion right here in the view-by-view database. For example, when producing the video elements of a cast of Muppets, we have to track not only which Muppets are in which shots, but which performers as well. By using this list in the database, we can plan a schedule to minimize the time each performer sits around on the set. Also, we can arrange the performances so that the characters perform in the preferred order. From the list we can schedule when they need assistance with a character so we can arrange to have another puppeteer on set. We often try to schedule one performer, then add a second performer for the shots where two Muppets appear together, let the first performer go, and let the second performer work alone. We find that including the character *and* performer names in the view-by-view database really helps us organize shooting schedules efficiently.

A List of Sound Effects, Music, VOs, FMVs, and/or Animations Triggered by Environment or World's Behavior

To bring a view of a world to life, you or the production designer will probably want environmental behaviors. This is a term I use for the list of sounds, music, and other multimedia elements that create the sense of a living, breathing view. Each is cross-referenced to its actual ID and filename. Some of these elements are triggered by the user's behavior and others by the specifications of the designer to create this living world.

Another part of this list is a specification of frequency. Later in the book I discuss random numbers and naturalness at great length. Let me say here that you, as the game designer, want to take responsibility for the use of the environmental behaviors, and this is the place to do it.

For each multimedia element or asset, specify the following:

- When does it start? Specify a random range of times in whatever accuracy level *you* want.

- When does it stop? Does it always play to the end? Again, specify any randomness.

- How does it stop? Does it simply stop, or does it fade out or cross-fade? This is especially important in music and is almost always forgotten until it's too late.

- How fast does it play? You can usually alter the playback rate of anything. Specify playback ranges here.
- Does it loop? Specify whether it is always, never, or if sometimes, what percentage of time.
- Does it repeat? This is different from looping, as it implies there is always a pause between repeats. Specify the randomness of the pause!
- Does it alternate with other elements? If so, specify which other elements and whether each element has to play at least once before any one element is repeated; if each element is played in order before repeating the cycle again (this is different from the first choice); or if each element is randomly selected from a list. If the last, be sure to be clear if you want to prevent any element from playing twice in a row, three times in a row, etc. (You'd be surprised what a big deal this is. Almost everyone forgets to specify this, and the programmers end up creating code where, inadvertently, the same thing is repeated over and over.)
- Are there any states in which it does or does not play?
- Are there any other changes during playback? Specify volume, color, language, pitch, or other things that can be varied by the computer during playback.

I can't stress enough how important it is for you *not* to give up the responsibility for environmental behaviors.

Creation and Modification Dates

This is actually a list of dates that the producers will want. Include

- Creation date and creator, so you know when and who created this view record.
- List of modification dates, modifier, notes, so you know a history of changes, who made them, and any reasoning behind the changes.
- Most recent modification date, so others in the group can look for recently modified views.

Production Status of the View

Finally, keep a status of the view (e.g., deleted, produced, approved). Even if you've discarded a specific view from the original design, keep it in the database marked *deleted* or some such designation, so there is no doubt as to its status.

Again, this section is mostly for the producer, but it can also be a useful tool for tracking the progress of a design. For example, you could have a state that says "design not complete" so you can quickly find all the views you have left to work on.

That's the View from Here

That about wraps up the view-by-view descriptions. Clearly this is a critical part of the design documents. As I discuss later, it's important to remember that this is a living, evolving document. So please create it in such a way and in such a spirit that it can grow during the course of production.

Flowcharts, Game Logic, Algorithms, and Rules

Whereas the view-by-view description is essential for producers, directors, and others, this section is one of the key sections for the technical director and the programming team. Nevertheless, it is, in my opinion, still the responsibility of the designer to do most of the work here. As with other sections, help may be needed, but, unlike in other sections, that help should only be in the form of consulting. It is crucial for game designers to understand the underpinnings of the interactivity of their product, and writing this section is one of the best ways to do that.

Almost every product can be tracked in a flowchart. A flowchart is a sort of map of interactivity. Not to be confused with the map of the worlds, this chart allows the producers, directors, writers, artists, and most importantly programmers to understand the sequence of events in an interactive product as determined by a user.

After creating the flowchart(s) for this section, you should provide all the game logic and algorithms. Sometimes these are one and the same, and at other times they are quite distinct from one another. Very often, the logic for the game is simply provided in the flowcharts.

If you choose another method of expressing the logic of the game, consult with your technical director so you can agree on a format. With the exception of puzzles, I prefer that all game logic be presented in the form of flowcharts.

A Puzzling List

If your product includes puzzles, list them right here, at the end of the game logic section.

⇒In an adventure game, a list of puzzles that specifies each step of the puzzle is needed. Be sure to name each puzzle and provide a numeric list of the steps to solve it. If there are alternatives within the puzzle, create a numbering scheme (I like to follow traditional outline form for this) that is easy to follow. If there is scoring attached to the puzzles or to the various steps within the puzzles, put it here. If the puzzles change, update the list. This list is used by not only the production team but also the customer service people, the reviewers (who might need to cheat), the telephone help line, the on-line Help area, and the person writing the companion book to your bestseller.

If you are doing an RPG, then in addition to the puzzles list, include the method for scoring the outcome of each "move," the number and type of obstacles, and the resulting impact on attributes of all the characters involved in the move. Again, keep this list up to date.

Table 3-7 is an example puzzle with a listing of potential points.

The Bad Guy, Good Guy List

In many products, especially action or real-time games, enemies and obstacles appear in specific places, at specific times, and with specific attributes. I think of these as real-time puzzles in that the user has to memorize the sequence of events to overcome, avoid, or otherwise get past these obstacles.

⇒If you are designing such a product, make a list for each world as to the sequence, time, type, and attributes of each obstacle and how the user can get past it. Also include any points scored or any states changed as the user succeeds or fails to pass the obstacle. Partial credit is often given for inefficient, but ultimately successful efforts; note that here, too. In the design vernacular, the last enemy at the end of each level is called the *boss monster* and is usually the "locked door" to the next level. First you have to get to it, then you have to figure out how to defeat it or get past it. Often, you need to collect some good things such as "power-ups" to be able to do this.

The list of good things a user can accomplish is similar to the enemies and obstacles list. The good things often behave just as the obstacles in that

TABLE 3-7

Goal	Find the right tiles to step on to cross a booby-trapped hallway.	No points as points already received from other (first test) puzzle
Consequences	If you step on the wrong tiles, you fall through the floor which *loses 5 points* and puts you in the Underground Trap puzzle. If you fail to get through the hallway, you cannot complete the second of four tests to finish your quest.	
Maximum points:	32 points	
Step 1	Find the hallway by solving the first test puzzle.	No points
Step 2	Discover that it's booby-trapped (by trying, asking about it, or reading about it).	No points
Step 3	Find the special book in the library that Mentor is looking for (that only Mentor can read).	5 points
Step 4	Give Mentor the book.	2 points
Step 5	Take Mentor to hallway.	2 points
Step 6	Ask Mentor for guidance in avoiding the booby trap. Mentor says, "Walk with God."	2 points
Step 7	You figure out that this means you need to spell out *God* with your steps on the tiles.	No points
Step 8	You realize the tiles are in Greek.	No points
Step 9	If you don't know Greek, go to the library and look up *God* in the Greek-English dictionary.	1 point
Step 10	Step on the letters in the hallway that spell out *God* in Greek.	19 points if scored one point for previous step. 20 points if accomplished without looking up in Greek-English dictionary.

they appear in sequence according to place, time, type, and attributes. And the user often collects the benefits of these good things by doing the right thing in the right place at the right time. List these under each world as well.

Al-go-rithm

⇒This section is what often separates the novices from the pros. As designers get more and more sophisticated, they use a higher percentage of algorithms than logic in their products. In my experience, users also somehow understand the difference in quality of a mostly algorithm-driven game. These games tend to feel more natural and usually have better replayability.

So what is an algorithm? It is a combination of logic, arithmetic, manipulation of data, and other computer programming techniques that determine what the computer does next. Very often algorithms are used to determine what the computer program does in direct response to a user's input.

As a rule of thumb, logic is usually faster for the computer to execute, but algorithms are more efficient to code (i.e., write programs) and usually make for smaller programs (in terms of bytes) and are far more flexible. With really good designers, it is even possible to make algorithms faster than logic. This is best illustrated by an example:

Twister Logic

Let's say we are going to design an interactive storytelling game based on the movie *Twister.* After some sequence of events, we need to have a twister appear for the characters to chase. We have a few choices:

1. Always make the twister appear at a certain time.
2. Wait for the user to make a certain sequence of moves, and then start the twister.
3. Specify a random chance that a twister will occur during a window of opportunity.
4. Select a starting time for the twister based on a statistical model.

Choices 1 and 2 are both logic-based. Choice 3 uses both logic and algorithm, and choice 4 is purely algorithmic. Let's look at the pros and cons of each method.

1. *Always make the twister appear at a certain time.* In this case, the programmer simply has the code check for a certain time or condition, and that triggers the twister.

    Pros: This is very easy to code, and the twister is very predictable for testing and storytelling

    Cons: The twister always occurs at the same time or under the same exact circumstances. Replayability and naturalness are lost.

2. *Wait for the user to make a certain sequence of moves, then start the twister.* Here, the programmer has the code keep track of the various states of the game based on what the user has done. When certain combinations of states are reached, it triggers a twister.

    Pros: This is relatively simple code, and the user's action will trigger a twister. It's still quite predictable for testing. Sometimes users like this amount of control.

    Cons: The twister always occurs under the same exact circumstances. Replayability and naturalness are lost. It's always possible that the user won't do any of the sequences of things required to trigger the twister. It is also possible that depending on the number of states involved, the programming logic might get very complicated and difficult to maintain.

3. *Specify a random chance that a twister will occur during a window of opportunity.* Similar to choice 2, the programmer looks at a set of states or conditions. However, instead of triggering at the moment that these conditions are met, the programmer uses a random number to decide if it's time to start the twister. Every so often (say once every 20 seconds), the program checks a new random number to see if it's time to start a twister. If not, then it keeps on checking until either a twister is started or a new set of conditions occurs, making it inappropriate to start a twister (i.e., the window of opportunity closes).

    Pros: This is relatively simple code, and the user's action will trigger the random number algorithm, which might trigger a twister. This creates a situation in which the user is expecting a twister but doesn't know exactly when it will start. This is an effective way of building suspense in the story. There is also a tremendous amount of flexibility in the product. If, for example, you have a random number generator that creates a number between 1 and 100, you can select the chance (in percent) that a twister starts every time the program checks the random number. If you set the threshold at 60, then any random number over 60 will trigger the twister, giving a 40 percent chance of a twister each time the program checks. It's trivial to change this threshold either during testing or, better yet, based on the user's actions, settings, and preferences.

Cons: The twister may not occur at all, because each time you get a new random number, there is a 60 percent chance (or whatever your threshold is) of not starting a twister. There is still a lot of logic involved in determining when to start looking for a randomly begun twister.

4. *Select a starting time for the twister based on a statistical model.* Create a statistical curve for when a twister can start. For example, create a simple bell curve that starts at time 0 (i.e., when the user starts the story) and ends at 15 minutes. At either end you have a very small chance of the twister occurring; but near the middle, you have a greater chance. Then use the random number generator once, and using the statistical curve, pick a starting time for the twister.

Pros: This is very simple code and is based on a data table. As this table is statistically based, it is very easy to change it or tweak it during testing and based on the user's setting and preferences. Also, the twister will always occur within the first 15 minutes of game play at completely unpredictable times. This creates a sense of naturalness and suspense each time you replay the game.

Cons: Since the twister may appear at any time in the first 15 minutes, there is no guarantee that the user will have done anything useful to prepare for it before it comes. This is remedied by combining this method with any of the above methods.

How to Write an Algorithm

Let's use the last example of a statistical table algorithm. Here is an algorithm for statistically predicting the start of the first twister:

1. It must start within the first 15 minutes of game play.

2. At the beginning of game play (or of the window of opportunity, as defined by such-and-such a game state), generate a random number between 0 and 99 (note: *not* 1 to 100).

3. Use Table 3-8 to identify the time when the twister begins.

TABLE 3-8

Random Number	Twister Begins at Time:
0	0:30
1	1:00
2	1:30
3	1:45
4	2:00
⋮	⋮
47	7:20
48	7:23
49	7:27
50	7:30
51	7:33
52	7:37
⋮	⋮
97	14:30
98	14:40
99	14:50

Notice how the times in the middle of the list are closer together while the times at the ends are pretty far apart. This table is very efficient (i.e., it's both fast to use *and* a small amount of bytes) once created and, in some cases, can be generated by a small computer program, so you don't have to enter these times by hand.

Oh No, Equations

At this point, some people get very, very afraid. However, equations *can* be your friend. If you need help, think of this help as similar to the help your writer or art director provides with back story or color selections. Often designers who can't create these equations treat their technical advisers as if that specialty was somehow not creative and that the foreign languages of logic and mathematics were somehow things to dismiss. Please don't.

⇒While it's easy to give notes and feedback and to offer suggestions about writing and art, at some level, many designers believe that they are speaking the same language as the writers and artists. In my experience, they generally are not. They are often commenting on demos of what the writer and artist are thinking. For better or worse, believing they are speaking the same language allows everyone to have quite extended conversations with the writers and artists about redoing, fixing, or approving their work.

Most designers don't believe they can have similar conversations about mathematics and equations. While this may seem realistic, try to show the same bravado used in critiquing an artist's work when analyzing the quality of a programmer's algorithms in order to make your product match your vision. If you can't summon up the patience (or nerve) to discuss equations, have the programming team write a small program that demonstrates how the equation functions based on a variety of conditions and inputs. They'll have to write this code anyway, so this is a good time to get it done.

It almost goes without saying that most game designers, producers, and executives have to see what the production designer wants to do through storyboards, conceptual art, and other graphical tools. Think of this art as a demonstration of the art, and you'll see that it's really just a way of creating a way for the two of you to discuss your ideas.

It is the same for demos of algorithms. I can't emphasize this enough. Always try to get demo programs of the equations and algorithms programmed so you can test how they work and adjust them. This means that in these demos the programmer has to build a simple interface to allow you to set the various states and user inputs that drive the equation.

An Early Example

As an extreme example, when I was working on Earl Weaver Baseball (EWB), I met with Earl a few times to discuss the way in which he selected his starting lineups. We discussed what information I had available, and fortunately for me, Earl is a great believer in letting the statistics of a player speak for the player's ability. So, armed with this information, I created a small demo program that chose starting lineups and batting orders from a small set of ballplayers based on a selectable opposing pitcher.

I brought a computer to Earl in an Oakland hotel room while he was waiting for the Orioles to play the Athletics, and I showed him how the algorithmic lineup selection worked with my demo program. We could specify an opposing pitcher and have the program either select a starting lineup and batting order or, by selecting nine players to cover each position, create a batting order out of our starting lineup.

After playing with it and examining the results, Earl, Dan Daglow, and I had a great discussion about how to improve my algorithms and equations. I was able to make some of these changes there via the interface I built into the demo (e.g., the weight I put on the batting average versus the slugging average for the #4 batter or how important speed was in the #7 hitter in a designated hitter lineup). He was able to see and comment on those changes right then. The rest I had to go back and fix at my office.

The end result was a far better set of algorithms and equations for the program. Also, this demo program process increased Earl's understanding of what I was doing to create a computerized version of himself.

OK, But What Can an Equation Do?

Equations are one of the best ways of looking at a lot of data simultaneously and creating a response from the computer. Since computers are so good at doing mathematics (of which logic is just one discipline), you can use equations from a wide range of mathematical disciplines. You can use algebra, geometry, statistics, linear algebra, the calculus, and so on to create a huge number of results that you couldn't possibly create with logic alone.

One of my high school teachers gave me a great piece of advice about story problems which holds true for just about any type of equation you would deal with in game design: "Follow the units." As an example, if you want to convert X miles per hour to feet per hour, set up your equation as follows. (Note that the asterisk $*$ means to multiply.)

1. Miles per hour is written mathematically as X miles/hour (or X miles $\div$ 1 hour).

2. There are 5280 feet per mile, which is 5280 feet/mile (or 5280 feet $\div$ 1 mile).

3. Follow the units. To get feet per hour, do this:

   - (X miles/hour) $*$ (5280 feet/mile)
   - This is the same as (X $*$ 5280)(miles/hour $*$ feet/mile).
   - From basic algebra, miles units cancel, leaving
   - $= (X * 5280) * $ (feet/hour)

By using this rule, it's pretty easy to know whether to multiply or divide two numbers to get the desired result. The final units always reveal the nature of the equation you need to create.

Sim Example

As an example, assume you are designing a simple sim-type game in which you have to choose how many people live in a town, what kinds of crops are growing, and you have to click on the clouds to make it rain on the crops.

Now, let's set up some parameters and equations:

1. Time is measured in weeks. Every 10 seconds, a new week goes by.

2. Each person requires 10 units of food per week. If the person has less, the person moves away or dies.

3. Each acre of corn can create as many as 200 units of corn per week.

4. Each acre of wheat can create as many as 500 units of wheat per week.

5. Each click on a cloud represents one-tenth the amount of rain required for maximum crop production per week. No more than 10 clicks can be counted in 1 second.

6. Both corn and wheat crops create the same percentage of maximum output as the percentage of rain per week (i.e., if there is 20 percent rain, then the crops produce 20 percent of the maximum yield).

7. The goal, or final units in your equation, is people. Can you set up and maintain the system so that you don't lose anyone from week to week?

So an equation for how many people live from week to week is

End no. of people = starting no. of people * (((no. of corn acres * 200 food units/acre * no. of user clicks of rain/10 maximum clicks of rain) + (no. of wheat acres * 500 food units/acre * user clicks of rain/10 maximum clicks of rain))/(starting no. of people * 10 units/person))

It does look scary at first, but let me break it down a bit. This is the big picture:

- Figure out how many units of food are needed (the required food for 100 percent survival).

- Figure out how many units of food there actually are (the portion of the required food grown).
- Divide the second number by the first to determine the percentage of required food created.
- Multiply this percentage by the number of people who started out the week.

Looking at the trees instead of the forest for a minute, we see that the amount of food created is a function of

- The number of crops of each type of food which is planted.
- The percentage of rain created by the user. To get this percentage, divide the number of user clicks by the maximum number of clicks (which is 10) required to get 100 percent rain.
- Following the units, multiply the number of acres of each crop by the number of units the crop should produce by the percentage of rain.
- Add the two food unit values to get the total number of food units created.

Do the Math

Using the above example, we do some math to see how it works. Based on the input from a user, in the first week we have

- 75 people
- 2 acres of corn
- 1 acre of wheat
- 8 clicks of rain (the user was pretty fast, but not fast enough for 100 percent rain)
- Thus we need 750 units of food to maintain 75 people.

People at end of week = $75 * (((2 * 200 * 8/10) + (1 * 500 * 8/10))/(75 * 10))$

$$= 75 * ((320 + 400)/750)$$

$$= 75 * (720/750)$$

$$= 75 * 0.96$$

$$= 72 \text{ people}$$

So 3 people left or died, and you have to either plant more crops or click faster.

Now, no respectable equation writer would leave the above equation in its current state. The value of the original version of the equation is that it's convenient for someone to look at how it works and to verify units. However, with standard algebraic manipulations, the equation (without carrying the units along in longhand) can become

$$\text{People at the end of the week} = ((corn * 2 * clicks) \\ + (wheat * 5 * clicks)) \text{ people}$$

or

$$\text{People at the end of the week} = (clicks * ((2 * corn) + (5 * wheat))) \text{ people}$$

Looking at the simplified equation in this way brings out a potential problem. It is possible for the number of people at the end of the week to be greater than the number of people at the beginning of the week. There are two simple solutions: (1) Let the population grow, or (2) put a cap on the equation with some logic (e.g., "If the number of people we can feed is greater than the number of people we started with, then no one moved away, no one died, and no one was added to the population.").

There is another aspect of looking at the equation in its reduced state. In the original equation, there were several divisions. This made it look as if it were possible to have fractions of people left. However, once the equation was reduced or simplified, it became clear that you can only have whole-number results! That means no families with 2.4 kids.

Logic Rules—Not!

It is my hope that in looking through the math of the example above and understanding a little bit about how algorithms work, you will come to appreciate their power and significance. Think of all the permutations you can handle within this simple sim game with this one formula. Imagine attempting to figure out all these with logic. I know I can't.

⇒It takes a while for most designers to wean themselves away from purely logical designs and to begin working more and more in an algorithmic design style. But it is worth it.

In the CD-ROM craze of the early and middle 1990s an unfortunately high percentage of products were created with purely or mostly logical designs. We're now seeing a lot of this on the Internet as well. My opinion is that this is due to the availability of prototyping tools which are, quite honestly, built mostly for logic-based interactivity. I truly believe that games and products of all kinds will be vastly better when they begin to use a higher ratio of algorithms to logic; this means improved tools, experienced or well-trained designers, and the reinclusion of the technologists on the creative teams. And this goes for all types of products, including games for kids, games on the Internet, home pages, info-tainment, and edutainment products as well as games for gamers.

Scoring, Winning, Losing, Saving, Loading, Starting, Stopping, and Playing Again

⇒This section is about data and overall game states. I like to keep this section separate from the interactivity section so that this information is easy to locate for the programming team.

If your product includes any kind of scoring, make a table here of each condition that creates a score and the resulting points (include subtracted points). Total the maximum number of points that can be scored, and you are finished. Be sure to consider optional scoring in the maximum point total. In some games there are multiple ways to progress through the same obstacles that, depending on the technique used, net different point counts. In these cases, pick the highest score of the set, but don't add the others!

Sometimes scoring is an internal device for tracking the progress of the user. If you're doing this, it's often a good idea to provide users with some way of viewing their progress or score. Points, of course, can be displayed in some status menu or another, but there are other ways. Progress bars, percentage-completed numbers, the health of a plant, and many other progress or status indicators can be used.

Almost all games are about winning or succeeding. Put the following in this part of your design:

- Which conditions (often the score) indicate winning
- The user's "reward" for each subsection of the game, if any
- What transition takes place after winning the subsection and the next part of the game (keep transitions very, very short, if possible)

- The user's reward for winning the entire game
- What happens after the user wins the entire game
- What happens after that

Depending on the type of game you're designing, what happens after the user wins can vary greatly. Try to put yourself in the user's shoes after she or he has invested a lot of time and energy (and possibly money on Hint lines or on the Internet) to win. If you've created a masterpiece of a linear ending, let them watch it over and over at the end of the game. If they've had to master some remarkable set of maneuvers, let them replay it; or better yet, let them save it to disk so they can E-mail it to their friends on the BBS* you've set up. And, if it's the kind of game that you play over and over, let them get very quickly to the start of a new game; making them wait is almost the same as telling them to stop playing now.

By thinking carefully about it and putting this in its own section, you're sure to get the ending produced just as you envisioned it.

One of the most difficult things to program in Earl Weaver Baseball was the instant replay of the last play of the game. It was worth the extra effort though, as many people turn off the graphics, allowing the game to play in a very fast simulation. When the nongraphics version of the game is over (which takes about 1 to 2 minutes), the user sees the box score. At this point the user has the option to watch the final play of the game. Users do this quite frequently, and this creates an unbelievable illusion that a real game has actually taken place.

In RTZ at the end of the payoff "movie," the user can choose to watch it again, end the game (which displays the credits), or start the adventure over from the beginning or from a saved game.

In Muppets Inside, after winning the game, you can go back to the "Bit Map" and see any of the video clips of the Muppet Show you've discovered during your adventure, play any of the games at any of 15 levels, or watch the final sequence again.

How you design losing is, in many ways, far more important than how you design winning. Your goals need to be clear if you decide the user can lose. In the adventure game world, there are two distinct schools of thought: (1) The user can die, and (2) the user must never die. In both cases, the user can, in a sense, lose. But only when the user's character actually dies is the user alerted to this fact.

---

*On-line Bulletin Board.

In any case, as with winning, make a list for the programmers and producers about losing:

- What conditions, if any, cause users to lose?
- What happens to alert users that they lost?
- What transition occurs after you've alerted them?
- If losing is different on different levels, list the differences.

Again, put yourself in the user's shoes. Users don't want to lose. And *you* want them to try again. If you really do, then you need to make losing a relatively painless event. In other words, be quick and clear about it.

⇒If you can, tell users what they did wrong and/or what they should have done to succeed. Do it quickly, within the context of the product's story line, and be done with it. Then have your programmers do everything possible to get the user playing again.

I would rather see a simple or even ordinary losing sequence if it means I'm allowed to get right back to the action. There's an Internet game that I downloaded that's really fun, but you lose a lot when you play it at first. There is no button after you lose to simply try again or start again! I even believe in giving users a "Start over Now" button that they can press in the middle of game play in case they know they're going to lose. Why make them suffer through the rest of a losing round? I can't think of any reason.

One of the best games to deal with losing is Lemmings. This game has several of these features built into the various versions. This includes the ability to simply skip all the information you've probably already gotten and to start a round over before the clock has run out on your current attempt.

In the early days of graphic adventure gaming, the two major producers of high-quality graphic adventures were Sierra On Line (especially with King's Quest and other Quest series) and LucasArts (with the Monkey Island and Indiana Jones Adventures). In Sierra's products, you died somewhat frequently in the course of playing. However, each time you died, you saw a very quick sequence followed by a hint to what you should have been trying to do. In the LucasArts games, you never died. You could end up wandering around trying the same things over and over, which, quite honestly, gives you a very mild sensation of losing; but you would always keep up hope! However, in both lines of products, you could call a Hint line when you got stuck.

From what I've heard, the LucasArts people were adamant that you shouldn't die, but at least they kept a sense of humor about this. In one of the Monkey Island games, you could walk off a cliff. If you did, you appeared to die with your character's "voice" telling you in the exact same style as in a King's Quest game what you "did wrong." Then, a few moments later, Guybrush Threepwood (your character and the protagonist) would rise up on a rock platform elevator, miraculously saved from death so you could continue playing the game.

In the traditional world of the Zork text adventures, dying was a key element. For the really clever game players, though, the original designers from Infocom put in a great twist. When you were dead, your ghost could continue to navigate the world but couldn't interact with anything. However, your ghost could go through any door regardless of whether it was locked. In this way, once dead, you could collect an awful lot of information to help you in your next "life." Another way you could lose was by doing something wrong whereby a thief would come and take away all your stuff.

In RTZ we tried to pay homage to this sense of history, fun, and product rivalry. In keeping with the tradition of the Zork universe, we allowed you to die (all right, sometimes we killed you). But sometimes, if you did something morally reprehensible (such as killing the school teacher), a thieflike character, The Guardian, comes and takes all your stuff. You can still wander around the world (stuffless). However, the really clever game players would drop all their stuff before trying something "wrong." The Guardian comes and has nothing to take. You can then pick up your stuff and go along your way. Also, at one point you can drown. Before you do, we floated by you a skeleton in a pirate suit with the initials GT on the jacket while we played a variation on the Monkey Island music.

Saving and loading is an option in many games. Sometimes products automatically do this, and sometimes the user has the option of saving and loading from a list of games at will.

There are several design considerations to address here:

- Which data are required to be saved? Things such as the score, states, user's name, the date, and other useful items should come to mind. Think this through thoroughly, as programmers can have a difficult time retrofitting a new piece of saved data into their save-game scheme.

- When is saving a game allowed? Sometimes you have to wait until certain sequences are concluded, and sometimes you want to only allow saves at specific moments (e.g., for prerecorded saves).

- How many saved games can a user have?

- What kind of names can the user enter for a saved game? The more letters and nonalphabetic characters they're allowed to use, the better (especially the Space key).

- Do the saved-game files appear as icons on the user's desktop (in computer games only)?

- Can different users have different sets of saved games (this requires a user to "log on" or register somewhere within the product)? This is a necessity for Internet games, but this can work well with kids' games in households with more than one child.

- When is loading a game allowed? This could be at the beginning of the game, from the operating system, during game play, only at certain times during game play, etc.

- When you start a game, can you quickly and efficiently resume a loaded game? (If not, I think there's a design flaw!) This is also possible for video games as well as computer games.

- When you play a game for the first time and you try to save your first game, is there a logical default name? Again, I think there should be. Many users keep clicking until a game is saved and don't think to type in a name.

- Is there a "quick save" function? In other words, is there a button or shortcut key that will save the current game to a special place?

- If there's a quick save, then there must be a quick load. Specify the filename for this file and a way to start up the game directly from the operating system (i.e., Windows, MacOS, or DOS).

- If you're doing a video game, is there a way to give users a "save code" that they can enter to resume a game? (Many games do this.)

Related to saving and loading games is the design of starting and stopping games. Much of this type of design happens by accident, which isn't necessary. Here are a few simple rules of thumb:

1. ⇒Let the user play as soon as possible; long introductions are not necessary. If you want to tell a story, do it interactively. Most users only watch an introduction once, so it's not usually a good use of production dollars. They bought the product to interact, not to watch. I keep the introduction under 2 minutes, if possible.

2. ⇒If the user has seen the opening, skip it. Or, at least, let the user skip it very easily.

⟱➤ **3.** ⇒If you must have an introduction each time the user starts up, vary it! And don't repeat one until all the others have been played. This is easy to do if you plan from the start.

⟱➤ **4.** ⇒Stagger any loading of game code and data so that the user is interacting as soon as possible. If you don't set this goal for your programmers before they start, it will never happen.

⟱➤ **5.** ⇒Remember the user's settings and preferences. This is pretty standard now, but still the list of elements needs to be specified early in the production process.

⟱➤ **6.** ⇒Let the user stop whenever he or she wants. This is a good place for an auto save feature so you don't have to ask, "Do you want to save this game before quitting?" Then when the user starts the game, automatically load it.

⟱➤ **7.** ⇒Allow the user to interrupt any multimedia or linear elements. Interruptions should take effect immediately.

⟱➤ **8.** ⇒Let the user restart at any time. Don't force users to continue to some "logical" conclusion. This wastes their time.

⟱➤ **9.** ⇒Scrolling credits are nice, but if users want out, let them out. I've found that a one-page credit screen while the game "cleans up" is a good compromise.

⟱➤ **10.** ⇒If you have an installer, make it simple and fast. Also, test all the multimedia technologies in the installer (e.g., play digital sounds, FMV, MIDI). Several games do this, and it's a relief to know that your sound and video work before you leave the installer.

Art and Production Design

This section contains a discussion of the art or production design for your product. Each world should have its own section, and there should be some example of full-color art to demonstrate exactly what the production designer is thinking. I've found the best way to communicate with visual designers is by looking at and discussing example art (similar to programming demos).

⟱➤ ⇒Interface elements are often forgotten until the last moment. If they are described in great detail here (if they have not already been covered in the interface section above), this avoids the problem. Often these elements are the same throughout the product. However, there is no reason why they cannot change to reflect new worlds and/or different modes within the product. These are usually very small physical assets (i.e., not many bytes per image or sound) and can be a very efficient way of indicating to users what world or mode they are in.

Next, give a brief description of all the transitions in the product. Cross-reference to the audio design, and include the opening and closing sequences, transitions from winning, losing, restarting, stopping, changing modes, etc. Be sure to indicate what transition effects you want (e.g., fadeouts, cross-fades, wipes, jump cuts) and your expected time frame for each (as short as possible!).

If there is to be FMV, then there needs to be a discussion of set design and decoration, lighting, and costumes. These may be done by specialists if you can afford to hire them. (Remember that you may have already specified costume information in the characters section. Simply cross-reference from here if you have.)

This is a good place to have the technical director work with the production designer to list the following technical details:

- Number of background images
- Number of removable art elements (for pasting on background images)
- Support of transparency for removable elements, animations, FMV
- Number of interface elements
- Number of animations
- Size of animations
- Frame rate of animation
- Average length of animation sequences
- Maximum length of animation sequences
- Animation effects (e.g., looping, repeating, alternative sequencing)
- Minutes of FMV
- Size of FMV
- Frame rate of FMV
- Average length of FMV clips
- Maximum length of any FMV clip
- Load-in times for each type of art listed above (from CD, from hard disk, from the Internet, from cartridge)

Finally, there needs to be a discussion of art engineering and palettes. Touch on the following topics:

- In what size and color resolution will original art be created? The bigger the image (height and width) and the more colors (color depth), the better-quality your final art will be. Shrinking images and reducing palettes are far easier processes than enlarging or increasing the number of colors because in the latter two cases either the computer or an artist has to fill in information that isn't there.

- What palette technology is your product going to use, if any? (High-resolution systems don't use a palette per se, but you can simulate a palette-style technology to save a lot of space.)

- What color depth (or bits per color) are you going to use?

- What is the maximum number of simultaneous colors you will use?

- Are there some colors that must be present in every palette (e.g., black, white, interface colors, skin colors)? Do some colors have to be in a certain order or location in the palette?

- How many colors are available in the palette to change from view to view?

- Can each backdrop use its own palette?

- Can each frame of an FMV have its own palette, or does the entire clip need to share one palette?

- Can the palette change occasionally in an FMV?

- Can art elements change some of or all their colors either by changing the palette or by changing the image slightly?

- Do palettes have to be arranged in any specific order to allow better transitions from image to image?

- Are off-the-shelf or company proprietary tools available to create images, sequences, and palette changes to your specifications? If not, can they be built?

- How will animations be "registered"? Can this be automated and stored with the animations themselves, or will work sheets need to be created?

- Are registrations absolute or relative? (In other words, is the animation only registered to work on one background from one starting point, or does each frame "know" where it goes relative to the previous frame's position so that the programmer only has to specify a starting animation location?)

- Are FMV and animations *programmable?* For example, can the same animation move twice as fast from left to right?

- Can animations and FMV be played backward? Can they skip frames or cels? Can they stop midstream? Can they freeze-frame and advance by a single frame? Can they start midstream?

- Can images be flipped or rotated during game play? At what angles can they be rotated? Can they be mirrored? Can they be resized in real time?

- Can images be layered in different orders?

These are a lot of questions and if the answer to any of the yes/no questions is no, you should pursue the technology director with a "Why not?" All these graphics techniques have been available for years on both computers and video games. Sometimes there are legitimate reasons for prohibiting a certain technique, but I've found it's usually due to a poor choice in tools or because no one asked for the technique to be included in the program soon enough.

Storyboards and Sample Art

If the view-by-view section is the heart and soul of the design document, storyboards are the blueprints. My preference for this section is to create storyboards as follows:

- Use black-and-white drawings

- Use the same exact aspect ratio (i.e., height to width ratio) as the screen area for the primary target platform

- Place on the upper half of a vertical page or on a complete horizontal page with wide margins allowing room for notes

- All elements appear exactly where they are to appear in the game (i.e., no approximate placements just to show the idea)

- All backdrops, removable art elements, and interface elements get their own storyboards.

- Storyboards are labeled with the exact names indicated in the view-by-view description with ID and filename of final art listed.

- Storyboards are scanned into digital format so programmers can begin working with placeholder art with exact placement of objects and navigational hot spots.

- A set of key storyboards is painted or otherwise colored in (e.g., using digital ink and paint on a computer after scanning) as sample art
- Storyboards of intros, "outtros" (endings and exits), credits, alerts, dialogs, and other transitional elements should be included (these should be the responsibility of the production designer)

⇒During the process of creating storyboards, the producer should check each storyboard with the game designer, director, technical director, and whoever else is necessary before signing off on the storyboard and including it in the approved design document.

I developed a technique over the years, starting with EWB and continuing through RTZ, of color-coding a copy of each storyboard for the programming team. We used the following scheme (with highlight markers):

- Use black and white for backdrop or background art.
- Outline all navigation (exit) hot spots in green (using the shape of the hot spot, not the shape of the art).
- Outline all nonnavigation (interactive) hot spots in red (again, using the exact shape of the hot spot).
- Outline any removable art destinations in yellow.
- Outline any animating or visually changing areas in blue.

We developed an enhanced version of this method which was to mark these colored areas on plastic sheets that we could then layer over the storyboards, so we could see the individual elements for placeholder art. Also we could see and approve the scene of the view as a whole and by its parts. In addition, we could scan the individual drawings of the removable objects directly from the transparencies.

The point of this exercise was twofold: (1) It gave us a method of instantly seeing if there was a layout problem with all the hot spots at once, and (2) it provided a tool for the programmers to know exactly what hot spots, animations, and removable objects they needed to program and where these objects belonged on the screen. Checking the layouts in such an efficient fashion allowed us to give immediate and visually obvious feedback to the storyboard artists. It also drove underscored to the art teams the need to be exacting in storyboards of backgrounds and removable objects. And, the programmers had early and accurate information about where to program all the screen locations, with confidence that the art wouldn't change simply because it was rendered or colored in.

This style of art direction requires some discipline, but it really pays off. However, it's almost impossible to make this work with photographic backgrounds or video-captured backgrounds. This is one of the reasons why so many producers choose to shoot video in chroma key (often referred to as blue screen)—so they can "drop in" computer-generated or drawn and scanned images behind the actors. It turns out it's very difficult to be this accurate when one is going from a hand-drawn storyboard to a 3D rendered image. However, this was accomplished in 1993 by JP Asperin's team for Return to Zork; it certainly must be easier now.

Transition Design

You will notice, if you've been reading carefully, that this section is redundant. There are discussions of transitions spread throughout the design document. However, to ensure that everyone on the production and design team remembers how important (and how often ignored) transitions are, I believe it's a really good idea to create a special transition design section simply as a reminder.

This is a great opportunity for you to use cut-and-paste. List all the types of transitions you expect to be possible in your product and the parameters for each type of transition.

Audio and Music Design

Two other, often-ignored elements of the design—audio and music—should each have its own separate subsection in this part of the design.

Although audio and music are great tools to enhance the immersion effect your game can have on a player, they can also be some of the most off-putting elements as well. The sign of a well-thought-out and -created audio and music design is that the user never chooses to turn it off (and you should always give the user two options here: to turn sound effects on or off and to turn the music on or off). Ask your testers how many have ever turned one or both off. If more than a few have, reconsider your design or implementation.

For the audio design, if you cannot afford a sound designer, select someone who has some experience, knowledge, and/or good sense about sound. Create a few paragraphs and get a tape of sample sounds, so everyone knows what is intended. Sounds, as with music, can go a long way toward enhancing the user's experience. They can also drive a user to distraction! You should create a general description of the sounds and how they are to be used. Include

- Environmental or background sounds
- Interface sound effects which let users know that the program received their input and what the program thinks of their input
- Special-effect sounds that occur in response to specific events in the game or story
- Animation sound effects which are tied to any or all animations
- Voice-over recordings or synthesized speech
- Sound tracks (including speech) for FMV clips
- ⇒No sound (At times lack of sound is an important, purposeful part of the design. Be sure to discuss when this will occur in your product.)
- Transition sounds which can be used to entertain, count down, or otherwise occupy the user during any type of transition (e.g., in the Apple and C64 versions of EWB, we used the sound effects of a construction crew while the user waited for the computer to construct the VR ballpark)

Also, the following technical issues should be addressed with the technical director here:

- Playback rate or rates. The ability to alter playback rates is very important for a flexible and natural sound design.
- Looping. If looping is meant to be used, be sure everyone understands the limitations of a looping sound. What is the maximum length of the sound, and what gap, if any, is there before the loop begins again?
- Repeating. If repeating is meant to be used (i.e., played over and over but with random gaps between plays), specify the expected random controls you wish to have, such as minimum and maximum gaps and range of playback rates.
- Average length of sound effects.
- Maximum allowable length of sound effects.
- Will you ever need to stream sound effects from disk, CD-ROM, or from the Internet? If so, can the computer do anything else while this is happening?
- How many simultaneous sound effects can you have? In today's games, you should be able to have several, but this is not allowed by

less sophisticated software tools and game engines. You may need to make redundant sound effects if you sometimes need simultaneous sounds.

- Volume controls. Be sure that the user of the end product has a master volume control switch and that there is some mechanism for adjusting and notating the volume of each sound effect in the game during testing. If planned in advance, this is easy to program so that the producer and director can balance the sound levels throughout the production process. If you attempt to do this at the end, it can be a big problem.

- Sound on/off. Even though one measure of a great sound design is that users never wish to turn it off, every game should provide the option anyway. You never know in what environment people will play your game or the technical difficulties that people will experience with sounds.

- Stopping sounds midplay. Do your best to have your technical team provide a way to fade out a sound effect if it needs to stop playing in the middle. Otherwise, sounds will stop midplay, which is abrupt, distracting, and generally unnecessary. Again, if you plan it early, it's not hard.

In your design, warn your programmers about repetition and volume problems. And warn the creator of your sounds about your desire to loop and repeat sounds. If everyone knows the technical tricks you intend to enlist, then they can work to avoid the big pitfalls.

⇒Avoid these audio pitfalls:

- Poorly looping sounds. If the end and the beginning of a sound don't match, then it will pop like a skipping record and will annoy just about anyone. Sometimes this is caused during the engineering phase and, as often as not, by technical limitations such as the seek time on a CD (*seek time* is the time it takes to go from the end of a sound to the beginning of a sound on the CD), inadequate RAM set aside for sounds, or downloading limitations.

- Poor randomization of repeating sounds. If the random repeats are too similar, it will sound like a poor attempt at looping with a sound that's not meant to loop.

- Volume level out of alignment. All sound effects for a view or scene should be balanced, not between every possible sound in the view (including VO or FMV that may play), but also balanced to the sounds for any previous or subsequent views.

- And the big one: a misunderstanding of where users will spend a lot of time thinking, waiting, working on a problem or a puzzle, or simply navigating. If you force yourself into the mindset of a real player, you should be able to anticipate where she or he will get stuck or simply spend a lot of time, and then you can listen to the sound effects in that area for 10 to 20 minutes. Then do it again with the volume turned up just a little too high. You'll know if you've designed a problematic sound effects use for that place. Often, the problem lies with the looping and repeating (with repeating being the worst offender). See the sections on randomization and naturalness.

Music to My Ears

⇒If your game is going to have music, hire a musician to consult on the music design. Music is great for setting the mood of a product, keeping the user engaged emotionally, and providing transitions from element to element as well as from mood to mood.

Many of the same issues for sound effects arise for music, especially in regard to looping and repeating.

First, a few words about digitized music, synthesized music, and MIDI music.

- *Digitized music* is sampled recorded just as voice-overs, FMV sound tracks, or sound effects are. It is sampled by the computer many thousand times per second (kilohertz, or kHz) as the music is played back from tape or CD. So the quality of the music played back in your game with digitized music can be as good as that of your original recording. This is usually the best-quality music you can get in a game. It can take a lot of disk, CD-ROM space or download time, and about the only things you can do to digitized music realistically is to change (1) the volume and (2) the playback speed, which, in turn change the pitch (how high or low) of the music. Play it back faster, and the music gets higher; if it's slower, it's lower.

- *Synthesized music* is created with a sound and music processor in the computer or game system. The programmer creates a set of instructions to this coprocessor which synthesizes instruments by creating sound waveshapes in very complex combinations. The instructions are a very small amount of data, which are extremely flexible as you can change the individual note's pitch and duration, the instruments, the volume, and the playback speed all independently. You can even fold in sound effects created by the coprocessor as part of your music. However, this is usually the most difficult environment for a composer to work in and typically creates the lowest-quality music.

- *MIDI music* requires a software "player" either in the computer or game system or in your program. MIDI is a music "language" that was created for electronic instruments, music synthesizers, and computers to speak to one another. It's very powerful and allows composers and engineers to create and edit music with simple software tools on computers. With MIDI, each note is efficiently notated for pitch, duration, and one of 128 instruments. As with synthesizer music, in real time, every element of the music can be changed. With the better MIDI players, the quality of the music can approach that of digitized music, as the instruments are often created by sampling real instruments. MIDI is the most efficient type of music for computer games in its size (it's very small), its flexibility, and its quality. Keep an eye out for an enhanced form of MIDI which uses DLS technology to improve the quality of MIDI instrumentation. This improvement will greatly enhance the reasons for using MIDI music.

In large projects, I often recommend a combination of two or more types of music technology. This allows you to balance very high quality with flexibility and data size. Whenever I can, I use MIDI music for the bulk of the work. I try to choose key moments in the user's game play experience for the digitized music: introductory sequences, endings, rewards, major transitions, and, most importantly, areas in the game where the user is going to be thinking, waiting, planning, or otherwise remaining in the same environment.

When you discuss the music design, be sure to include what you expect the technology to be able to do with the music. Include these things in this list (which are all possible and have been for years):

- In key views of scenes, load in all the nonmusic elements to memory so you can stream digitized music from CD, hard disk, or from the Internet.
- Change the instrumentation.
- Change the key of the music.
- Alter the playback rate of any kind of music.
- Alter the volume of any kind of music.
- Fade in and out of any kind of music (especially based on user interactions).

- Loop music. (Different types of music have different technical limitations. Learn them and work with them.)

- Repeat music. (Specify real-world random ranges for the programmers.)

- Attach intro and ending phrases to otherwise looping or repeating music. In this way you can more gracefully and artfully start and stop music.

- Special volume control keys enable producers and directors to adjust volumes and record them during testing.

- An interface switch enables the user to turn music on or (heaven forbid!) off.

If you're putting music on the CD, consider putting it in a form that can be played by a regular music CD player. There are two reasons for doing this: the grandparent factor and the sound track album.

Consider using actual CD music technology (this technology is variously referred to as Red Book, multisession, enhanced CD, and CD+) especially when you are doing consumer product-style products in support of major motion pictures or television shows or the like. As an example, if I were producing a CD-ROM to go along with a film, I would put several songs from the movie on the CD so they could be played in a regular music CD player. Why? Consider the marketing of such a title. It's what I call the *grandparent factor*.

Imagine a family member who doesn't know what (if any) type of computer is in a child's house wants to buy the latest (and often slightly expensive) tie-in product for the child's current favorite characters. It's often not clear to a non—family member and/or non—computer user what a CD-ROM is in comparison to a music CD or that you cannot play a CD-ROM in a fancy stereo system. So when the gift is opened, the child cannot use it if it requires a computer. If there are regular music tracks on the CD-ROM, then at least there is some actual way to use and enjoy the product (assuming that there is a better chance of there being a music CD player available than a CD-ROM drive in the right kind of computer).

As for the sound track album, assuming you've spent considerable time, thought, and money on creating a really great sound track for your game, there is no reason not to allow users to enjoy this music through their stereo system. On the Return to Zork CD-ROM, there are almost 20 tracks of recorded music from the game that you can play on your music CD player.

To this day, I believe that the score that Nathan Wang wrote for Return to Zork is one of the most complete, complex, interesting, and highest-quality scores ever created for a computer game. In discussing all the elements that were considered in creating the RTZ sound track, I hope to give you a sense of the kinds of things that go into the highest-quality music design.

Nathan was provided with a list of all the music pieces or cues he was to write for the game. There are 80 or so views in RTZ, and as the game progresses, the music for many of the views becomes darker and more forbidding (in three stages). In all, the list was about 180 items long. He was given a list of cues that included, for each view in each stage of the game,

- Name of view (or event, such as the opening, credits, death scenes)
- Mood for current stage of game
- Brief description of type of music or example (e.g., like the theme from *The Magnificent Seven*)
- Length of the cue
- Whether the cue repeated or looped
- A filename for the cue
- Whether the cue was to be recorded live or used only as MIDI

In addition to this list we provided him with videotapes and storyboards, a synthesizer that allowed him to simulate the computer music devices that RTZ would play on, and a budget for the live recording session. He composed the 180 or so cues in his studio directly into a series of MIDI files. So as he was creating the score, we could use (and test) placeholder music.

Nathan used a technique from the world of classical music and opera known as the *Leitmotiv.* You can think of this as a small musical theme for each character and for each major geographic location in the world. If you are familiar with Prokofiev's "Peter and the Wolf," you can see how this is used in an orchestral piece (it's also used in the sound tracks to the *Star Wars* movies). The great thing about writing music this way is that you are forced to create rich and complex melodies and counterpoints when two or more of these characters and locations are juxtaposed. For example, as you navigate from location to location in the world of Return to Zork, you hear themes shift in and out, indicating where you've been, where you're going, whom you've just been with, and whom you might run into. It's a subtle yet sophisticated way of communicating information to the player, in setting a mood, and creating anticipation. Imagine trying to combine the theme for a silly, off-beat character as this character is about to enter the deepest, darkest recesses of the Great Underground Empire!

Another great element of the RTZ music is the way in which it repeats and loops. The repeating and looping cues were written specifically with the technological limitations in mind. If a cue was to be looped and that cue was to be played back only via MIDI technology, then Nathan wrote a longer-than-normal piece of music and often added a special intro so the music looped back to the second or third bar to skip the intro.

However, if there was a chance that the music was to be digitally recorded and played back or that the cue needed to be short, or if we felt the user would be hearing this music many, many times, Nathan wrote what I now refer to as *music with white space* (white space is normally used to refer to spaces and tab characters in word processing documents and such). This type of music is rhythmically very unusual and/or complicated and often has many pauses and stops throughout it. To most of the world, it is virtually impossible to tell when the cue repeats, so it's perfect for often repeated or looped music and for dealing with the vague timings of trying to loop music from a CD-ROM or hard drive. He attempted to eliminate any "hooks" in these cues so that the user could not catch where the repeats occurred in the music. Altogether we got these great cues that could go on and on and, to most, never seem as if they repeated. Also, when looped from the CD-ROM, this music with white space didn't appear to suffer from out-of-rhythm disc seeks.

⇒The message here is to create repeating and looping music in a very special way. Don't count on exact timing during the looping, and you won't create a sound track that sounds as if it has a terrible sense of rhythm. Use unusual rhythm patterns, pauses, stops, and other compositional techniques so that users can't follow the construction of the music without making a concerted effort. Finally, listen to the music repeat and loop a lot to see if you've actually achieved these goals.

When a MIDI sound track for a cue is made, musicians can actually perform the music directly to a MIDI file on a computer. Then the composer can use the computer to repeat sections, alter the pitch and durations of notes, and add other musical effects. In addition, the composer can do something called *quantizing* the music. Quantizing uses the computer to make the timing of the attack and release of each note exactly right on the beats of the music. It sounds like a great tool, doesn't it? Don't use quantization. Please! Stop your composer both in your design documents and when the music is being created! Quantizing removes all the humanlike performance quality from the MIDI file and creates a subtle but noticeable robotic effect in the music. If the composer isn't comfortable releasing music with his or her performance, hire a high-quality musician to play it! I cannot stress this enough. Don't quantize.

Finally, the digitized music that was created and used in RTZ was specifically composed and recorded to take advantage of the medium. First, my philosophy about digitized music is that if you are going to the trouble to use digitized music instead of MIDI or synthesized music, record acoustic instruments! It is self-defeating to record electronic instruments, electric guitars, electronic drum kits, and other synthesized musical instruments, since you can drive them all via MIDI which is much smaller and more efficient. In RTZ, Nathan was given a budget for both the cost of the musicians and the number of minutes of live music. He chose to not use string players in his orchestra for financial reasons (it can require as many as 15 players to make a string section) and, instead, wrote all his music for brass, woodwinds, and percussion. To be honest, he did use an extremely high-end synthesizer to simulate an organ in one piece and a string section in two places, but it was a matter of financial necessity. In any case, using acoustic instruments in the sound track provided a very different and affecting set of musical numbers in the sound track. We used these pieces in the opening and ending sequences of the entire product and in two or three key transitions between sections of the game, and the rest were set aside for places in RTZ where the user was to spend a lot of time. We used this very expensive, very high-quality music in the mazes, in rooms where there was a lot of research to do, and in locations where there were complex and time-consuming puzzles or strategies to consider.

A Word about Interactive Music

Although some companies, such as LucasArts, put a high value on music technology, most do not. This means that if you want to create a score that "writes itself" based on the user's actions, you must design and build the technology yourself, license it very inexpensively, or make it such a fundamental part of your game that it is indispensable. Although this type of feature should and can, in the future, enhance the quality of the user's experience, the senior management and production executives in most companies will ask, "But will this feature sell more units?" Unfortunately, it is difficult to answer an unqualified yes in most cases.

I think that algorithmically created music technology will come in time, and it is most likely to happen with MIDI or synthesized music as opposed to digitized music. Both MIDI and synthesized music are efficient and small languages that allow a programmer to manipulate music by using the well-established rules of music. Digitized music is neither efficient nor a language, and as such, there are no musical rules that really can be directly applied without a lot of research followed by a lot of coding and a lot of processing power. The only exception is the ability to change the playback rate and volume, but I think those hardly qualify as the tools to create a self-writing musical score.

My hope is that someone *will* create a technique and a licensable (or free) technology for interactive scoring. It should allow a composer to write a score in such a way that the score can modify itself as the user interacts. I'm sure this will happen, and I look forward to the day. In the meantime, however, be prepared to adjust your music design so that it can use a prewritten score.

Physical Production Elements or Assets List

This is almost everyone's least-favorite part to create in the design document. This is a comprehensive and complete list of each and every asset used in the product. At a minimum, for each asset you should list

- The filename of the asset
- A "real name" for the asset (creating a long description here can be a lot of work, but very useful)
- The category and subcategories of the asset (e.g., art/FMV/mayor's welcomes, music/MIDI/suburbs/final act)
- The status of the asset: final, version number, storyboard, temporary, deleted, to be done, submitted, approved, tested, etc.
- The date for the latest version of the asset
- Where the asset is being kept (the computer, server, site, folder, subdirectory, etc.)

Some optional items for your list:

- Who is responsible for creating the current stage of the asset
- Where in the product is this asset used
- Duration, cel count, and other measures of the asset's length
- On-screen size (for art elements)
- Data size (for all elements)

■ Playback information: playback rate, location, size, volume, randomness, etc.

■ Repeating information: looping, repeating, pauses, different start and stop locations, etc.

■ Reusability information: can be resized, repositioned, used in alternative order, recolored, etc.

■ Localization required: for art that includes text or local symbols, VO, FMV, text

There are several ways to make this list easier to create and maintain. First, realize that, like the view-by-view description and other major sections of the design document, this is a living, evolving part of the design. Give yourself time, room, and mechanisms for adding, deleting, and altering elements in this list. As with the view-by-view, when you eliminate an element from your product that was originally on the list, don't remove the item from the list; strike it through and/or indicate that it is deleted with a status indicator that's very easy to see (e.g., bold red).

⇒Use either a spreadsheet or a database program just for the creation and maintenance of this list, and put any printouts in a binder. You want people to have fast and ready access to what is ultimately a large document. You don't want people to have to either load the entire design into their computer software or thumb through dialogue, view-by-views, storyboards, and other things just to use this list.

Finally, if you have a large enough product, hire an "assets" manager to function as a librarian. This person should help create and then maintain this list of assets as well as manage the storage and retrieval of these assets.

What's in a Name? A Rose By Any Other Name Will Smell as Sweet

⇒Regardless of whether you hire an assets manager, include a page or two at the beginning of the physical assets list which dictates a naming convention for the data files that contain the assets for the entire production. Trying to retrofit a naming convention to a set of assets can be a huge waste of production time as well as potentially disastrous. Once established, the naming convention can make your life easier throughout the design process. These are some of the advantages:

■ When creating the view-by-view, you don't have to spend time making up names for files, as the convention will dictate what the name must be. You can even use some database tools to help you name them.

■ When creating the art, sound, music, FMV, or other physical assets, the artists, engineers, and other folks involved will already have a specific name or naming style under which to save their files.

■ The programmers can begin creating your program with no assets at all. By using the actual, official, and final names for each asset, they can instantly create all the placeholders or use other methods to build the product. When the producers provide them with files with the real assets, the program to load and use them is already completed! It turns out that sometimes certain styles of naming conventions can actually reduce the size and increase the efficiency of the code, when the programmers algorithmically create names for the files the program needs to load.

■ When you search for files for a specific purpose, it's a handy device for quickly identifying groupings of assets.

■ When you move files between operating systems (especially from Macintosh to Windows), the naming convention can prevent names that are illegal on one system from ever being used. You'd be amazed at how insensitive most computer users are to this unfortunate reality of computer operating systems. Having a naming system in place avoids this problem.

■ If a file shows up that someone isn't expecting, the person has a chance of figuring out what it is by decoding the name.

■ When you are in environments where the user is forced to see the filename, such as the World Wide Web or in make-it-yourself programs, you can provide useful and sometimes even entertaining information in the filename.

Naming Conventions

⇒If you are working on a large project with lots of physical assets to track and many filenames to remember, I cannot think of a more important production technique for dealing with the hundreds or thousands of files and dozens of people creating and using them. This portion of the design document may need to be written with or by the producers and technical directors; but, in any case, it should be written early.

As I mentioned earlier, one problem in coming up with a naming convention is the necessity of creating filenames that will work on all your production equipment. This usually means that DOS filename rules are the least common denominator. It doesn't matter if your artists and sound engineers and composers are all creating files on Macintoshes or other systems that support long filenames; if your final product or any major step in the production process requires that the files be on a system that only supports DOS names, that's what everyone should use.

DOS filename rules are pretty simple. You have up to an eight-letter first name with up to a three-letter last name separated by a period (or "dot"). The first name can use any alphanumeric character plus a few other characters such as !, -, _, but I would avoid these. The last name or file extension can likewise be any three alphanumeric characters. In both the first and last names, spaces are not allowed.

Decoding DOS names can be a bit like reading vanity license plates. Hence, we get clever but not particularly useful DOS names such as IM2QT4U.txt and Inhis.age (that is "in his dotage").

Regardless of what filename format you have to deal with, let me make a few suggestions:

Name your files so that they form groups based on the view in the product in which they are used. For example, if you have a location in your world called the *Dugout,* you could begin the filenames for art, sound, animation, FMVs, and anything else that happens in the Dugout with the letters DO or DG or DUG. If you are going to have multiple views of the Dugout, you might want to number or letter these sublocations, for example, DUG8, DGb, and DO0. Since many computer systems don't do a great job of distinguishing between the letter O and the number 0, it is very dangerous to use them both in a naming convention. And as you will see later, you need the number 0. My suggestion is that you either always use lowercase letters (a small o is easily distinguished from a 0) or avoid the letter O. Also, the fewer letters and numbers required to identify a location, the better. If you think you might have more than 10 sublocations (i.e., where 0 to 9 is insufficient), consider using letters only; then you have 26 subdivisions, which is usually more than enough and helps keep the filename shorter.

Use the computer standard naming convention of a three-letter *extension.* This is a three-letter combination that follows a period at the end of the filename. On many systems this helps the software identify what type of data is in the file. I strongly recommend using this, as it can help you when you have a variety of types of files in one location. For example, *.txt, .gif, .wav,* and *.mid* are standard extensions for plain text, an Internet graphics file format, a popular digitized audio data format, and MIDI music files.

Between the location and subview and the three-letter file type extension, you can do many things. I like to add a two-letter initial or abbreviation for the name of the type of object that's represented in the file. If it's a xylophone, I might use the letters XY or XP. Keep in mind that I might have a xylophone piece of removable art, a xylophone animation, and several pieces of xylophone music. In this case, the filename extension helps to distinguish which xylophone asset is which.

Finally, I like to reserve three spaces in the filename, right before the extension, for a number between 000 and 999 (notice it's *not* 001 and 999). If a product isn't too big and I know I'll never have a series of similar or related things of more than 26, or 100, then I can reduce these to one or two characters and give myself more room for either the name of the location or the name of the object. For example, if I have an animation of the xylophone that's 200 frames long, each individual frame could require its own filename, and therefore we'd need the entire three spaces in the filename to handle this.

When you are using any kind of numbering or lettering where the naming convention requires more than one letter or number, always insist on leading 0s or a's in the filename. The filenames should all be the exact same length (i.e., the same number of alphanumeric characters). So even if you have only three pieces of xylophone music, the numbers should be 000, 001, and 002. If nothing else, this makes sorting the files much easier and much less complicated to read. Always counting from 000 leaves no doubt as to the first filename in any sequence.

Using the above examples as a guideline, I might have a naming convention that looks like this:

LLVoo###.eee

where LL = location name abbreviation
      V = view of location as a letter from a to z or as a number from 0 to 9 (there is always at least one view in each location)
   oo = object name abbreviation
 ### = object count from 000 to 999 always beginning at 000 (and always three digits)
 .eee = file type extension

Table 3-9 contains some filenames based on the above example.

TABLE 3-9

Filename	Description
Dgaxp000.bmp	Dugout, view a, xylophone BMP or bitmap art image file
Dgbxp000.a03	Dugout, view b, xylophone animation #03 (which is the fourth animation sequence, counting from 0). I use this extension filename to indicate multiple animation sequences.
Dgbxp000.c03	Dugout, view b, xylophone animation #03 frame (or cel) #00 (which is the first frame or cel in the fourth animation sequence). Again, this is an extension that I've made up to allow some clarity about which files are attached to which animation sequences.
Dgbxp001.c03	Dugout, view b, xylophone animation #03, cel #01 (the second cel or frame).
Dgbxp010.mid	Dugout, view b, xylophone MIDI music selection #10 (the eleventh selection counting from 0).
Dggxp000.fmv	Dugout, view g, the first (#000) full-motion video sequence of the xylophone.

Assets List

Now that you know how to specify and name each asset, here is a list of the kinds of assets you need to exhaustively list for a multimedia title:

1. Art
   A. Complete backgrounds or backdrops
   B. Partial background art
   C. Transition elements (e.g., black screen, shrinking frames)
   D. Removable objects
   E. Animation
      (1) 2D animation sequences
      (2) 2D animation components
      (3) 2D animation registrations
   F. 3D animation
      (1) 3D animation sequences
      (2) 3D models
      (3) 3D surfaces
      (4) 3D motions
   G. FMV
      (1) Uncomposited clips and components
      (2) Completed clips
   H. Interface
      (1) Cursors and pointers
      (2) Wait cursors

          (3) Icons for desktop
          (4) Other interface elements
      I. Frames, borders, other layout elements
      J. Fonts
      K. Palettes

2. Sound effects and audio
      A. Interface sounds
      B. Environmental sounds
      C. Animation sounds
      D. Voice-overs
      E. FMV "sound tracks"

3. Music
      A. Digitized music
      B. MIDI music
      C. Synthesized music
      D. Sampled instruments
      E. Synthesized instruments

4. Data
      A. Text
      B. Default settings
      C. World, stats, and other data
      D. Downloads

5. Code
      A. Installer
      B. Launcher
      C. Main executable
      D. Overlaid code
      E. "Plug-ins"

As I'm sure you can imagine, if you include all the minimum information for each and every single element that needs to be produced, named, and tracked, this becomes a huge spreadsheet or database file.

Competitive Products

At last, a simple section. Here you should list every single product that you or anyone else can think of that might be competitive. Point out briefly what's good or bad about each product and how your product will compare. This will help you keep an eye on the ball in regard to creating a product that will compete well. It also goes a long way to helping your critical thinking as to what you want to accomplish and avoid in your product.

Finally, keep this section upgraded throughout the life cycle of your game, as the producers, directors, and marketing team will need to keep up to date on how your project is going to compete with the latest games.

Marketing Ideas

This may be your only chance to communicate all your great marketing ideas to the marketing team (whom, depending on your role, you may never meet!). This section combined with the competitive products, high concept, dust jacket story, platform, genre, target audience from the design, and the unique features and selling points from the preliminary design will go a long way to help you state the product's case for the sales and marketing staff.

⇒Without the help of your knowledge and ideas, they will have to do all the research that you've already done.

Follow-up Products

As a final thought in your design, spend some time discussing follow-up products and sequels. Many of the best-designed products are constructed in such a way as to allow the creation of an aftermarket. This can be done with add-ons, data disks, mission disks, plug-ins, and the like that add new features, characters, worlds, puzzles, data, statistics, and so on. Regardless of whether your product can support these ancillary products, consider the possibility of creating a sequel.

By considering ancillary products and sequels here, the technical director and many members of the team will be able to focus on creating a product that is *extensible* (i.e., allows add-on or ancillary products) and extendible with sequels. Most of this work can be accomplished by carefully designing the computer programming to anticipate these features. Some work, however, might need to be done by you in order for the story to have room for a sequel once your product has topped the charts.

The Myth of the Complete Game Design

Throughout my career, just about everywhere I've worked, someone has said at the beginning of a project, "Before we begin production, I want to see a complete game design!" This is usually said after this person has just experienced the frenetic behavior of the production team during the last project. Watching as the production team improvises solutions to game design problems or adds new features based on new information about the competition, or simply discovers that they need to add something crucial that no one thought of until the last moment, this person believes this could have all been avoided by a complete and final design before production ever began.

⇒Frankly, I believe that the notion of a complete game design is a myth. It's normal for a producer or executive to believe in complete game designs and to fantasize about how easy it would be on everyone if the game design were simply perfected before production got underway. However, the nature of the interactive business is that the customer is part of the entertainment experience. Until you create enough of the product to test it on a real person, you cannot know whether your design will ever work.

This is true in every other creative medium, so I don't see why it shouldn't be true in the interactive business. The creative process is an evolutionary process. As with workshops for plays, screenings for movies, on-set rewrites and improvisation on a TV set, rechoreographing a dance when a substitute dancer is inserted into a cast, and so on, the producer can insist on the original version or can acquiesce to the larger artistic picture and let it improve.

This is not to dispute that some interactive projects have more or less stuck to their original design documents. Smaller products and non-game-style products have an especially good chance of having completely static game designs.

But during the course of any production, all sorts of things change—the competition, the platform, the world of entertainment, world events, the ideas of the production team, and so on. If you allow these things to influence a design during the course of production, as I believe you should, you stand a better chance of creating a product that everyone will be happy with. And don't forget your testers. Use outside people who are in no way related to the production. The more creative and innovative you want to be and the more willing you are to incorporate the input of your testers, the more willing you must be to making changes in the design during the course of production. For me, in the end, the point of making the product is to create interactive entertainment at the highest possible level of quality, not to produce a product that simply matches my original script.

Principles of
Game Design

7

Principle 1:
Great Rhythm

⇒The core of any great entertainment experience, interactive or otherwise, is great rhythm. The rhythm of the experience will hook you, lead you on, tease you, tantalize you, frustrate you, and reward you. Interactive entertainment is no different, but as you might rightly suggest, the users are in control of the rhythm of their own experience. This makes the design task difficult, not impossible. Ignoring this key principle is, in my opinion, the main reason why most designs fail to lead to compelling interactive titles.

Baseball: A Simple Paradigm for Great Rhythm

⇒I think baseball is one of the best models for the kind of game play rhythm that works well. It's what I call the "hits, outs, and innings" approach to game design. In baseball (real or computerized), each section of the game is punctuated by a ball, strike, hit, out, or inning (I'm taking some liberties here for clarity). The beauty of this structure is that an out or a hit happens every few minutes, and half of an inning usually takes only about 8 to 10 minutes. Watching just one more batter takes so little time that you are usually willing to stay for just one more batter or one more half inning. Before you know it, you've been watching for an hour. Major League Baseball is so aware of this fact that several attempts have been made to speed up the time between pitches.

In this model, the less time the hits, outs, and innings take, the easier it is to capture the attention of and, to be quite frank, to addict the player. A few seconds is a small investment in time if there is a satisfactory reward. Compare this to a game in which each reward requires 15 to 30 minutes of play time; you know before you sit down to begin that this amount of time is possibly too long to consider even playing.

In designing Earl Weaver Baseball (EWB), I was considering this time issue in the rhythm and flow of game play. EWB was designed to work as a simulation of baseball, so that balls and strikes were realistically shown pitch by pitch for each batter before the play resolved (with a hit, walk, or out). However, since it was built as a true simulation, the graphics were only a visual manifestation of the underlying game being modeled by the computer. By turning off the animation graphics during the pitches leading up to the final pitch for each batter, we created something called *one pitch mode*. In this mode, you see the final ball-strike count appear on the scoreboard for each batter before the deciding pitch is thrown with the animation graphics turned back on. The batter reacts to the pitch, and the play is visually resolved in one pitch, all the while retaining the statistical and physical integrity of the full-pitch simulation. This feature reduced the time each batter takes at the plate to a few seconds. Games in one pitch mode were reduced to 15 to 20 minutes, whereas full pitch mode games (in which each pitch was graphically shown with pitches, throwbacks from the catcher, foul balls, etc.) took from 90 to 120 minutes. After this change, I discovered that people were willing to play not only additional innings, but also more games.

This rule works for more than just baseball. I believe part of the great success of Where in the World Is Carmen Sandiego is due to this design model. If you consider each clue a pitch, each answer a hit or an out, and the solution to each crime a half inning, you can see how people could get hooked on playing for long periods. Each question (out) takes only a few seconds, and each crime (half inning) can be solved in a matter of minutes. Add to this the extra reward of getting promoted (full inning), and you really have a great rhythm going. Answering just one more question (out) is such a small investment that you're likely to go ahead with an answer. Before you know it, you've been playing for half an hour or longer and have been promoted several times.

Although a bit more abstract, other examples of this design technique are found in just about every side-scrolling video game and trough game. Obstacles are placed in your path as you move, and you have to get them out of your way or die (hit or out). Get enough obstacles out of the way, and you either face the "boss monster" or "clear the level," which is, of course, the inning. The better the rhythm here, the better the game play.

Football: An Alternative to Baseball

⇒If we stick with sports to provide design models, football gives us another great paradigm for a rhythm that people like: *Think, then do.* While adventure games, RPGs, and strategy games are often based quite naturally on this design principle, they often miss the mark in creating a compelling rhythm by not consciously applying the Think, Then Do model.

In football, the offensive team thinks up a play while the defense creates a strategy to stop it. Then at the signal from the quarterback, all players attempt to do their assigned tasks. Depending on the rules, you have about 1 minute to create your strategy and 10 seconds or less to execute it. You do this over and over, but with the limit of a ticking clock, the subgoals of gaining first downs, and the major goal of outscoring your opponent. This rhythm provides a great challenge for both the intellect and the body; the thought of outthinking or outperforming (or both) your opponent is a very potent hook.

In other uses of this design, the action done after thinking is only the execution of your strategy and not a test of skill or physical prowess. In this way, chess as a game design fits into the Think, Then Do model.

While you could squeeze football into the Hits, Outs, and Innings model, the fixed time and ability to mathematically eliminate an opponent's chance to win before the end of the game really help delineate these models. In baseball, a game can go on indefinitely or can be very short, and the team that is behind always has a chance to win in its final at-bat. More importantly, the rhythm is defined by the hits, outs, and innings in baseball since technically the ball is always in play until the end of a half inning. In contrast, the football rhythm is one of alternating pauses to think while the ball is dead and brief spurts of intense action.

The all-time best example of Think, Then Do is Lemmings by Psygnosis. In this highly entertaining and addictive game, you are presented with a problem—get a certain number of Lemmings from point *A* to point *B* in a fixed time—with an unlimited amount of time to create your strategy.

I believe it was an interesting design choice by Psygnosis to not limit your time for considering strategy. I've watched many people play (and have played it myself for far too many hours), and often people have their own, internal ticking clock measuring how long they will think before jumping into the action. Once you decide to move your lemmings, then there's a real ticking clock and you must have the dexterity, presence of mind, and discipline to execute your strategy.

Adventure games are also often designed as Think, Then Do products. You are presented with a problem to solve, either explicitly or implicitly, hints as to how to solve it, and then time to consider a strategy. When you're ready, you attempt to solve the problem. These games often bog down in the timing of the solutions that you can do. In Return to Zork, we attempted to adjust the design so that the first puzzles both were easy to solve and required the use of the entire interface. In the following puzzles, we attempted to "train" the user to use the tools from the first puzzle solutions to solve increasingly complex puzzles. Then, just when the player thought he or she had solved the final puzzle of the game, we opened up the entire world of the Underground Empire. At this point in the game, we switched into a design that allowed the player to simultaneously solve many small and large puzzles all at once. What this created, in my opinion, was a rhythm in which people were thinking of several solution strategies at once, which allowed them to solve puzzles or discover new things on a regular enough basis to always feel that they were moving forward in the story and the game.

Skiing: Fall Down or Pause

In contrast to the Hits, Outs, and Innings and Think, Then Do models, there is the downhill skiing model or Do, Do, Do, or Die. While the Do, Do, Do, or Die model, in which the user is constantly doing something, is the ultimate in interactivity, it is the most difficult in terms of creating great rhythm.

When you're skiing, you can simply keep the same speed and direction and you're sure to have fun for a brief time (right until the moment where you hurt yourself). More likely, you will change direction and speed to adjust for the snow, the terrain, other skiers, and the type of overall experience you want to have (such as a high-speed or a more peaceful run). However, unless you choose to stop or fall down, you simply continue to ski. Naturally, you develop your own rhythm of changing speeds and directions, and this is a reward in and of itself; there is no scoring.

Allowing players to develop their own rhythms while being pulled along (as gravity does to the skier) is the key to these kinds of games. Getting this right is one of the greatest tricks in the business and, I believe, can best be done by a combination of insightful anticipation by the designer and lots and lots of testing and tweaking by the development team. Without the anticipation by the designer, the right kind of elements that drive the action and allow the user control won't exist as tools for the development team to adjust.

While side-scrolling platform games and trough games such as Doom and Quake fall into this category, they can also usually fit into the Hits, Outs, and Innings design as well. Some of the first and best attempts came early on in two of the text adventures from Infocom: Planetfall and Suspended. In each of these, time was a design element so that the clock was in some ways always ticking. Whether counting time as a number of moves or as real time, both games forced the player to make strategic choices and to live or die with the consequences. As time marched on, the pressure increased to make better and better decisions; the tension and suspense were created in the player's own head. This tension and suspense created a rhythm that really motivated the player to keep playing to see if she or he could beat the clock or die trying.

More recently, Voyeur, Johnny Mnemonic, and Psychic Detective have attempted to make "interactive movies" that continue playing with or without your interactions. In these games the clock keeps ticking as you move from full-motion video (FMV) scene to FMV scene. Johnny

Mnemonic offers some interesting action designs for a first effort, and Psychic Detective does a better job of involving you in the story and the interactivity. My only question about both of these is whether players have enough time and control to create their own rhythms or whether they're simply pointed straight downhill with only enough time to avoid the really bad bumps and trees.

I'm still waiting for the breakthrough design that will keep a story or game going while allowing the players to control the rhythm of the experience through their interactions.

Beyond Game Play

⇒For a truly great title, the entire product must have great rhythm. It is not enough that the game play rhythm works; every component must be carefully designed with the rhythm of the *overall* product in mind. Having these extra elements well designed is often enough to have them create an overarching rhythm to the experience. However, often these icing-on-the-cake items are left to others to design or, worse, are not designed at all. Here's a list of some of these key elements that impact the overall rhythm of the experience and that are often ignored during the design phase. The elements most often forgotten in terms of the rhythm of the game are

- Installation
- First-time intro
- Subsequent intros
- Attract mode
- First interaction
- General player interactions
- Lack of player interactions
- Load and calculation time
- Transitions
- Quitting
- Linear sequences
- Endings

Installation

⇒Often ignored, this is the first impression your product makes with the user. Anything you can do to entertain, create a sense of excitement, and cover the time for installation makes an enormous impact. There is no reason not to include something entertaining! These are some essential ingredients that you should really design yourself:

- ⇒Don't require installation if possible.
- ⇒Otherwise, make installation as short as possible.
- ⇒Make the installation look and feel as if it is part of the "world" that the game belongs in (rather than the world of computers and operating systems).
- ⇒Tell part of the story of the game during installation.
- ⇒Keep the user posted on the progress of the installation without using non-English terms (such as filenames).
- ⇒Keep something moving so the computer doesn't appear to be stuck.
- ⇒Count the progress so that the end is predictable (e.g., count down toward 0 or up to 100 percent).
- ⇒Prove to the user that the sound and graphics systems are working with your product by playing a clip or animation that uses sound and music.
- ⇒Automatically detect settings and useful files that your program needs.
- ⇒Offer a complete and easy uninstall.

First-Time Intro

⇒**Rule 1:** Make it entertaining and informative.

⇒**Rule 2:** Keep it as short as possible.

⇒**Rule 3:** Don't expect anyone to want to watch it more than once.

⇒**Rule 4:** Don't bother the user with buttons to continue a saved game if it's the first time playing. Get to the opening.

⇒**Rule 5:** Look to experienced professionals in different forms of linear media to help you with creating a great rhythm in this piece. Explain to them that it needs to be very, very short.

⇒**Rule 6:** Remember, the user bought this game to play it, not watch it, and wants to interact sooner rather than later.

⇒The function of the first-time intro is to hook the user into the world you're creating, not to impress the user with your experience in creating linear media or to show off technology that doesn't appear elsewhere in the product. Remember, the user should be expected (or forced) to watch it only once. From then on, users will (and should) skip it.

Because of this, care should be taken not to spend *too* much money or effort on the intro, as it is the part that the user sees and interacts with least. Spend your time and money on great game play. Even if your intro is 10 minutes long, compared to a highly engaging 80-hour experience, it's a small and probably forgotten part of the product. Creating a great attract mode (see below) is far more valuable.

For me, the best intro of all time comes from one of the Indiana Jones Adventure games, as it is instantly interactive (or at least gives that illusion) while supplying the context of the story, titles, and credits all at once.

Subsequent Intros

⇒Depending on the product, you should design a separate introductory sequence for players who've played before. This is something the computer can easily track and detect, so use it. Sometimes, the best solution is no introduction at all. Simply show the title card while loading the product, and get right to it. If you cannot do any of these things and for some reason still want to show the first-time introduction on every subsequent start-up, be sure to allow the user numerous ways to skip the first-time introduction without having to get the exact right input. In other words, allow the Esc key, the space bar, the mouse button, the Q key, and/or possibly any other key press to skip it. You'll have happy players.

In *The Muppet CD-ROM: Muppets Inside,* each time you start the game by double-clicking an icon with your name on it, you get a different welcome from the Muppets. Kermit and company know how long it's been since you last played and tell you so (e.g., Kermit comes on screen and says, "It's been 4 whole days...let's get going already..."). Also, they look at the system clock to see what time of year it is. If it's your birthday, there's a birthday greeting from Fozzie; and if it's around Christmas, the whole gang shows up in a bus decorated for the holidays.

I can't say enough about the impact of this on players. It draws them right in and makes them feel as if they're in the world of the Muppets

instantly. In terms of the rhythm, these segments were written and produced by the same folks who write and produce the Muppets for television, and it shows. And very importantly, all these sequences are quite
short.

⇒If you're dealing with a game that has options at the beginning, consider making different ways to launch the program or clever ways to integrate these options into the subsequent intro sequences. The options often
include these:

- Load or continue a game in progress. This is the most used start-up
  selection for just about every game. Design the subsequent intro
  sequence with this in mind.
- Start a new game (which might play the first-time intro, but probably
  shouldn't).
- Replay the intro sequence (if it's great, it's conceivable the user might
  want to show it to a friend).
- Reconfigure the game (difficulty level, etc.).
- Reconfigure the system (sound systems, graphics resolution, etc.).

Attract Mode

This term comes from the stand-up video game arcade world. This is the
self-promotional, linear, self-running demo and advertisement for the
game. Most video games and the better-designed computer games have
this feature. I think it's best if the game designer and director design the
attract mode early on and insist that the programming team build this
very early in the production process.

Typically the attract mode will run in a video game if you plug in the
cartridge, turn on the machine, and don't interact at all for about 30 to 60
seconds. For computer games, it usually starts by running a separate program; by pressing a special cheat key combination while the game is running; by using a special command line switch when starting the program;
or by waiting 30 to 60 seconds after the user launched the program and
detecting that the player has not interacted at all.

In any case, *attract mode* is a way to show what the game's worlds look
like and to give a viewer a sense of the type of interactivity and experience involved in playing your game. You should use actual elements and
assets from the real game; and room permitting, you might want to add
special voiceover audio to promote and explain the product to the viewer.

On top of all this, if you design the attract mode with random behaviors, it can be different every time you see it. If you've had the programming team create a "replay" function for testing in the program and there are a series of cheat keys for skipping around the worlds, these can be powerful tools for quickly creating your attract mode.

Attract mode is also great for use in trade shows where retailers can see your product but often there isn't anyone demonstrating it who really knows how to play it. Likewise, it can be a great tool for use in a software store for potential purchasers to see the game in action.

In the original EWB, the attract mode played a few innings of one pitch baseball with famous old-time players (such as Babe Ruth and Ty Cobb) with "supers" or title cards between the plays and innings. After a few innings, we'd cycle back to the start with a super for Earl Weaver Baseball and start up a new game with new players in a new stadium. Because the normal game simulation was running during attract mode (as opposed to preprogrammed plays), each round of the attract mode was different. It got to be pretty addictive to stand there and watch it. It is a very effective tool.

First Interaction

⇒As I've said many times, the player's first interaction cannot come soon enough. So after watching your really brief first-time intro, the player should be given the first chance to interact. Design this so that the user has something obvious to do with a clear purpose and instant feedback. Better yet, provide several opportunities for this sort of instant-gratification experience on the first screen. This will set a rhythm for the first experiences that will help entice the user to keep playing.

⇒While you are designing the experience for the first interaction, create mechanisms for feedback that will train the user to use the tools and make progress right away. If it's an action game, perhaps you can start in a training exercise with a helper, teacher, or guide talking the user through the experience. If it's an adventure game, it's often a good idea to set up obvious and easy puzzles in the style of, and using the same techniques as, the more complex puzzles to come. In either case, wrap any story to be told around the interactive choices of the user, not more linear sequences. Doing these types of interactive things helps start the game play rhythm.

One of my big gripes with the standard RPG design that most people use is that the first interactions are long, involved sequences of setting up your party, defining your character, and equipping your group to go out into the world. And these days it always seems to follow a lengthy linear intro sequence informing you of your mission. This can detract from the interactive rhythm of the experience. Just when you're ready to dive in, you're forced to learn a once-in-a-while interface and you aren't doing anything in the normal rhythm of the interactivity to come. I'm waiting for (and perhaps designing) a different type of RPG first interaction in which what you do and how you do it define your character, the party members you'll travel with, and the first set of supplies you'll need. Your name can even be bestowed upon you, completely eliminating the need for you to come up with something clever that may or may not fit within the fantasy world created for the game.

The Player Interactions

⇒Whenever the player interacts, consider the rhythm of the experience and specify it for the production team. If a sound, FMV, animation, or some other feedback is to be used in response to the player's input, specify what type, how fast, and how long it should play. Also, be sure to indicate how to let players know when they've done something inappropriate.

I think that anytime the user attempts to interact, the product should supply feedback. If your product has any needle-in-the-haystack type of hunting around, you should still provide this feedback; but it should be very subtle. If, for example, you use a big, loud foghorn sound and users are constantly clicking everywhere, they will become annoyed and will at least turn off the sound or at worst quit the game. Sometimes you can indicate an "illegal" or inappropriate click by visually changing the cursor with no sound whatsoever. However, if you do this sort of design, simply change the cursor to something that indicates a legal hot spot whenever the users "roll over" the spot with the cursor. This is fairly standard on the Internet, and many people seem to deal with it well.

Be sure the technical director knows how important instant feedback is and provides a technical solution to have ready access to the assets required for each and every type of feedback in a view. This often requires preloading of assets in anticipation of their use, but this is rewarded in terms of maintaining a great game play rhythm. If possible, keep track of the player's input tendencies and use that information to anticipate moves. Nothing keeps a player intrigued and into the rhythm of a product like a surprise, specific response from the computer indicating that it is learning about the user's behavior.

Lack of Player Interactions

⇒My rule of thumb is this: Treat *not* interacting as an interactive choice, not as a mistake. I like to think of this as one would think of music: Silence is as much a part of musical composition as the notes.

So, how do you maintain the rhythm of the game when a user doesn't interact? This is one of the great philosophical debates carried on in production teams around the industry. It's as popular a topic as the question, Should the user ever die? In particular, many people believe that in a children's game, nothing should ever happen if the player doesn't do something to make it happen. In other words, the world of the game should always be under the user's control.

I disagree. I think that having the world completely under your control sends the message that *it is possible* to be in complete control of your real world. Regardless of the age of the player, there are moments in most games when, in order to maintain the rhythm of the game and to advance the story of the world, the program should initiate some action which is manifested with music, animation, FMV, etc. This is certainly true in action games in which not acting is a sure way to die or end up in jail.

However, these kinds of responses to noninteractivity can pose a problem: What if users aren't interacting because they are distracted or away from the computer? There is nothing worse than catching the end of some FMV that looks and sounds as if it contains a vital piece of information. There are two solutions to this problem: the Pause key and the Repeat key.

If users are distracted or have to leave the computer, they can press the Pause key to indicate that they are not interacting because they cannot pay attention to the game at that moment. When the Pause key is pressed, nothing should happen until the user clears the pause mode. When pause mode is in effect, there should be an obvious indicator of this with an easy way to clear the mode and continue the game.

The Repeat key can allow a user who was momentarily distracted to replay the last response from the game. This response could be the result of the user's input or the program deciding that something has to happen without the user's input.

⇒In any case, keeping a world alive during noninterative moments by introducing animations, running FMVs, and doing the like can help engage the player in the rhythm of the game.

Load Time and Calculation Time

Like it or not, almost every type of game has some sort of load time to "cover" or hide from the user. Likewise, long, involved calculations need to be covered. Video games, computer games, and, worst of all, Internet experiences have to deal with loading new information into the system's memory or huge calculations; and the best designers deal with this "delay of game" problem from the beginning. If the designer is not technical, the technical director should be closely involved in planning the techniques used to cover the load time.

⇒If the load time is covered effectively and creatively, you can actually incorporate this time into the rhythm of the experience. Unfortunately, most game designers, and therefore most game producers, ignore this fact.

⇒From a technical point of view, to really do a good job of covering the load time, the programming team must attack the problem from the first days of coding the game. Often it is a matter of setting aside memory and other assets to be used solely for the purpose of covering loads. In the operating systems' world, the hourglass and wristwatch "wait" cursors are used to indicate that something is taking time. However, the cursors usually don't indicate how long, and so all they're really telling users is that they have to wait. If good rhythm for users' experiences is your goal, you have to give them some indication of how long they have to wait. If you cannot tell them how long it will take in seconds, quantify it by counting down with an on-screen counter to zero from some nonzero number.

⇒Covering loads, however, can be achieved a lot more creatively than by providing a wait cursor. You could design a character that talks during loads or sends printed messages, all to advance the story. You could put up a simple game such as tic-tac-toe. You could create a series of musical interludes or sound effects that lead into the next scene of the game. You could display hints. You could create small training sessions. You could print a brain teaser for the user to work out on paper.

Whatever you do, don't do nothing!

Transitions

⇒Like the task of covering load times, creating great transitions is something that's rarely thought about except by the best designers. Also, as

with covering load times, unless the technical director instructs the programming team to deal with transitions from the beginning, there is a
very good chance that there will never be satisfactory transitions.

Often transitions from view to view are the very moments during
which you have to cover the loading of files, downloading of information,
and the massive calculations that take noticeable time. If this is not the
case in your game, reconsider the technical design as you can often kill
two birds with one stone when this is the case.

⇒Try to create the type of transitions that are purposeful and that fit
into the world you are creating for the user from an audiovisual point of
view. Don't settle for transitions that are a result of what's simple for the
computer to do.

⇒My first rule of transitions:

No black screens.

⇒You should have black screens in your product only if there is an actual
design and creative reason to do so! I repeat,

No black screens.

⇒If you need to fade to black to create a cinema-style effect, that's one
thing. If your technical team members say they cannot create a different
style of transition, have them reevaluate their tools and technical design.
Too many games in every genre on every machine don't have to resort to
this; neither should yours. I say, once again

No black screens.

If the lights go completely out and you really don't want to see subtle
shapes in the dark, well OK. But sudden cuts to black screens (usually to
cover a load and/or change of palette) just are not necessary. Worst of all,
black screens subtly destroy the visual rhythm of the game (especially if
there's ambient animation), and the user is snapped back to the world of
computers for no apparent reason. Use cross-fades, fade-out and fade-up,
wipes, jump cuts, and other video effects.

These film or TV-style visual transitions can be useful for getting characters and animations on and off screen. Fade them up or out; or better
yet, have them move on or off in some creative, yet logical way.

⇒My second rule of transitions:

No silent transitions.

There is *no reason* for the music and sound effects to stop just because you are changing views or covering a load. Again, early on the technical design team must plan to keep either music and/or sound going during a transition or loading sequence.

⇒The transitions between sounds, like the transitions between visual elements, need to be smooth. Cross-fading, musical endings, and fading out or up are all usable effects. Nothing is worse than a transition in which a piece of music comes to an abrupt stop in midnote just because the game has to switch to a new view or load something! This is true for sound effects, too. Be sure the technical director is planning for graceful audio and musical transitions from the beginning. It is possible to do, with careful planning and regular reminders from the producer.

⇒In my opinion, the only time to break either rule is to achieve a purposeful, dramatic effect. Jump cutting to a black screen, creating an instant silence, or fading music out so you hear only the ambient sounds can create great entertainment moments. However, this is only possible if these moments fit within the drama of the current moment and don't happen in every single transition. Save these effects and use them wisely.

⇒My third rule of transitions:

Make transitions as short as possible.

⇒Create the video effect, change the mood, get users to their new view. Just get it over with. Don't disrupt the rhythm of the experience by making users sit through a long transition, just to show off what you can produce in linear media. Occasionally a nice transition sequence of a minute or so is justifiable as a reward for a big job well done or even as a breather in a highly intense action game experience. But in the end, keep this third rule in mind, and be sure the programming team knows how important this is to the overall design.

⇒My final rule of transitions:

Don't fall in love with your transitions, as players won't.

⇒If you have transitions that the user will see over and over (even if *you* don't when testing or playing yourself), give the user the option to turn off these transition effects. If in your game players want to get to the upstairs door for the 10th time, they don't want to have to wait for even a 5-second transition between the time they click and the time it takes to see the door. They've been there, they've seen it, just get them to the door. The best solution is to skip transitions once you detect that users are playing in such a way that they are in a hurry (it *is* detectable). The next best idea is to allow users to skip transitions either through game settings or by clicking past them. In any case, anything that slows down players from a task that they are hurrying to complete is an annoyance. There is a delicate balance here between providing transitions that set mood and transitions that cover loads. Take charge of this aspect of the design, or else be prepared to deal with the 3 A.M. Green Syndrome!

It is true that in some of the games I've produced or executive-produced, these rules have been violated. In every case, honestly the games would have been better had these rules been followed.

Quitting

⇒No matter how good your game is, players want to quit at some point. So, instead of being crushed by the possibility, accept it and make it part of the experience. Remember, the quitting experience is the last thing users see when they leave your product.

I suggest sticking with the standard Quit keys associated with the type of game you're designing. In computer games this is often handled by a menu that comes up after the user presses the Esc key. Sometimes, simply pressing the Q key will start the quitting sequence. With video games, it's simpler; you usually just turn off the system.

I strongly believe that when a player wants to quit, she or he wants to quit right now. So I've come to the conclusion that rather than ask users several questions as to their true intentions, make quitting simple. Automatically save the current state of the game (assuming that you even have that feature), and put up a simple dialogue that says something to this effect:

Game will be saved as "Current Game." To save the game and quit, click the Quit button.
QUIT   RETURN TO CURRENT GAME

In this way, users know that their games will be saved; they know the name of the game in case they want to return to the current game when they restart; they can easily figure out that the previous game saved with the name *current game* will be overwritten when they click on OK, and they can simply continue the game in case they inadvertently got here. It's fast, it's understandable, and it only requires one click to deal with.

⇒Once users have specified that they want to quit, get them back to the operating system immediately, don't scroll credits; it's the last thing users want to spend time looking at and trying to figure out how to skip. This is especially true if their boss shows up or, heaven forbid, the user has to do something right away on the computer that's truly important other than playing your game.

⇒If some credits cannot be skipped, find the smallest number required, put them on one screen, and put up the screen during shutdown procedures for the game.

Linear Elements

I have four rules for using linear multimedia elements:

⇒**Rule 1:** Keep linear elements as short as possible. The user wants to interact, not watch. Interactivity is the difference between this business and all other forms of entertainment. ⇒Linear sequences are necessary. Long linear sequences are not.

⇒**Rule 2:** Make linear sequences skippable. This is especially important if the game is structured so that the user experiences a linear sequence more than once. If your programming team cannot figure out a way to detect it, know that the user will. Give the user the ability to skip by clicking a button or turning off repeated sequences.

⇒**Rule 3:** Make linear sequences change. It's not impossible, just difficult. If the linear sequences are different when the user expects them to remain the same, you stand a good chance of really catching and keeping the player's attention. It will also make the game seem more responsive to the individual user.

⇒**Rule 4:** Create graceful and purposeful transitions into and out of linear sequences. As linear sequences are usually necessary and are part of the design from the beginning, use every possible transition trick to make the switch from interactivity to linearity smooth and natural. Abrupt starts and stops, long waits, black screens, cut-off music, and music that changes abruptly are all signs that the technology team wasn't thinking about transitions to and from linear elements soon enough. And they are usually not thinking about transitions because transitions are not part of the design documents.

Endings

Although starting and quitting should be short and sweet, endings are an altogether different matter. If users invest hours playing your game, they want a great payoff. Surprise them, entertain them, reward them. In my opinion, this is one of the best places to spend your resources on linear sequences. If you can make personalized or individualized ending sequences, all the better. And in any case, be sure to leave yourself an opening for the sequel!

CHAPTER 8

Principle 2: Naturalness

⇒Designers should always "naturalize" their games to create a better experience for the user. Lately, the term *immersion* has become the buzzword used to describe a desired type of computer game environment that surrounds players and draws them into the experience. Of all the principles that create a sense of immersion, none is more important than naturalness.

Now, creating naturalness doesn't necessarily imply that the environmental elements are created from naturalistic representations from our own world. I use the term to mean that the behavior of the game environment is such that it feels as if it could be real, as if it could exist. In other words, naturalness creates the illusion of a believable world. Any sense of artificial behavior or complete perfection can burst this illusion.

⇒Three design techniques work together to create the illusion of naturalness:

- Randomness
- Statistics
- Artificial intelligence (AI)

The use of these techniques throughout your product's art, sound, music, dialogue, animation, programming, and other elements will create the kind of experience that the user will intuitively understand is of higher quality without being able to say why. Often, this is why these techniques are not incorporated into products: it's very hard to quantify the result of what can appear to be extraneous effort to naturalize a product.

A Sense of Perfection

⇒Most people have a good sense of when something seems perfect. In the world of game design and production, this is especially true in regard to graphics, animation cycles, movement, sound effects, music, and any other behaviors of a computer program. If a line is perfectly straight, a 3D surface is perfectly smooth, a sound effect repeats in exact intervals, or a musical piece is played in exact rhythm, most people can tell. Even if these things are close to or almost perfect, they seem perfect to most people.

⇒In most cases, perfect rhythm, perfect surfaces, and so on create a sense of artifice or unbelievability. Worse yet, things that repeat in close-to-perfect intervals, such as sound effects, actually irritate and distract players.

The problem is that it is really easy to create these almost-perfect elements and behaviors on a computer. In fact, computers are really good at this perfection. Designers have to work to keep the production team from using tools and techniques that create perfection by designing in randomness, statistics, and artificial intelligence.

The Secret Life of Quantized MIDI

MIDI music files are most often recorded directly into a computer by a musician performing the notes on a keyboard. The recorded or MIDI-notated music is actually a representation of the performance of musicians on hand. This is why it is very important to have composers who are good performers create your game's music. If the composer isn't a great performer, the producer should hire a different musician to "record" via MIDI the composer's music. In my experience, the best solution is a composer who can perform along with a percussionist who plays a synthesized drum kit directly into the MIDI file. The cost of the percussionist is well worth it.

In any case, the composer has several tools on the MIDI editor to adjust, realign, add to, and otherwise edit the performed MIDI score. One of these tools is the *quantize* option. This tool uses the computer's capacity for calculation to adjust the performance so that every note is exactly on the beat. In other words, it creates a rhythmically perfect performed piece of music.

However, quantizing removes the almost-imperceptible rhythmic errors that all musicians make when they perform. Good musicians are usually quite accurate; but between the purposeful altering of the rhythm, the physicality of pressing keys or striking drum pads, and the occasional mental mistakes, there are statistical errors in the rhythm of any performed piece of music. These errors are what makes the music sound performed by a human.

The problem is that most people can tell the difference between a piece of music that's quantized and one that isn't. It's subtle but powerful. The art of performing music is so much a part of the human experience that we've come to appreciate the nuances and imperfections of it quite deeply. Having the computer eliminate this takes the heart, or naturalness, right out of the music.

The Master Renderer

Naturalness can also be applied to graphics. As 3D graphics have become easier and more cost-effective to create, more and more products are relying on *rendered* graphics composed of 3D models with textures applied to the surfaces during rendering.

Unfortunately, so many producers, designers, programmers, executives, and artists are in love with the tools of 3D art that they slip into what I call the "Master Thespian" school of 3D art. A few years back, John Lovitz played a character called the Master Thespian on *Saturday Night Live.* When demonstrating or performing a scene, he would grossly overact (often referred to as *chewing the scenery*) and then, at the end, would throw his arms up in the air and shout "*Acting!*" This was clearly meant as a parody of overly self-conscious and overboard actors that always need to remind the audience that they are acting.

In the same way, 3D artists often fall into the trap of doing every 3D graphics trick they can to let us know that they are *Rendering!* They use shiny surfaces with lots of reflections, perfect geometry in physical objects, perfectly placed light sources, and unbelievable details that all demonstrate their knowledge of the tools they are using. What's lost is the art.

The computer can do all those things, and it's an interesting exercise. But is it in any way aesthetically pleasing or, more to the point, in any way immersive? We don't live in a world or expect to find worlds where lines are perfect, surfaces are perfect, reflections are perfect. In addition, focus isn't perfect. Yet, so many people feel compelled to use the computer to create images with that attribute.

In fact, the computer is capable of unbelievably subtle effects through the application of naturally captured assets (such as MIDI or digitized photographs) as well as statistically generated "errors." By using these techniques, and by not focusing on creating shiny reflective surfaces that scream out "I'm rendered," artists can create 3D images that look otherworldly and natural at the same time.

In Return to Zork, because of the design plan, the artists were not allowed to create plastic or shiny surfaces unless it was an actual design element of the scene at hand (which was rare except for a few mirrors and water). They were forced to use or create natural-looking surfaces on all their 3D renderings. For those of you who may not know, all the locations of the text-based Zork series were comprised of extraordinarily different styles and looks. As you move from room to room and place to place, the look and feel changes dramatically. To accomplish a similar feel for RTZ, the art team used different surfaces and textures as you moved from place to place.

Because of these production rules and the design style of the worlds, RTZ has a wide range of 3D modeled imagery. Not only did the artwork live up to our goals of looking naturalistic in this weird, almost unthemed world, but also most people couldn't figure out exactly how we created the art. The art team used only off-the-shelf tools. However, the art team went the extra step of using hand-created or photographic surfaces that featured a lack of perfection.

Now there are computers that can render with statistical errors built in. So lines can look hand-drawn by specifying the amount of error to create as the computer draws each portion of a line. Likewise, surfaces can be generated with statistical errors so that the bumps and edges aren't perfect patterns in the texture. And on top of all that, these techniques are being used to create realistic (i.e., naturalistic) fog, dust, fire, water, hair, and so on.

What Is versus What We Believe

⇒Be careful not to get too caught up in creating a world that is absolutely accurate. In certain situations it is more important to create a world that will fit the users' perception of the world or its behavior rather than the actual look or behavior of our everyday world.

⇒Often reality is slightly different from the perception that people have of it. In creating environments on the computer, I recommend leaning toward the choice of people's perception over reality. However, I recommend this only when there is a perception issue involved, not for an important rule or behavior of the world.

Once in an EWB design discussion as to which hand the umpire should hold up for strikes and which for balls in displaying the count between pitches, it was suggested that we switch the hands so that the balls and strikes would "read" from left to right "ball *x*, strike *y*" when, in fact, real-world umpires hold their hands in the opposite way. I argued that if we used the nonreal but left-to-right positioning of the umpire's hands, we would have trouble. The people who purchase baseball games are often true fans and students of the game and would (1) automatically read the ball-strike count incorrectly and (2) give us endless grief about such a mistake.

On the other hand, once when using a video-captured sequence of images of a hawk in flight, everyone seemed concerned that it looked as if it weren't actually flying. It turns out that hawks (or most birds, for that matter) don't really flap their wings in a manner that we've come to expect from cartoons and our intuitive understanding of bird flight. The art team had to "break" the wings in the middle images (i.e., make a vee shape of each wing), creating a downstroke that matched what the viewers *thought* it should look like. Instantly, the bird looked as if it were flying. Now, some people will notice that a bird doesn't really fly this way, but most everyone else will perceive that the bird is flying "naturally."

Going Natural

⇒In the end, creating a natural feel to a game is simply an illusion. However, it is often the difference between a good game and a great experience.

Just about any product can benefit by using some of or all the techniques for creating the illusion of naturalness.

The Illusion of Naturalness— Technique 1: Randomness

⇒In many respects, randomness is at the heart of all techniques for creating the illusion of naturalness. Randomness can create a sense of unpredictable behavior and provide a basis for the user to come to believe that the world you've designed is a living, breathing, realistic world. This is pretty easy to understand, and it is up to the designer to specify when, where, and how randomness is to be used throughout the product.

As true as I believe this is, it is rarely done. Design documents often say things such as "Animation A will randomly repeat" or "Event *P* will occur after a random amount of time has passed" or "The maze will be randomly generated." While these statements are more or less sufficient to pass on to the programmer, they completely undercommunicate the designer's real intent. This leads inevitably to either the code's having to be rewritten after the designer sees the implementation (see the 3 A.M. Green Syndrome) or, worse, the designer's vision of the use of randomness is not implemented at all because the designer doesn't check it or it's too late to change once it's been noticed.

When you are dealing with the design of random numbers,

⇒*Be extraordinarily specific about the design of random events.*

Production designers would not say in their plans, "Make the leaves on the trees green." They would either provide an actual image or specify the exact color of green. Likewise, game designers should have some expectation of the actual randomness in their designs and should say exactly what they mean. Creating randomness is one of the things computers do very well, and good use of randomness is a significant factor in creating a natural feel for both the environment and the interactivity.

Here, however, is the rub: A random number to a programmer is very different from a random number to a designer. To a programmer, a random number can be a choice between 0 and 1, a range from 0 to 100, or a range from 0 to 16,000,000. It's all under the programmer's control. To the rest of the world, a random number is usually a whole number between

1 and 100. Further, to programmers, the units of measurement, such as time (e.g., nanoseconds or milliseconds), are usually far smaller than the units everyone else uses (e.g., seconds or minutes). So, left without guidance, a programmer might choose a random number between 0 and 500,000 as the "random pause" between the playing of a sound effect. After the sound has played, the program selects the number and pauses that many "units of time" before playing the sound again. The problem is that the units of time are often millionths of seconds. Therefore, even with this wide range of random numbers, the pause is always very, very short. In addition, there are no instructions for the programmer to ensure that no two pauses in a row are the same exact length. The designers probably had something else in mind altogether when they said "random pause."

⇒The solution is to have each member of the design team specify exactly what is meant by randomness. In the above example, the sound designer might have said

> *"There should be a random pause before these sound effects are repeated. The pause should be no shorter than 3 seconds and no longer than 20 seconds. No two pauses in a row should be within 3 seconds of each other. In other words, if the first pause is 9 seconds, then the second pause must be either shorter than 6 seconds or longer than 12 seconds."*

This is an extreme example. But it is an example born of experience, intended to illustrate the importance of specificity in regard to randomness. In the programmer's version, the sound will repeat in almost perfect rhythm in a very short time interval and won't sound at all like what the sound designer had in mind. The difference between the two interpretations of randomness by the programmer and the sound designer above is often the difference between a good product and a great product. Sometimes it is also the difference between a product that is completed on time or is late due to constant adjustments in the code.

Don't Repeat This Anywhere

⇒As I alluded to in the above example, one of the key design elements in the use of random numbers is the rules for repetition. Often forgotten about until it's too late, any design element that is driven by random numbers should be evaluated for how it might repeat.

In some cases, the repetition of a random element is not a problem. However, in most cases, the designer never wants an element repeated exactly the same way twice or, worse, three or four times in a row. In spite of the designer's vision that elements don't repeat the same way twice, it still happens a lot.

⇒The designer must specify when and how repeating is allowed. There are several scenarios for this. Here is a small set of examples. The designer might say

- Don't repeat this twice in a row.
- Repeating twice is OK, but not more than two times in a row.
- Don't repeat any of these until you've done them all.
- Use at least five different versions between repeats.
- Don't use any from group A (or any other group) twice in a row.

Creating a product with these or other rules requires a little bit of planning by the technical staff. So if the designers don't provide this information until after they've taken a stab at implementing the random features, they might very well be faced with some awful amount of work to retrofit the actual design vision.

Random Assets

While randomness can obviously be used to naturalize the behavior of the environment, characters, or feedback from the game's world, it can also be used to construct a wide range of visual and audio elements while the game is being played.

You could use this technique to create a new house in a town that users are exploring so that every user has a different-looking house located at the same address. You could specify a random range of sizes, colors, and features. Also, you could use randomness to draw the leaves on the tree and to change the pitch, volume, and length of the birds' songs.

A Bit About Random Numbers

There are many techniques for generating random numbers for use in a product, and it's often useful to understand the different qualities associated with each technique. Sometimes you need a predictable sequence of random numbers, sometimes you need a specific range of random numbers, sometimes you are using so many random numbers that processor speed is an issue, and at other times you need to ensure that each number in the range is used before any number is repeated.

⟰ ⇒I suggest working with the technical director to define the kind of random number that you need. First, identify the range of numbers that you'll require. Remember how important counting from 0 is and what special computer values there are. If you think you'll need a random number between 1 and 10, consider using a random range from 0 to 15. Likewise, use 0 to 255 instead of 1 to 100. The computer will work faster and is easier to program if you work with its numbering system.

This is an interesting trick: If you need a random number that gives you a 50 percent chance of an event, you can simply look to see if a number is even or odd. It turns out that this is accomplished by looking at one of the bits in a byte (the least significant bit is simplest) in case you're wondering. This is a very fast operation for a computer.

Next, using the techniques described in Table 4-1, determine which technique is best suited for your purposes. All these methods serve different purposes, but each is effective in its own way.

TABLE 4-1

Random number generator	An algorithm that uses the last random number or seed to calculate the next random number.	These are predictable but often slow equations. You can also "seed" the equation for testing, replays, attract mode, and other effects. You can often change the parameters of the equation to give different ranges of numbers.
Random number list	A list of numbers in a specific range. Using an *index* each time a random number is required, take the next number in the table.	This is very fast but can be very repetitious. Also, you are generally stuck with the range of numbers in the table. You could, of course, skip numbers until you found one in the required range.
The clock	An old standby: using the computer's system clock or some other counter in the computer, grab the most frequently changing value (usually the milliseconds) and use it as a random number.	The range of random numbers is limited, and you cannot repeat sequences of random numbers unless you store the random numbers in memory as you use them.
The code	A very old method. By looking at the data that make up the computer program at a specific memory location in the computer, you can use the program code as a random number list.	Sometimes not all the numbers are there, and repetition can be a real problem.

Initial Conditions

When you look at the list of techniques for generating random numbers, it may seem obvious that some are better than others. However, to ensure a random experience, the most difficult random number to generate in any program is the first one. Once that's selected, if it's indeed random, then it's clear sailing. The problem is, when you start up a game, all the initial conditions are the same. The user hasn't done anything, and there's nothing different from the last time the user started up the game. On a computer, the clock and code methods (see Table 4-1) are useful for selecting a first random number (because programs are often put into memory at different, almost random locations). Also, if you saved the last random number used by the game on the hard drive, you can pick up the random number sequence where you left off.

Video games, though, pose a different problem. Unless the game system has a built-in hardware random number generator, there is generally no system clock and no way to remember the last random number from the last time they played your game. So, what to do? Often, this requires the programmer to start a "clock" ticking when your program starts up. When the first random number is required, you see how long the game was running (in milliseconds) until the first moment the user interacted.

⇒Once the initial random number has been selected, switching to the better forms of random number generation, such as the generator or the list, makes sense.

Another word about initial conditions. Initial conditions are the data that define the state of the game at the beginning of each user's game or turn. In addition to the other initial conditions, you could have the programming team store the first random number to be used in the upcoming turn. When the turn actually begins, the computer can store these data along with this "first" random number. When the turn is over, you can grab all the initial conditions data and have the computer recreate the same exact situation. This ability to store and recall the initial conditions is great for testing, for use as an option during game play, and as a way for users to share their game-playing exploits with friends.

Random Cheating

In preparing to work with any design element of a product that includes randomization, the producer should ensure that there are cheat keys that allow the production management team and designer to quickly test the quality of the random behavior of the program.

The Illusion of Naturalness— Technique 2: Statistics

Most designers never think of using statistics. I think they're missing out on a great opportunity to use a very powerful design tool. Statistics and randomness are very closely related. I differentiate them as design tools as follows:

- *Randomness* allows you to create events that are completely unpredictable.

- *Statistics* allows you to specify behaviors that occur within certain predictable guidelines.

Both techniques require the use of a random number generator. The technique of statistics, however, I treat as a special category because it uses the random numbers not as a result, but as a jumping-off point.

Let me give a quick example:

The premise:	You want a frog to jump each time the user clicks on the screen. You want the frog to look as if it is not perfect, and so each jump should be different from the last. Your random number generator returns a random number between 0 and 255, and no number repeats until all 256 numbers are used.
Using randomness:	Each time the frog jumps, the frog jumps as far as the random number plus 1. In other words, the frog jumps between 1 and 256 units (let's say inches) each time the user clicks. The frog will jump a different distance each time, and there is no way to guess about how far any jump may be. This is a completely random experience, and while it is much more natural than the frog jumping exactly the same distance each time, it probably won't look all that natural.

Using statistics: Each time the frog jumps, the random number is fed into a simple statistical equation that "knows" that the frog jumps between 100 and 200 inches with most jumps being about 150 inches. This equation is based on the statistical principle of the bell curve using the average jump as 150 inches. Therefore, most jumps will be around 150 inches. So each time there is a click, the user can expect a jump of about 150 inches and will be surprised at the occasional 100-inch or 200-inch jump. This is a much more natural experience.

Stealing Second

One of my favorite examples comes from baseball. Here's the setup:

> It's early in the game, the score is tied, and you have a fast runner on first base with one out. His statistics say that he steals second base 80 percent of the time (which only the very best base runners can do). The user knows this and, since it's early in the game, figures it's a good risk.

> The user instructs the runner to attempt to steal second, and the runner is thrown out! The user bangs the table and says, "That was a 1-in-a-million play."

> Later in the game, it's the ninth inning, the same runner gets on base with one out again, and the user's team is down by a run. The user says, "Well, there's no way that this guy is going to get thrown out twice in one game; he's an 80 percent base stealer, and the catcher already got lucky once." So the user sends the runner, and the runner is thrown out again.

What's happened here? Well, the user is playing the odds or, more simply put, gambling. The user's response of disbelief is a case of "heart over head." The odds at 80 percent were actually pretty good in both attempts to steal. In fact, the odds were exactly the same: 2 out of 10 times the runner will get thrown out! Most people, even if they know this fact in their heads, don't believe it in their hearts: "Twice in one game? It'll never happen!"

⇒This type of use of statistics causes users to create their own internal drama: the battle between what they know (or think they know) and what they believe.

This is a simple example where the user can actually tell the entire statistical situation simply by looking at information about the base runners. Imagine what happens if you also begin to factor in the catcher's throwing ability, the wind, and the state of the running surface! By adding a few key extra ingredients to the statistical equation, you make it just complicated enough that most users will be forced to go with their gut—then you've got them emotionally invested in your game!

Legacy of Statistics

Many games rely on statistical techniques, not just sports (and frog-jumping) games. This gaming technique can be traced to board games, card games, dice games, and other games where people gamble on the odds. In particular, board- and card-based sports and role-playing games use giant tables that contain statistically based outcomes. Based on the roll of a die (which generates a random number), the initial conditions of the player's turn, and the player's choice of strategy for the turn, players look up the results of their turn.

If you're having trouble understanding how statistics can work in your design, I strongly suggest you play a few of these board-based sports and role-playing games.

Statistics and Naturalness

⇒I believe that in just about every type of game, statistics can play a role in creating the naturalness of the experience. Even simple statistics can be used to "guide" the random behaviors of characters and environmental elements so that users generally get what they expect but are occasionally surprised. More complicated statistical equations can be used to control the behavior of the world or even the story.

The great power in using statistics as a design element is that you can revisit the same situation over and over, and you will usually have a slightly different experience. Looked at over time, the average experience will happen often, but those occasional surprise experiences will continue to entertain and intrigue the player.

Statistical Behavior

As a simple example, say that you have designed a character who has poor eating habits and a high statistical chance of having indigestion. Whenever the user encounters this character, a random number is generated which is used to determine if indigestion is part of the character's current condition. If so, the character might be very cranky or might ask for some medicine. If the character doesn't have indigestion (which is rare), the user might encounter a much more pleasant character with more interesting things to talk about than cures for a sour stomach.

By using statistics in the design of this character, you can "guide" the chance or probability that the character will have a certain condition, which, in turn, creates a certain behavior. The user may or may not be aware of the underlying condition that causes the behavior but might be able to find out. Also, the user will eventually realize that your character doesn't always have indigestion, and this might influence the user's feelings about your character's behavior. And all this with just one character with poor eating habits!

The Religion of Statistics: Believe It or Else!

⇒Once you choose a statistically based design for some of your game, don't compromise and don't give up on the robustness of the principles of statistics. It's easy to panic (especially for executives) if a product exhibits extreme behaviors a few times in a row. However, if a product has statistically based elements and the equations are true to statistical theory, things will work themselves out over time and over the playing of many, many games.

Streaks of good, bad, or no particular luck at all are all part of normal statistical behavior. In rare cases, you need to program in streaks. In fact, it is my belief that you end up skewing the behavior of the world and making it unnatural if you force a streak pattern on an otherwise robust statistical equation. If there is a compelling, real-world reason that streaks are occurring, then the conditions have probably changed that impact the equation.

⇒You have to have an almost religious belief in statistics, or you'll go crazy and drive everyone else crazy. If you can't believe in the principles of statistics, especially the idea that only over time will the true patterns of behavior, streaks and all, emerge, then don't use statistics. However, you will have a less interesting product.

I heartily recommend closing both eyes and jumping in with both feet in regard to using statistical design elements. If you don't quite understand statistics, be sure the producer, technical director, or one of the programmers does. Then be sure to track the statistically guided game behaviors over a long time (computers are really good at this kind of track-ing!). If the expected average behaviors don't emerge, have the program-ming team fix the algorithms. Build it, and it will sum!

The Illusion of Naturalness— Technique 3: Artificial Intelligence

⇒In the future of interactive gaming, I believe that artificial intelligence (AI) will become the most important of all design features. With improve-ments in AI, the relationship between the user and the computer-generated characters can take over as the primary element in interactive entertain-ment. And yet, many designers give short shrift to AI considerations.

Here is my interpretation of what AI actually is:

> *Artificial intelligence is the computer programming technique of using logic, algo-rithms, randomness, and statistics to create behaviors that gives the illusion that the computer is thinking.*

Notice a few things about my definition. First, the point of AI is to create an *illusion* that the computer is thinking as opposed to simulating think-ing. Next, AI is about creating behaviors; these behaviors could be text on screen, spoken words by a computer-generated character, a chess move by a computer opponent, improvisation of a new fighting move by a com-puter bad guy, and so on. Finally, AI is a combination of computer pro-gramming techniques.

As with randomness and statistics, the use of AI in your design can improve almost any kind of product. It brings a level of naturalness that cannot be accomplished in any other way. It brings characters to life and creates opponents, game play situations, and environmental behaviors that are otherwise impossible to program.

Even games such as Tetris, Lemmings, and Shanghai benefit by AI pro-gramming. These games have no computer opponent per se. But if you have played them, you could envision these programs keeping track of and studying your moves and strategies in order to create game play lev-els in response to your style of play. Each game's adaptation to your style of play creates a series of levels adapted specifically according to the game's experience with you. This is a very personalized way of playing a computer game, and it can really only be done with AI designs.

Designing AI

As AI is a science unto itself, I have never attempted to master it for use in a game play design. It would be a massive undertaking. But in the gaming world, creating the illusion of a computer thinking and creating behaviors can be accomplished without having a Ph.D. in computer science.

On the opposite end of the spectrum, many first-time designers create extensive logic trees for their AI model. Logic programming is great for identifying very specific situations that dictate a certain type of behavior in a character. However, in a game of any complexity, there are so many individual situations that this type of logic programming can be enormous. Also, I believe the completely logical approach to AI is too simple a method for creating AI, as it creates a very predictable behavior pattern from the computer which is not natural in any way.

⇒My approach to AI is to build a combination logic and statistical model of the behavior of the people or characters who are to look as if they're thinking. Since the statistical model uses random numbers, I've already established in my mind that there will be a feeling of naturalness in the building blocks of the AI. The naturalness created by the statistics balances out the absolute predictability you would get if you used only logic in the design of AI.

⇒Using a mixed model, you can create characters who usually are predictable within a certain range of behaviors but who once in a while do something unpredictable. I think this type of behavior sounds a lot like the behavior of real people.

⇒Another advantage of the mixed model of logic and statistics is that you can use the same program code for more than one character. Simply by changing some of the parameters of the statistical equations, you have a different set of typical results for similar situations.

Thinking Baseball

In EWB (what else?) I designed the computer AI version of Earl to work in three phases: the logic or analysis phase, the player evaluation phase, and the statistical behavior phase. In the analysis phase, the program determines which game play situation is "called for." There are surprisingly few moves to make in baseball, but they revolve on instructing the batter, base runner, pitcher, and fielders and making substitutions.

After identifying the situation, the Earl AI evaluates players that might be involved in the play or substitution. This code is a set of equations that compares (arithmetically and logically) the statistical and physical attributes of the players and creates a numerical rating indicating the "level" of interest in executing the play or substitution. The rating value is usually a number between 0 and 4 or −2 and 2.

The final stage of Earl's AI uses a random number and a statistical equation based on the situation and the level-of-interest value to dictate Earl's likely behavior. So in any specific situation, there is always a chance that Earl will not exhibit his normal behavior but will surprise you. For example, even in a level 4 steal situation (i.e., the highest indicator that the steal is a good play), Earl may call the steal play only 70 percent of the time. Likewise, if the steal situation creates a 0 level of interest, Earl might still have a 3 percent chance of calling the steal and will, from time to time, surprise everyone by sending the catcher to second base.

This combination design is extraordinarily flexible and allows the code to be modified quickly to change the ratings of the level of interest as well as the statistical chance that affects Earl's behavior.

Ned's First Rule of AI

Ned's first (and I believe only) rule of AI design is as follows:

⇒ *Don't let the computer character do anything dumb.*

This may seem simple and obvious but, in fact, it's quite powerful. Having computer characters do simple things or nothing at all can often give the illusion of great thought and AI going on in the computer. However, the moment that a computer character does something stupid, it bursts the bubble of the illusion.

> *I met Ned Lerner at one of EA's A.U.G.U.S.T. meetings when he was working on the original Chuck Yeager's Flight Simulator. He's a programmer of extraordinary talent and insight into design. He went on to become a principal at Looking Glass Software in New England and has now started up his own game company in the Bay Area in California.*

When designing AI, I find that most of the logical part of the design revolves on Ned's first rule. I suggest the same for your design.

People Have Great Imaginations

The second great principle of great AI design is

⇒*Allow the player to assume behaviors that are not there.*

Why? If you don't overdesign your AI, there will be many moments when your characters simply don't do anything. As in the movie *Being There*, allowing people to fill in the blanks for a mostly silent character gives players the freedom to imbue your computer character with unbelievable intelligence.

There are many examples in computer gaming. In EWB, people would sweat over what Earl was "thinking" when he wouldn't act in situations as they thought he should. But the best example comes from Dan Bunten's M.U.L.E. In the game there are four mules, each with its own bright color: red, yellow, green, and blue. In the computer program, they are exactly the same and behave in exactly the same way. However, many wrote letters to Dan and EA saying that they discovered through hours of game play that the red mule was by far the best mule to choose. This, of course, wasn't true, but players convinced themselves and other players that it was.

Natural Thinkers

⇒I strongly recommend that AI be a part of the naturalization of your designs. Keep the design simple and slightly unpredictable, and it will probably come off as somewhat natural.

As I said earlier, I believe that in the long run AI will be the central design element used in creating naturalistic products. In many respects this may be because AI is the ultimate combination of randomness, statistics, and logic. In any case, the ability to create the illusion of natural thinking will allow designers to focus on products where the fundamental activity is the interaction between the human player and the artificially intelligent computer character.

CHAPTER 9

Other Principles

Highly Interactive Interactivity

This is a simple principle:

⇒ *The more the user does, the better. The more the user watches, the worse.*

Since computer games are an interactive form of entertainment, design your game to feature *lots* of interactivity. I don't believe that simply means lots of choosing and clicking. There needs to be a sense of cause and effect, action and response, and risk and reward between the user and the computer program.

I don't consider CD-ROM encyclopedias to be interactive entertainment. They are interactive in that you can click through menus and type in searches to find what you want to know. However, the interactive experience is not responding to you in a way that presents a risk-reward situation.

The risk-reward element is what creates the interactive drama in computer games. It is often an internal drama created by the self-gambling that players create in their head. Sometimes, the interactivity triggers consequences in the game world that create drama in the story in which the user is playing.

⇒The more opportunities exist to experience the risk-reward element of the interactive experience, the more the user will become wrapped up in the game, world, and story. So the more the user has an opportunity, the better. Thus the user has to have lots of opportunity to interact almost all the time.

The Two-Rules Rule

⇒The two-rules rule is as follows:

In computer games, the user must know two sets of rules: (1) the rules of the game being played and (2) the rules of the interface required to play the game.

Whenever possible, try to design products in which the user has to learn only one set of rules. Eliminating the need to learn two sets of rules makes a product much more accessible.

Many games eliminate the learning process for the first of the rules ("The user must know the rules of the game") by basing the game on an existing game, for example, all sports games, card games, board games, and so on. In these games the user has to learn only the interface.

A few games have either such simple interfaces or interfaces based on existing computer input metaphors as to make the second of the rules ("The user must know the rules of the interface") not a learning exercise for the user. The 7th Guest, The Manhole (by the same team that created Myst), Myst, The Neverhood, and most text adventures all have very simple interfaces that, for the most part, the user doesn't need to learn.

Of course, when you're dealing with certain kinds of products such as action video games, RPGs, and other genres with well-defined interface standards, you have a built-in audience who understands the interface rules already. The problem with these "standards," though, is that they are not readily understood by newcomers to these genres of games.

⇒So, unless you plan to design a game for the already initiated, I can't emphasize enough how important it is to make learning both sets of rules as easy as possible.

In the perfect scenario, the user doesn't need to learn either set of rules. I would venture to say that the most popular game of all time on the Windows platforms is Solitaire. Not only is it distributed freely, but also just about everyone knows the rules of the game and the rules of the interface are so simple and obvious that there is virtually no learning curve.

Gambling

⇒As discussed in the section on statistics and naturalness, one of the more powerful design principles incorporate is gambling. People generally enjoy playing the odds. If you can create a game in which interesting things are at stake and the user has a pretty good sense of the percentages, you have a good chance to draw players emotionally into the experience.

There are many ways to create a "bet" in a game, and this is the easiest way to incorporate statistics and/or statistics-based AI into your design. For example, let's set up a simple game in which players are supposed to catch balloons falling from the top of the screen and red balloons are the most valuable balloons to catch. If the behavior of the red balloons is based on statistics (as opposed to being completely random), then the better players will watch and learn the usual behavior of the red balloons. Given the right balance of consequences for guessing *in*correctly, these observant players can then decide when it's worthwhile to bet that they can predict when a red balloon is going to fall and gamble that they will reap the benefit of their "research."

Creating a gambling situation in this way is a powerful hook for a game. But why not simply create a predetermined, but hard-to-recognize pattern for the red balloons? There is nothing wrong with the predetermined pattern method. However, players will eventually (often a lot sooner than you think) realize that the pattern is the same each time they play, and they will try to learn the pattern to master the game. Predetermined patterns are perfectly fine for game design, and many video games use this to hook players completely. Once a pattern is learned and mastered, the game is more or less over for the user.

With a statistically based gambling design, users learn the odds instead of an exact pattern and have to create strategies for balancing their "bets" with the consequences. Creating strategies based on the balance between the odds and the consequences means there is no right or wrong way to play. Forcing players to gamble in this manner engages not only the players' minds, but also pits players' minds against their gut instincts. Getting users to engage in this personal emotional battle creates a great interactive experience that is rarely the same for any two players. It is also very simple to change the parameters of the statistical behavior so that once players have mastered one level, the game program can easily "make up" a new level.

Patterns

While gambling is one of my favorite design principles, the predetermined pattern is an often used, easily understood, and well-liked game design principle. The best examples of predetermined patterns are found in action-based video games, computer games, and arcade games. If you have not seen or played many action-based games, I suggest a trip to the local video arcade. Stand behind someone pushing quarters into a side-scrolling game or a trough game machine, and watch carefully what the player is doing.

In the predetermined pattern design, you create a sequence of obstacles and goodies that players encounter and attempt to avoid, dispatch, collect, or otherwise deal with in a prescribed order. The obstacles and goodies (the game objects) are usually presented to players in specific locations at specific times. In addition, the manner in which the player has to avoid, dispatch, collect, or deal with the game objects is often a singular, specific action. For example, in a side-scrolling game in which you have to avoid overhead obstacles, dispatch angry bad guys, and pick corn off tall stalks, you have to duck, punch, and jump, respectively.

Games designed with predetermined patterns are among the most addictive and fun games of all. There is clearly a part of us that enjoys learning complex patterns and testing our memory of them. The fact that there is often a high-speed hand-eye coordination element of predetermined pattern games seems to heighten the experience for many game players.

Of course, it is not necessary for this style of game design to be used only for high-speed action games. Games based on strict story lines, many

RPGs, flight simulators, and very simple adventure games can all benefit from predetermined pattern designs. In every game genre, time is an element of the pattern whether the time is measured in turns or in real seconds and minutes. *When* a game object appears is just as important to the predetermined pattern as *where* it appears.

The Dance with Death

Interestingly, most players learn to master predetermined pattern games just as dancers learn choreography. As there is no widely accepted form of movement notation, dancers learn choreography by memorizing vocabulary words and stage directions as they relate to time. A dancer might memorize a pattern by saying to herself "Walk, jump, run, duck, turn, kick, stop, reach, spin, punch." This is remarkably similar to the way video game players (gamers) memorize the sequence for mastering a game: "run, jump, punch, punch, kick, run, duck." While dancers use a mix of "normal" or "pedestrian" vocabulary mixed with dance-step vocabulary (often in French ballet terms), gamers use a similar mix of pedestrian vocabulary mixed with game controller words such as "up, up, right, a button, b, b, b, c, a, left, down" and so on. Of course, if a gamer mis-steps, the gamer's character often dies.

There is an entire generation of gamers who have learned patterns in this way as well as of dancers who learned choreography in a similar fashion. I'm hopeful that some scholar will look into this relationship and study what impact the memorized pattern style of learning has on dancers and gamers alike.

Matching Expectations and Completeness

In designing any kind of software product, it's important to anticipate every possible thing users may do and then to create responses and behaviors that live up to the users' expectations. In more complex games, it is often hard to figure out all the things that average users will do. In addition, the production team often gets caught up in playing the product they are building in a certain specific manner and often forget that consumers will do a wide range of other things.

⇒Users have great expectations of computers and therefore your game. If there is a big button on the screen, most users will click on it. Be sure it does something to live up to that expectation.

⇒Always try to look at your product with fresh eyes during production. Look for things that players will do because they are curious. Look for things that users do over and over, and make them simpler and faster. Most importantly, look for things that the computer should remember about the way the user is playing, and design that ability into your game; most users have come to expect this.

In RTZ player's had a knife in their inventory so we had to allow the knife to be thrown at every character in the game because that's what the players expected. Realizing this, the game design was adjusted to have certain characters die, some fight back, and in every case create some consequences for the users to deal with.

⇒Ensuring completeness is the cause of a great deal of redesign and improvisation during production. Until you can see the screens and interact with them, you will not be able to anticipate every possible user interaction. As long as everyone is prepared for the discovery of unanticipated user actions, being flexible enough to add responses and behaviors to ensure completeness will make for a much better gaming experience.

To give you an idea of the sort of unanticipated interactions you might have to face, here is a short list:

■ The user clicks multiple times on the same hot spot when the program is expecting only one click per hot spot.

■ There are visual elements on the screen that scream out to be clicked on, but no interactions were anticipated for that on-screen "object."

■ Users delete elements (such as players on a team) until there is not enough information for the game to play.

■ Players are asked to enter their names, and some people find it amusing to use "dirty" words. (In other words, your program should check for inappropriate names, words, and sound-alike spellings of such words and prohibit them if the name is to be used on screen.)

■ You expect your product to be around for many years, but the programming team decides to enter 19 as the first two digits of the year.

■ Some users have unusual audio cards that play music and audio too loud or too soft. The user should be able to adjust this in your product rather than have to figure out the operating system's volume control method.

- Some users are left-handed and cannot use the keyboard controls as originally designed.

- Some users are color-blind and cannot decipher a certain puzzle because certain colors are used as key elements of the graphics.

- Some users are tone deaf and/or have never learned music, yet your product requires them to use musical elements to accomplish a task.

- To play your game, players have to view information and possibly do calculations. But the design doesn't allow quick viewing of data in the modes where users really need access, and an on-screen calculator wasn't included in the original design.

Surprise and Entertain

⇒I'm a firm believer in surprises for the game player. This means that users aren't in complete control of their own experience. We are, after all, in the business of entertainment. So, to that end, I think that there should be a healthy dose of entertaining surprises throughout your product.

To surprise people, you can take advantage of the computer's ability to track users' behaviors, patterns, and current activity. If the user is moving the mouse around on the screen and not otherwise interacting, you could send out a surprise piece of entertainment. If the user is clicking on the same thing over and over, you could create a surprise response to the repeated clicking after, say, the fifth click.

⇒My only word of caution is to design these surprises to be small, fast, and with minimal delay to the game play.

Keep Their Eye on the Ball

⇒Design your interface to minimize hand and eye movement. If possible, "pop up" the interface right where you know the user is looking. This notion has become popular in word processors, other desktop tools, and the Internet. As you are rolling your cursor around, a little box often pops up to tell you what will happen if you click there.

The advantage of keeping the eyes and hands from moving too far to use the interface is that it speeds up the rhythm of the game and tends to keep the user immersed in the world you've created. The moment the user needs to look away from a specific spot on the screen and move the mouse to a "special" location, the user is brought back to the world of the computer.

Many game companies have begun to use this method. Tsumanmi's adventure games, Full Throttle from LucasArts, and Return to Zork all are good examples. In each the interface pops up around the spot where the cursor was pointing when the user clicked. This means the user is looking right at the interface when it pops up and that any mouse movement to use the interface is really minimal. It's very fast and effective.

The Three-Times-and-It's-Important Rule

⇒ *If a user does something more than twice, the user will want a simple way to do it.*

When designing your interface, think carefully about which tasks users will *really* do over and over. The more they do a task, the simpler it should be (i.e., the fewest possible keystrokes and mouse clicks).

In a way, when you determine which commands in the interface are easiest, you are telling the user what you think is most important. I find this true in software tools where the Save As function never seems to have a shortcut key. I think this is an important feature, and I get tired of pulling down the file menu to get to it. Clearly a group of designers didn't feel this was a very important function.

Use keys like the Space bar, the Tab key, and letter keys without modifiers (i.e., without CTRL, ALT, Open-Apple, etc.) for commonly used commands, and let the user know what these keys are.

Also, I'm waiting for the product that will send up an alert that says

You've used the "Shoot to Kill" command from the menu many times. Did you know that pressing the "s" key will invoke "Shoot to Kill" directly?

Shortcut Keys

⇒ Because you want a simple interface so the user can move at lightning speed through the product, provide shortcut keys. Don't count on the users reading the manual! Try to figure out a way to inform the user of shortcut keys (see the above section). If nothing else, provide an on-screen list of shortcut keys.

The shortcut key list might be good to use during transitions (at least until the computer detects that the user actually knows the shortcut keys). One advantage to displaying the entire range of shortcut keys is that the list might inform users about commands that they didn't know were available. The disadvantage of showing this list is that it is usually quite long and complicated and, quite frankly, intimidating. If you do choose to display a list of shortcut keys, work with the production designer to do it in a way that works visually.

Skill Levels and Age

As many people have figured out, there isn't necessarily a correlation between the skill level and age of game players. Often younger people are the more advanced users, but adults can overcome this stereotype and be far more sophisticated than kids and teenagers. In any case, you should design your product so that it can adjust for the age and/or skill level of the player.

As a rule, I offer age settings only if there is a real reason to differentiate players by age. Except for "mature theme material," there really aren't too many cases in which an age designation is appropriate.

⇒Skill level is another matter. In most games, a skill level setting can be a great help in making your product appeal to the broadest possible audience. A skill level option allows players to decide how difficult they want the game to be and how sophisticated they are as game players. In head-to-head games, the skill level feature can create a level playing field between two players of different abilities.

When designing a product with skill level options, you must plan which elements of the game will be adjusted to make the game easier or harder. This is referred to as *adjusting the difficulty* of a game. Difficulty can be adjusted by changing the

- Speed and pacing of events
- Number of obstacles
- Availability of hints
- "Smartness" of the computer AI

- Parameters of random elements
- Equations of statistical behaviors
- Required accuracy (e.g., how close to the ball do you need to swing in order to hit it?)

The 2-Foot Principle

⇒*In computer games, the user is sitting less than 2 feet from the monitor.*

Note that this principle is true only for computer games. For video games, the user is often 8 feet or more from a TV screen.

If you are designing a computer game, including Internet games, keep the 2-foot principle in mind. Now, keeping this in mind, think about how you feel when someone stands this close to you and speaks to you. It's an intimate experience.

⇒In other words, when interacting with a computer game, the characters in the game are in the user's personal space. They should speak, act, and interact in accordance with their physical proximity to the user. Television, theater, and film all have different viewing distances from the audience and are written and directed accordingly. So, too, computer games should be designed, written, and directed with the 2-foot principle in mind.

Manage Screen Real Estate Appropriately

When you lay out the visual design for your product, use the screen realistically. If it is a computer game, keep the 2-foot principle in mind. If it is a video game, remember that the user is often many feet away.

For computer games, the user is sitting too close to watch the entire screen at once. Since the user cannot watch everything at once, design the screen layout so that the user can see everything crucial in one-quarter of the screen or less. If you are entertaining the user with a piece of animation in the upper right, do not expect most users to catch an important message or change of image in the lower left. Most of us do not have peripheral vision quite that good.

> *When I joined Jim Henson Productions, I traveled to all their offices to brainstorm about interactive games. In the introductory remarks in one of these meetings, I was pointing out how, due to a technical limitation of the time, all FMV was usually shown in one-quarter screen sizes. I made a big deal of this as a limitation of the current technology.*
>
> *Michael Frith, one of the creative geniuses involved with the Muppets and other Henson enterprises, said that he didn't really see a problem. When we look at a TV, it only occupies about one-quarter of the wall that we're looking at, and we cannot possibly focus on more than that amount of visual information at one time anyway.*

Video games are more of a problem in that the viewing distances vary. I believe you have to take the 8-foot distance as the average situation. This has other implications than the 2-foot principle does for computer and Internet games (until the Internet is readily viewable on TV). The 8-foot distance means that text and small objects are very hard to see accurately. You can, however, animate the entire screen with a reasonable expectation that the typical game player can watch almost everything at once.

In either case, if you need to move players' eyes, move them on purpose: Move a graphic element from where they are looking to where they need to look, or create a large, impossible-to-miss animation (possibly accompanied by a sound) that will refocus their attention.

Use Colors Wisely

While it may seem that you have as many colors as you want in designing your game, you should actually be quite conservative in your use of colors. The number of simultaneous colors displayed at a given time in your product can impact the speed and rhythm of the user's experience.

If you design your product to use fewer colors (at the same time), then the technical director can take advantage of your design foresight and use techniques to reduce the size required to store and the time required to display the graphics. This is true in every type of game platform, from computers to video games to the Internet.

Note that this issue is about how many *simultaneous* colors you can display, not *which* colors you can display. The simultaneous colors are the complete set of colors or palette that you can use on one entire screen at any time. The number of simultaneous colors available is almost always one of those special computer-type numbers (i.e., powers of 2) such as 2, 4,

8, 16, 32, 256, 32, 768, 65,536, 16,777,216, and so on. As far back as I can remember, computer and video game systems allowed you to choose between palettes of colors. In those and today's systems, you can switch between palettes as you switch screens. So while the reduction in simultaneous colors may mean you can't use every color at one time, you can still use a wide variety of colors as you move from screen to screen.

If, for example, you were designing a game that took place early in the 20th century, you might choose to present many of the images in a sepia tone wash (that brownish gold wash of many old black-and-white photographs). If the only images on the screen were in sepia tones, you could reduce the number of simultaneous colors to 16. You could do this because, in the world of computer graphics, you can usually create enough shades of a single color in 16 shades. This is called *color scaling* and is most often used with a range of 16 colors between white and black called the *gray scale*. Using the sepia tone scale, you can create very small and therefore very fast images.

At this time, this wise use of colors is most necessary in Internet products. The Monty Python Web site (www.PythOnline.com) is a great example of economy of color. For the most part, this is a black-and-white site with one or two other colors. In other words, most of their images are in two or four colors. This allows the images to be greatly compressed (requiring only 1 or 2 bits per pixel).

Extending the Product: Extensibility, Add-ons, and Sequels

⇒Your product will have more value in the marketplace if there are *after-market* products that extend the life of the original product. These after-market products can be in the form of additional data, add-on functionality, and sequels. While creating a sequel is pretty straightforward, in order to sell additional data and functionality, you must design your product to be extensible.

Extensibility, in the computer games world, means the ability to extend a product without having to create and sell a new program. In other words, an extensible product can grow simply through the purchase of more information and functions. Examples are word processors to which you can add fonts, dictionaries, and templates; database programs for which you can purchase front-end programs for data entry for a specific business; art programs such as Adobe's Photoshop in which you can purchase or download "plug-ins" that add functionality to the core program; sports games for which you can purchase new player statistics from season to season (or even day to day); and war strategy games in which you get new "mission disks" that include new enemies and territories to conquer. Print Shop was one of the very first entertainment products that was extensible by providing seasonal artwork for greeting cards.

⇒If you want your product to be extensible, design it appropriately from the earliest possible stages. Almost any game can be made extensible, yet not really that many games are.

⇒There are two ways to make a product extensible: through well-defined file data structures and through hooks in the program that allow new subprograms to attach themselves to the main program through what's now called an applications program interface (API).

In the early phases of your design, create data structures for all the game play elements for which you might add subsequent "data" disks or downloads. After you've identified all the game play elements, quantify them so that each can be described by a data file or set of data files. For example, in an RPG, the characters in the world might consist of a name, a physical set of attributes, a set of other attributes, and statistically notated behaviors. All these items can be reduced to numerical representations and stored as a file on disk. If, on top of all that, you want a series of animations of that character, create a second file that contains all those animations. Then, either by using the filenames for the data file and animation file or by including the name of the animation file inside the data file, your program can add this character to the world.

Creating hooks in the game to allow add-on functionality is more difficult. The programming team has to provide a way for this to work, and you have to design an interface element that allows the user to specify that there is a new add-on to hook into the original program. This requires a lot of up-front planning and testing. This technique hasn't yet become popular in game programming, but it has taken off in the on-line world. This is the technique that allows Java Apps, ActiveX controls, and other browser plug-ins to work. EWB II provided this feature, and we were going to publish the programming interface so that third parties could create EWB plug-ins. Unfortunately, due to a change in EA's commitment to the property, this feature was never promoted.

Another method for giving aftermarket functionality to a game is to provide *utilities* for the game. These programs allow the user to modify or create elements for game play. This method assumes there are data files that can be shared between the main program and the utility. This is another reason to create file data structures for your game elements.

⇒The success of games that feature add-on data disks certainly demonstrates the value of aftermarket products. I'm hopeful that there will begin to be more entertainment products that support the idea of add-on functionality.

Work with Experts

Whenever the opportunity arises, work with an expert in creating your design. Find experts in the type of product you are making, in the subject matter, in the type of algorithms you want to use, and so on.

⇒Experts almost always raise the level of product quality. But be prepared to teach. Most experts don't have any idea of what interactive gaming is about. The better informed the experts are in the medium you're working in, the more help they can be to you.

⇒Sometimes, though, experts just don't want to spend the energy to learn about interactivity. Even if this is the case, the experts will be valuable.

Arrange to have the expert available throughout the course of the production. Show the expert small example programs that demonstrate your implementation of her or his ideas, thoughts, and other expertise. It's especially productive if there are cheat keys and other mechanisms to adjust algorithms based on the expert's knowledge right in front of the expert. This makes the expert feel involved in a hands-on way and is very motivating.

Ensure that experts understand what the game is and how to play it, and most importantly, ensure they respect the technical team. There is nothing more awkward at a press event than celebrity experts who cannot answer the most fundamental questions about the game they've supposedly contributed to and, worse, make fun of the industry and the people (programmers especially) who work in the industry.

I've had the privilege of working with celebrities and experts several times. If there is a chance for you to bring in experts, jump at it.

PART 5

Production Information for the Interactive Designer

CHAPTER 10

Production Plan, Team, and Process

Production Plan

As this document is usually written by the producer and could be an entire book in itself, Table 5-1 is a list of some typical elements of a production plan.

TABLE 5-1

Assets creation plan	Discuss how art, animation, FMV, audio, VO, music, dialogue, on-screen text, and all other physical assets will be produced. Include how each element will be engineered and stored. Indicate if work is to be done by in-house staff and contractors or outside vendors and third parties. Specify who's responsible for which steps in the design, creation, approval, and engineering of all assets.
Personnel list	Include all staff, contractors, etc.
Equipment list	Include all equipment to be purchased and/or rented.
Tools list	Include all software and hardware tools that will be purchased and/or upgraded.
Backup and storage plan	Discuss how your assets will be stored and how the code will be maintained. Consider off-site backups and redundant systems for crucial elements during production.
Production schedule	Include production, testing, manufacturing, shipping, and marketing.
Budget	For all versions to be built at once (often only one or two)
Hiring plan	For staff, contractors, and outside services
Licensing plan	For licensing of technologies
Testing plan	For quality assurance as well as market-testing and focus groups
Localization plan	For moving the product to other languages
Port plan	For moving the product to other platforms

Who Does What and When in the Design Team

Although opinions and company procedures can vary widely on this subject, some general guidelines exist for most large projects. The team of people involved in this process consists of

- Game designer
- Writer
- Production designer or art director
- Producer
- Technical director or lead programmer
- Sometimes, a game director
- Other specialists as needed

Also, remember that, in my opinion, the design document can never be completely finalized. So this group should plan to work together on a regular basis from the preliminary design phase all the way through the final release of the product.

Nonetheless, the primary participants during any one phase can be quite different. Table 5-2 is a list of who is primarily responsible for the creation of the design documents for each phase.

The role each person plays seems obvious, but I've found it not to be true. For whatever reason, some people lose sight of the big, team picture and are very sensitive about their job titles, their production titles (which are very often different), roles, and amount of contribution they made to a project. It is almost the most difficult thing to manage in producing a title.

Give Credit, Give It Once

⇒Make it clear to each person who joins the production that each is expected to do his or her job, help others with their jobs, give freely of her or his ideas, and receive one (and only one) credit in the product. This credit is almost always nonnegotiable, as it is the actual production job for which the person was hired. If a company programmer were enlisted for a project as a writer and yet still contributed as an occasional program-

TABLE 5-2

Phase	Design Document	Primary Participants in Design
Idea or pitch	Design proposal, treatment	The game designer or the person who has the idea for the game
Pre-green light or preliminary design phase	Preliminary design	Game designer, writer, production designer, producer
Preproduction or predesign phase	Game or product design	Game designer, writer, production designer, producer, technical director, art director, audio director, music director, game director
Preproduction	Production plan	Producer, technical director
Preproduction	Technical design	Technical director
Production	Design revisions and sequel design specifications	Director, producer, game designer, technical director, testing or QA director
Postproduction	Localization specifications	Producer, technical director, audio director, art director

mer, I would simply list this person as a writer. Once in a while, make an exception to this rule, but not often.

⇒Using the one-person, one-credit rule helps, but it doesn't solve everything. Due to the nature of the beast, many people work lots of hours for many months, sometimes in relative isolation from others on the project (mostly programmers). Since there are many phases of preliminary design, design, production, and either postproduction or maintenance and since in each of these, different people work different amounts, it's almost impossible to say whose contributions were greater than anyone else's. Yet, people do this, and, unfortunately, it falls to producers to deal with this issue.

Design the Old-Fashioned Way

In the old days of computer gaming, the game designer was the sole person in charge of the preliminary design, the design, and the maintenance of the design during production. Often this person (or group) was programmer or producer. Once in a while it was an art director or writer. But in all cases, this person was closely associated with creating the product as well as designing it. Also, in the old days, freelance designers who only designed were almost never heard of.

Still today you see one-person design "teams" and even designs that change little or not at all during production. But, quite honestly, these are usually smaller productions or products with little sophisticated interactivity, as is required for most games.

Throughout the 1980s a more formal approach to game design teams was being developed simultaneously and independently throughout the industry. Products increased in scope and required higher quality. People who were originally brought in as workers for hire during the production process started getting involved earlier and earlier, until they became unofficial members of a design team or committee.

Hollywood and Silicon Valley, Alley, and Gulch

As the games industry continued to grow, members of the "traditional" entertainment community started participating in small ways. Writers, production designers, artists, actors, directors, producers, camera crews, and every other kind of entertainment type started to work on projects. The long-predicted marriage between the Hollywood entertainment community and the interactive/computer games community seemed as if it would come to pass. And to some degree it has.

In several companies during the early 1990s, a new visible trend was beginning (I say *visible* as there were earlier instances but not in a high-profile way). Companies started hiring design teams that included a game designer and technical director from the interactive community and a writer and production designer from the entertainment community. While I was at Activision, this marriage was attempted several times in many ways and finally began working and has continued to work for them and others throughout the industry. It was a difficult transition to make. For me, the big surprise came in how hard it was to coordinate the work of the game designer and the writer.

In some cases, the difficulty in getting the writer and designer to work together was due to the traditional visionary role of the game designer in controlling the entire design. In other cases it was due to a lack of gaming experience and knowledge on the part of the writer. And in yet other situations, it was due to misunderstandings as no one really knew (or believed) who was in charge of the project and who had the final word.

For some reason, there rarely seemed to be much difficulty with integrating the production designer into the process. Most of the time, this person went about her or his business of creating the look of the worlds and characters as described by the other members of the team.

As these issues got worked out, certain patterns began to emerge. It became clear that there is great potential for these two creative communities to work together. Although I like a specific type of arrangement, it is always good to evaluate the roles on the design team on a project-by-project basis.

Who's in Charge?

When I put together a design team, first I establish who's in charge. I prefer that it be the producer or (if the production is going to have one) the game director. After assigning the leader, I assign the other design roles listed in Table 5-3. With the producer or director in charge, the game designer and writer have to make their often-conflicting design elements work together. This is tough, but it can be done with great success.

TABLE 5-3

Game designer	Interactivity, integration of the story into the game, genre, interface, and rhythm of the experience.
Writer	Story, worlds (including maps), characters
Production designer	The look of the worlds and characters. Also, the look of the interface elements

The Technically Creative

After a while, I invite the technology director or lead programmer to participate in the design process. This is as much for a reality check of what's technically feasible as for having a fresh person with interactive ideas to add to the team. Whatever you do, do not underestimate the creativity of people who do technical work for a living. They are just as likely as anyone to have creative bones in their bodies.

Scott Page at the game company 7th Level often tells of his reliance on technical staff for creative contributions to products. While he admits that this wasn't what he originally thought in his early days at 7th Level, it is clear by the quality of its products that his faith in the creative talent of the technical staff is well founded.

How Long *Does* This Take?

Once a design proposal has been accepted and a project has moved into the preliminary design phase, projects can take on a somewhat predictable schedule. Table 5-4 lists the basic phases of a product's life.

Tables 5-5, 5-6, 5-7, and 5-8 show typical schedules for different kinds of projects. There are a wide variety of design and development times for projects. Keep in mind that it is an unpredictable business. You never know what will delay or advance a project's schedule. There are fairly well-accepted norms for schedule delays, and the best developers and programmers keep well under them. But the majority usually don't. Successful publishing companies have accepted this as a way of life, built this into their production scheduling, and stopped worrying about this overly much years ago.

TABLE 5-4

Preliminary design	Creation of preliminary design document.
Design	Creation of design documents and preproduction. Preproduction tasks include hiring, arranging equipment, and so on.
Main production phase	The computer programming and creation of all physical assets.
Alpha phase	Programming continues. The product is completely playable with 60 to 75 percent of all assets in final form. Outside, "real people" testing begins.
Beta phase	Programming continues. The product is complete except for final tweaking, debugging, and last-minute changes and additions to the final assets. Outside testing continues, and professional testing begins.
Final testing	Programming and asset changes only on an as-needed basis as professional testers look for "nonshippable" bugs. (All products ship with some known bugs, called *shippable bugs.*)
Maintenance	Some products, such as on-line game and Web sites and those with follow-up products, begin support of these ongoing services and/or additional production.

TABLE 5-5

Schedule for Large Multimedia and Video Games

Preliminary design	1 to 2 months
Design	2 to 3 months
Main production phase	6 to 9 months
Alpha phase	2 to 3 months
Beta phase	1 to 2 months
Final testing	2 to 3 months
Total time	14 to 22 months

TABLE 5-6

Schedule for Medium-Size Multimedia Games and Products and Large On-line Games

Preliminary design	1 to 2 months
Design	2 to 3 months
Main production phase	3 to 4 months
Alpha phase	1 to 2 months
Beta phase	1 to 2 months
Final testing	1 to 2 months
Total time	9 to 15 months

TABLE 5-7 Schedule for Small Multimedia Products and Small and Medium-Size On-line Games		
Preliminary design		$1/2$ to 1 month
Design		1 to $1^1/2$ months
Main production phase		2 to 4 months
Alpha phase		1 to 2 months
Beta phase		$1/2$ to 1 month
Final testing		1 to $1^1/2$ months
Total time		6 to 11 months

TABLE 5-8 Schedule for Web sites (Professional Quality and Use) and Other Small On-line Interactive Entertainment		
Preliminary design (sometimes skipped)		0 to $1/2$ month
Design		$1/2$ to 1 month
Main production phase		$1/2$ to 1 month
Alpha phase		0 to 1 month
Beta phase		$1/2$ to 1 month
Final testing		0 to $1/2$ month
Total time		$1^1/2$ to 5 months

There are ways to shorten these schedules, and once again, it works against the myth of the completed design. Some technical directors have programming staff begin work on a project as early as the preliminary design phase. If this is too big a risk, the staff may begin sometime during the design phase. In either case, this can shave months off a long main production phase. But this means they are working with a design that is possibly far from completion. This works if there is a good system in place for communicating changes and updates to the design while it is being finished.

Pacing the Design Team

In this way of doing things, the game designer, writer, and production designer really don't form a design team until the beginning of the design phase. Once they start working together on the design, I employ a

TABLE 5-9

Design Pacing Schedule*

Meet	Work Alone	Meet	Work Alone	Meet	Work Alone	Meet	Work Alone	Meet
3 days	4 days	2 days	5 days	2 days	12 days	2 days	5 days	2 days

* Total time: 6 weeks, 2 days.

specific method for pacing the design team that seems to be successful. I believe this method is necessary if team members have never worked together before or if one or more members have a lot to learn about the interactive business. Table 5-9 demonstrates how this design pacing works.

When the group meets, there are intensive brainstorming meetings led by the producer or director. As group members adjourn to work alone, assignments are given by the producer to each member of the team. During the work-alone days, each member of the design team is in regular contact with the producer and/or director and with any other team members via phone and E-mail.

One reason why this works is that team members brainstorm and think together and each member has a specific responsibility and time to work on it. Also, the time alone allows for a cooling-off period between intensive sessions, so that team members can "let go" of ideas they might be passionate about but that the rest of the group has turned down.

After the Design Is Completed

The key members of the design team—(the game designer, writer, and production designer)—usually become less involved once production begins. Unless they have some other ongoing role (such as technical director, producer, art director, programmer, writer), they more or less become consultants to the product. During the alpha and beta phases, it is a good idea for the game designer to take a more active role in testing the product and making additions, corrections, and other improvements to the game design.

The writer is often a part of any video or voice-over production sessions and must be available to work with the actors, producers, and directors in these productions. Also, the writer is often asked to write elements of the on-screen text, manual, box copy, and other product and marketing materials. Many writers are willing to do some or all of these things, but some aren't.

If the production designer does not take on the task of the art director, then there is often little involvement beyond consulting on art design-related issues and approving art during production.

⇒Once production begins, the torch of the design vision is passed on to the producer, director (if there is one), technical director, and regular members of the production team. This is why I feel that unless the game designer is going to be with the production on a daily basis, the producer or director should have final say over the design decisions during the design phase. This is also why I feel that it is important that designers know how to work with those most intimately involved with the creation of products—the programmers.

11

Working with Technologists

Include Programmers and Engineers

⇒ One big mistake that a lot of new designers make is to exclude the input of technologists from their designs. It is almost impossible to write a comprehensive design document without paying some attention to the technical aspects of creating the product. It usually requires the assistance of the technical members of the production team to write these sections. Inclusion of this information is important as it provides not only a blueprint for the production team, but also another tool for the inspiration and creativity of the designer. Teaming up with these technologists during the design phase gives the designer input that can transform the design from a naïve, simple design to a complex and highly innovative one.

Who are these technologists? In addition to programmers, there are audio engineers who transform all the sound and music to a usable format for the computer; the artists (or art engineers if the producer has junior artists who do only this job) who scan, digitize, touch up, palletize, resize, and compress art files; and sometimes even asset managers who coordinate the collection, engineering, and distribution of physical assets to the production team.

Designers usually never meet most of the technologists who work on their products. In many respects, though, the technologists are the very people most responsible for the creation of the product. What the designer has left out of the specifications is usually up to the production team to figure out. In fact, for programmers on most projects, there is usually so much left out of a design document that they have a tremendous amount of control over the quality of the final product.

This in itself is not bad. Programmers are usually game players, and many are designers, producers, or directors in training. However, if the design team does a thorough job, then there can be a good balance between what is left to the programmers and what is not.

⇒It is important to accept that programmers will be forced to solve design and other creative problems throughout the life of the production. On products of reasonable size, there is no possible way to specify everything for programmers. Programming a computer is like planning a paper route. Give the list of houses to receive newspapers to 10 kids, and you'll get back 10 routes. It's even worse for programmers. You're likely to get multiple solutions to a single problem from one programmer! Even if a designer wants to specify each algorithm down to the smallest detail, the design will still have holes in it for the programmer to fill.

⇒One of the designer's jobs is to know what to leave to the programmers and what not to leave.

What to Leave to Programmers

⇒Once design team members realize that they can't specify everything in the design, they should set up guidelines for programmers to follow and trust the programmers to come up with good solutions. The producer and director must maintain good communications with the programming team during production so they can approve the team's choices of solutions. One way to give guidelines is through default behaviors in the design.

⇒*Default behaviors* are those responses from the computer that happen when nothing specific has been planned, for example,

- What happens when the user doesn't interact?
- What happens if the user doesn't type in a filename before clicking on the Save button?
- What happens if the user clicks on the screen where there is no hot spot?
- What happens if the user double-clicks and only one click is required?
- What happens if the user tries to go through a locked door?
- What transition is used to go from mode A to mode B?
- What range of random numbers is used to determine repeated events?

⇒If these kinds of general questions are answered throughout the design document, programmers know what to do in a lot of situations. Also, when other similar situations come up, programmers have an idea of the type and tone of the solution desired.

I also recommend not being *too* specific about most algorithms in the design. First, it's hard to write a complete algorithm without actually programming it. Second, the programmer will probably be much better at creating an appropriate algorithm than the design team. The design should list the parameters of the algorithm and the expected results.

What Not to Leave to Programmers

In the old days, programmers often wore many hats. They designed, programmed, created the art, wrote the music, and produced every element of their products. Today, especially in products of any size, there is a team of specialists to create the assets that go into a game or product.

⇒Where this system of specialists often falls apart is in the area of *implementation* of the physical assets. It is not enough, in my opinion, to have artists create art, the composer write music, the video director create the FMV, and the sound effects designer record the sounds for the game. Yet, this is what typically happens: The physical assets are created and handed over to the programmers, who are expected to implement them in the product just as the artists who created them intended. I don't think this is a good method at all.

⇒Design documents should specify for the programmer the design or implementation of

- Transitions (type and timing)
- Algorithmic art (e.g., drawing shapes as opposed to using precreated pieces of art)
- Selection of palettes
- Animations (use, reuse, timing, looping, repeating, and especially registration)
- FMV (use, reuse, starting frame, stopping frame, transitions in and out)
- Audio effects and VO (use, reuse, volume, stopping, overlapping, looping, repeating, stereo balance, transitions)
- Music (use, reuse, volume, starting and stopping, looping, repeating, transitions)
- Use of interface elements (changing pointers, cursors, wait cursors, menus, dialogs, alerts, etc.)
- On-screen text (color, content, placement, and duration of error messages, success messages, scores, status, hints, etc.)
- Randomness (random events, random use of assets, naturalness, etc.)

⇒If you followed my guidelines for creating the game design document, you probably covered all these issues and more.

⇒Programmers, especially game programmers, are unusually talented people, but they are not artists, film directors, professional musicians, animators, or sound designers. They shouldn't be burdened with these other responsibilities; they have enough to do just to implement the interactivity and the algorithms and to hunt programming bugs.

In previous sections, many elements of the design documents are meant to be used by the programming team. These lists will guide the programmers through the implementation of the physical assets so that the assets are deployed in accordance with the design team's vision. By contributing to these sections of the design documents (even during the production phases), artists, musicians, and others can communicate exactly how they want their work to be used in the product. In addition, the game designer, art director, music director, sound designer, FMV director, and others should be available to the programming team when the first physical assets are about to be implemented in the game. The producer or director should be present, and notes should be given as additional guidance to the programming team for those times when these directors are not available for consultation.

Using the design document as a communication tool between designers and programmers, the game designer and producer can feel more comfortable about who is making the aesthetic decisions of when, where, how, and why the physical assets are used in a product.

In RTZ, we assigned the artists who created each view to review the implementation of their art and animation with the programmers. Many mistakes were found and easily corrected. However, time was wasted as programmers had to go back and rewrite their code. This was especially true for the use of animations. Where, when, and how often an animation were used and how it might be reused were inefficiently communicated to the programmers. By the time we realized this, it was too late to deploy several animations that were specifically created to be reused throughout the product in a variety of ways. We had better luck with the implementation of the navigation hot spots, removable art objects, sound effects, music, and FMV due to the extensive spreadsheets in the design documents. We had our best luck with transitions as Bill Volk, our technical director, made a great list of default behaviors for transitions.

We had our worst luck in providing game messages to the user (through text messages) when the user tried unsuccessfully to solve a puzzle. We had underestimated the number of places and ways in which a user could fail to succeed, and we had specified a method and style of response without having a writer create the text. The programmers created a lot of new on-screen text for this purpose, of which we were lucky to be able to use a reasonable percentage. Nevertheless, we had to go back through the code, find every instance of a programmer-written line, check it, and possibly rewrite and reprogram it.

What's Random to Me?

⇒One special area of design that should not generally be left entirely to programmers is the use of randomness. There was already a full discussion of randomness, but it should be restated here:

Randomness should be the responsibility of designers, not programmers.

As true as I believe this is, it is rarely the case. Designers and programmers have two very different perspectives on randomness. To designers, on one hand, randomness is a tool for creating the naturalness they want and often express themselves (e.g., "This should repeat randomly to create a natural feel"). Programmers, on the other hand, often approach randomness as a simple, statistical selection of a number. This is not to say that programmers cannot make good choices about the use of random numbers. But without clear, concise direction from designers, the chances of the programmer's creating the natural feel that the designer wants is, well, random.

It Can't Be Done!

In dealing with programmers, inevitably they say, "It can't be done!" However, in my experience, this statement shouldn't always be taken literally. During the design phase, any design element that elicits this response should be treated specially. The producer should ask for a programmer to actually think about it and ask that programmer to try to create a demo. (Sometimes the best time to suggest this to a programmer is on late Friday afternoon.) Talented programmers are usually up to a great challenge, and working alone with no one to bother them is the best way to tackle a tough problem.

⇒What "It can't be done" usually means is "I don't know how I would do this" or "It will take more time than I'm interested in devoting to it." There are many, many things that computers are capable of, and brainstorming with programmers on how to solve a problem or create a similar effect is better, I think, than simply letting them off the hook. If brainstorming doesn't help, consider searching for information on the Internet through news groups, freeware of example code, and other programming resources on-line. If after all this they really believe that something cannot be done, make them explain why not in great detail to the producer, director, or technical director.

⇒Another major reason for this statement by programmers is the limitations in the tools provided to them or selected by them to create the product. Again, I encourage all designers to not accept these limitations as an excuse. If a tool deficiency is spotted early enough in the project, then tools can be changed or improvements to the tools can still be made.

Some tools really do create limitations in what interactivity and algorithms a programmer can create. However, if you ever hear a programmer say "It can't be done" because of tools in regard to random numbers, either insist that the programmer change tools or consider carefully the impact of such a limited tool on the overall product quality. Then, start to reduce your design expectations then and there.

12

The 3 A.M. Green Syndrome

Many years ago, a programmer working with me had a typically weird programmer's schedule. He'd come to work in the early afternoon and work through to early morning. He got his best work done between his dinner break and 6 a.m.

One afternoon I confronted him about a particular scene that he'd programmed the night before, in which part of the screen was filled with an awful shade of green. The art director and I took one look at this screen and knew it was wrong. I also noticed that he was all of a sudden running behind schedule on some other things that were supposed to be done by the morning. He described what had happened:

The design document called for this view to be created with green in a specific view. He got to programming this view around 3 a.m. and couldn't call anyone because it was too late (or early) to discuss which green to use. So he programmed a green that he thought would look good. When he saw it, he didn't like it. It takes only a few minutes to reprogram the color, so he tried another green. Before he knew it, he had tried dozens of greens and had been at it for $2^1/_2$ hours (see the section on the baseball paradigm for rhythm in game design: try the green, wait to see how it looks, try the next green, etc.) and had to go home to sleep. He left the last green he programmed in the game and never got to the rest of his assignment for the night.

Not only did the programmer waste several key productive hours playing with his choice of green, but also the art director knew exactly which color green it was supposed to be. What took 2 to 3 hours of the programmer's time and made him late in his schedule should have only taken him 3 minutes.

This sort of thing happens all the time. No matter how detailed the design documents, it will still occur. The best one can hope for is to minimize the 3 A.M. Green Syndrome by providing as much easy access to design details as possible. Also, it is a good idea to convince programmers to talk to the producer before going off on an adventure like this.

Finally, the programmer also made a crucial mistake. The moment he realized that he was going to experiment with the color (i.e., when he tried the second or third version of the green), he should have created a cheat key that would allow him to change greens right in the middle of the program without having to reprogram the green directly each time. In this way, he could have written a small bit of code and tried dozens of greens in only a few minutes. Also, the art director could have used this cheat key to try colors for the final selection.

⇒Try to avoid the 3 A.M. Green Syndrome by providing detail in the design, setting up good communications with programmers, and insisting on cheat keys to help decide on unspecified design elements in real time.

What's So Important about These Special Numbers?

⇒One last topic needs to be addressed about designing with the technologists in mind: numbering systems. Computers, and therefore programmers, can count in a variety of ways. Some numbering systems are more appropriate for software designs than others. While it is great for designers to be familiar with hexadecimal (base-16) numbering, it is more important to simply realize that there are numbers of special importance to programmers.

Most personal computers and video game systems in the 1970s and early 1980s were based on 8-bit processors which forced everyone to think (as you'll see below) in ranges from 0 to 255. At the time this was fairly foreign to most people, even programmers. At Mattel, the Intellivision was based on a 10-bit processor which, if you figure out the binary arithmetic, provides data in what we called "decles," which had a range from 0 to 1023. This allowed most of us to think in the range of 0 to 1000, which is much more accessible to everyone. However, it never caught on. Everyone is still working in bytes and words (0 to 65,535—now there's a catchy number to remember!).

Designers must decide for themselves how much they need to know about binary and hexadecimal numbering systems. There are many reference books on the subject. However, every designer should be familiar with the counting and numbering system concepts in Table 5-10.

Once you know some of these numbers and counting principles, you have a better chance of understanding why programmers and other technically oriented people often design things to have ranges from 0 to 15, maximum choices of 256 items, or coordinates on a graph from −32,768 to 32,767. Knowing these things yourself can give you the ability to maximize the use of data required in the memory, downloads, and files associated with your program designs.

TABLE 5-10

▮▮▶

0	⇒Always attempt to count items from 0. First, it's easier for the computer; second, it leaves no doubt about the lowest number. If you count from 1 once, it places doubt in the mind of everyone from the programmer to the user. Finally, as you'll see in the next item, it gives you an extra number to count from.
	Zero has another special meaning to a computer and to many software programs. Zero is the easiest and fastest value to "test" for. Clearing out data, blanking a screen, setting transparent portions of images, and creating silence in an audio file are almost always accomplished by setting, inserting, or changing values in memory or in files to 0. In this way the computer and the programs running on it can most quickly deal with the most common data setting: no value.
Highest number versus number of values	If you are counting from 0 (which you should be now), the highest number you can count to is always 1 less than the total number of values you're counting. For example, if you count from 0 to 9, then you have counted 10 values, but 9 is the highest number.
2	The number values in 1 bit of data
0, 1	The only two values that 1 bit can count or record (used in binary arithmetic)
256	The number of values in 1 byte of data (1 byte is 8 bits "wide.")
255	The highest number that can be counted or recorded with 1 byte of data (i.e., the value of a byte is a number between 0 and 255)
16	The number of values in 1 nybble of data (2 nybbles make 1 byte, and 1 nybble is 4 bits wide)
15	The highest number that can be counted or recorded with 1 nybble of data
65,536	The number of values in a "word" of data (which is 2 bytes or 16 bits wide)
65,535	The highest number that can be counted or recorded in a word
Negative numbers	Numbers represented in computers can be "split" into positive and negative values. This is done by specifying one-half the numbers as negative. So for the above nybbles, bytes, and words, you have new ranges:

Data type	Range
Nybble	−8 to +7
Byte	−128 to +127
Word	−32,768 to +32,767

Notice that there is one fewer positive number. This is partly because of the way that computers typically notate negative numbers. It is also because 0 is often treated as a positive number (more accurately, as a nonnegative number) which therefore makes an equal number of positive and negative values.

TABLE 5-10   *(Continued)*

||||➡

1 K or kilobyte	⇒While many people believe that K in Kilobyte stands for 1000, they are only close, but not correct. In fact, in the binary counting system, which is what most, if not all, computers actually count in themselves, 10 bits of data give a range of 1024 numbers. Because of this and because programmers need to be able to deal with data counting accurately and quickly in low-level systems programming, when the computing world began to deal with larger amounts of data, it began assigning the shorthand K to stand for a group of 1024 bytes.
	This means that 200K bytes is 204,800 bytes, not 200,000. While this may seem trivial, often those extra 24 bytes per 1000 come in very handy. Also, it will impress your technical friends that you know about, correctly calculate, and take advantage of all the memory at your disposal in your designs.

Technical Issues
for Designers

13

Computer Systems

Here, for the game designer, is an overview of how computers work. If you know a good deal of the inner workings of the computer, you can probably skip this chapter. I would suggest skimming it in any case, just to make sure you understand my vocabulary and shorthand when it comes to talking about game technologies.

First, a review of Part 2, Chap. 3.

Computer Components

The five basic computer components are

- Input devices
- Processing devices
- Memory or storage devices
- Software and data
- Output devices

Table 6-1 provides some examples of each type of device.

TABLE 6-1

Component	Examples
Input devices	Keyboard, mouse, joystick, microphone, stylus, paper cards, touch screen, buttons, dials, modem
Processing devices	CPU (e.g., Intel Pentiums, Motorola PowerPC), math coprocessors, graphics coprocessors, audio processors, synthesizers, video display cards
Memory or storage devices	RAM, ROM, hard drives, CD-ROM, tape drives, paper tape or cards, DVD
Software and data	System software, programs or applications, firmware. Data usually exist as files created by or for programs or applications
Output devices	Screens, speakers, printers, modems, joysticks

The Basic Computer

(See diagram on page 44.)
Nowadays, the basic computer consists of the following:

Input:	Keyboard, mouse, often a modem, and possibly joystick and/or microphone
Processor(s):	Intel Pentium or Motorola PowerPC, a video adapter, and possibly a 3D assist chip
Memory or storage:	RAM, ROM, flash memory, a hard drive, a floppy drive, and often a CD-ROM drive
Software and data:	An operating system (Windows, Mac OS, etc.), utility software (word processors, spreadsheets, databases, etc.), and data for your programs
Output:	Screen, speakers, printer, modem

The Typical Video Game Console System

(See diagram on page 45.)

(See diagram on page 45.)

Input:	Game pad (a specially made device with a direction indicator and buttons)
Processor(s):	RISC processor (CPU), video chip, sprite (i.e., animation) chip, sound chip, and usually a 3D chip
Memory or storage:	RAM, ROM, a CD-ROM drive, or a ROM cartridge slot
Software and data:	Usually only the software that is on the currently installed CD-ROM or ROM cartridge. In the old days, an operating system was often found on a ROM in every system.
Output:	Screen and speakers

The Processors' Jobs

Computer and video game systems usually consist of several processors. A processor (of just about any kind) does the following things:

- Reads instructions
- Looks at data
- Loads data
- Stores or saves data
- Sends an electronic signal
- Manipulates data
- Reads more instructions

So, let's follow the flow a little more closely:

When a processor ***reads an instruction,*** it is reading the *next piece of a computer program.* That's what a computer program ultimately is—a series of instructions for a specific processor or set of processors. In computerese, there are many expressions for the processor's reading an instruction. Two of the most common are the processor loads or fetches an instruction. The key element is that the processor gets its instructions sequentially from somewhere in the computer system.

The processor reads the computer program instructions from RAM or ROM only. It cannot read from anywhere else, such as a hard drive or a modem. For a program to tell the processor what to do, first the program must be loaded into RAM or identified in ROM.

A processor can *look at data* in memory. Data can be in memory in *only one of three places:*

■ RAM (random access memory) or, a better way to think of it, read-able-writable memory. This is by far the most abundant and flexible type of memory as it can always be changed. However, once the system is turned off, all contents are lost.

■ ROM (read-only memory), that is, fixed memory that cannot be changed, ever. This memory is used for permanent portions of the system; for programs and data that cannot be lost when the power is turned off. This is about the same speed as RAM but comes in smaller quantities because it is so inflexible.

■ Registers. Each processor has some internal memory which comes in very, very small amounts. This is by far the fastest type of memory.

Looking at data is the simplest of all types of programming and is the first thing all interactive designers think of when considering what computers do. Looking at data means examining a value in memory to see whether it is something specific, for example,

```
if data in RAM-memory-location-#47 equals 0
        then do this
        otherwise, do that
```

Surprisingly enough, some computer programs actually look very similar to the example above. While executing the first part of this instruction, the processor looks at the data in RAM to check for the value 0.

A processor can *load data* from memory (a more quaint term we used earlier was to *fetch* data). As with looking at data, a processor can load data from *only one of three sources:* RAM, ROM, and registers. Data that are loaded into the processor are kept in a register. With so few registers and given the high speeds at which they work, you can imagine how valuable a resource a processor's registers are.

For example, in my pseudo-programming language:

```
load data in RAM-memory-location-#29 into Register A
```

So now we have whatever value was in a specific memory location in one of the processor's internal memory locations or registers.

A processor can *store or save data* or put data into memory. Where a processor could read data or look at data in three types of memory, a processor can only put or store data into *two types of memory:* RAM and register memory. ROM cannot be written to by a processor under any circumstances.

To continue my examples:

```
save data from Register A into RAM-Memory-location-#357
```

Saving, storing, or putting data into memory is used for either temporary storage (when the processor runs out of registers) or, most often, to record results once data have been manipulated (see below).

Processors can **send electronic signals** to various parts of a computer system. This usually *requires a specialized processor* that understands what sort of system it is in. The signals can be simple, along the lines of flashing lights, or complex, along the lines of creating the sound effects coming out of a speaker.

As an example, imagine a series of instructions to a graphics drawing processor that puts pixels (or points) on a screen, using color and location information stored in RAM. They might look like this:

```
load data from RAM-Memory-location-#100 into Register A
load data from RAM-Memory-location-#101 into Register B
load data from RAM-Memory-location-#600 into Register C
draw point at Register A, Register B in color from Register C
```

In this example, the screen coordinates are stored in pairs in RAM, starting at location 100, and the corresponding colors are stored as single entries, beginning at location 600. This means there is room for $(600-100)/2$ or 250 screen location coordinate pairs. This is enough information for a screen 25 pixels wide by 10 pixels tall.

This is a fairly inefficient way to draw pixels from memory onto the screen. However, a lot of general-purpose processors draw in more or less this fashion. A more efficient way is as follows:

```
draw point at RAM-Memory-location-#100, RAM-Memory-location-#101 in
    color from RAM-Memory-location-#600
```

This means far fewer instructions to pass along to the processor. The only question is whether the processor allows you to go directly from RAM to the screen in this way (that is, without "loading" the register memory first). Surprisingly, many computers don't allow this. Because of this shortcoming of the system design, drawing graphics on the screen at reasonable speeds can be almost impossible on computer systems.

Still, this is not all that efficient. Even though we've reduced the number of instructions from four to one, it still needs to be done 250 times just to draw that small 25×10 rectangle! A more concise solution is

```
draw screen at RAM-Memory-location-#100, 25 wide, 10 tall
```

With this one instruction, we've drawn the entire rectangle specified by the coordinate pairs starting at 100 and the color *table* (which is *not* a palette) at memory location 600. This type of processor instruction assumes a very specific data layout. Specific data layouts for graphics have become quite common in video game and computer systems.

⇒ *Familiarity with data layouts, especially for graphics, can be one of the most powerful pieces of knowledge a designer can have!* The number of tricks you can do to change images, how you draw images, and how you store images are some of the most important technical things a designer can know. And yet, many wanna-be designers don't learn this.

Now we get to the good part: a processor can **manipulate data.** This is where processor types differentiate themselves. Most processors can manipulate data *from any* of the three memory areas. Once the manipulation is finished, the result *can only be put* into either RAM or registers, as ROM doesn't allow you to write to it (hence the term *read only*). Since processors typically perform these manipulations significantly faster in register memory and because processors can only write to RAM and registers, most programming tends to focus on manipulation of register memory only. A programmer has to be careful not to manipulate ROM so as to try to write the result back to ROM. While attempting that won't crash a computer system, the results will never be found because the ROM memory locations will not change.

These are some types of manipulation:

- Addition and subtraction.
- Multiplication and division.
- Translation (one value is turned to another value as found in a table of values).
- Compression/decompression [a series of data values are "shrunk" (expanded) to a smaller (larger) set of data values].
- Physical manipulation (operations that change the actual representation of a value to make it another value, such as turning individual bits on or off, shifting bits, masking bits). This is the stuff of heavy-duty, bit-level programming, which is why I sometimes refer to "real" programmers as bit-twidlers.
- Identifying where to get the next instruction.

The types of manipulations, the complexity of the available manipulations, and the speed of the manipulations all combine to give processors different power and capabilities. Combinations of specialized processors often outperform single, powerful multipurpose processors. This is one area in which video game systems have often gotten the jump on the next generation of interactivity by providing a set of specialized graphics and sound processors to help create a great-looking and -sounding experience at very high speeds of interactivity. It usually takes a while before the speed of the general-purpose main processor of a computer is fast and powerful enough to emulate what all those special processors can accomplish.

Hail to CPU

While typically many types of specialized processors are found in today's computers and video game systems, there has been, and always will be, the need for one general-purpose processor in every system to control the machine. This general-purpose processor is called the central processing unit (CPU). Most computers are rated for speed according to how fast the "clock" on the CPU goes. The clock works as a metronome and ensures the coordination of the data moving through the CPU. If a CPU's clock "ticks" 1 million times per second, the CPU is rated at 1 megahertz (MHz) or 1,000,000 hertz (Hz). (Hertz is a unit of measurement that means "times per second.") This is approximately how fast an Apple II, an Atari 2600, and an Intellivision could go. Nowadays, computers go hundreds of times faster.

Keep in mind that there is *not* a linear relationship between the "clock speed" of a computer (i.e., at how many megahertz the CPU's clock ticks) and how fast a computer really is. Typically there are two things that increase the speed of the CPU:

1. How fast the CPU can perform its simplest instruction (sometimes as fast as 2 to 4 clock ticks)

2. The average speed of the most commonly used instructions

Companies who make CPUs study extensively which instructions to optimize for speed. They have to weigh the information about the current programming practices indicating which instructions are currently used most often against the impact on the programming community of increasing other sets of instructions. For example, if optimized instructions for arithmetic are added, programmers will surely change their styles of programming to take advantage of these new instructions. When this happens, the effective speed of a CPU increases beyond the simple increase in clock speed. For example, when the clock speed goes from 1 to 2 megahertz, the new computer might go as much as $2^1/_2$ to 3 times faster.

This is a motivation for many people in the industry to focus on a special breed of CPU called a *RISC chip.* RISC stands for reduced-instruction-set computer. By reducing the instruction set (instead of adding more and more instructions, as is typical with the creation of new CPUs), each instruction can be so optimized as to be virtually as fast as the simplest instruction. This means that just about every instruction in a RISC chip is performed at the clock speed of the CPU.

Example Manipulations   Here are two examples of instructions to manipulate data in my pseudo-language:

Example 1A:

```
multiply data in Register A by 15
```

Example 2A:

```
multiply data in RAM-memory-location-#489 by data in ROM-memory-
       location-#33
```

The multiplication in example 1 will be done many, many times faster than that in example 2. This is because (1) the data being manipulated are in register memory and (2) the multiplier (the second value in the equation) is actually part of the multiply instruction (i.e., it is not "fetched" from memory independently of the loading of the instruction).

In example 2 we multiply data in RAM by data in ROM. So, after loading the instruction, the processor must load data from RAM and then look at data in ROM. So where does the result go? This is typically resolved by the *syntax* of the computer language. In this case, I've made the assumption that the memory location of the multiplicand (the first number in the equation) is also the destination for the result. So, in example 1, the result is put into register A (overwriting the original contents of register A); and in example 2, the result is put into RAM memory location #489 (again, overwriting the original contents that resided there).

I could have made many other syntax choices for my pseudo-language. For example, I could have required the specification of the destination of the result. In that case, the two examples become as follows:

Example 1B:

```
multiply data in Register A by 15 into RAM-memory-location-#357
```

Example 2B

```
multiply data in RAM-memory-location-#489 by data in ROM-memory-
       location-#33 into Register B
```

In these two examples I've provided a destination memory location which allows me to multiply the two numbers yet preserve them in their original memory locations.

What's the point of all this? I've gone through all these steps to show, in simple examples the ramifications of understanding some of the fundamental issues in the technical design of a product.

⇒ *From a technical point of view, the two most valuable commodities are the size and speed of the program that performs the creative design.*

Understanding what influences speed and size in a program can greatly enhance your ability to communicate priorities to those who write or assist you in writing a technical design for your product.

These are two of the most straightforward ways to reduce size and increase speed:

⇒Use fewer instructions (this reduces size and often increases speed).

⇒Create efficient algorithms (this increases speed).

If you leave all these efforts to other people, you will often be giving up the opportunity to understand what they are doing and the ability to influence the way in which they do their work.

A Real-World Example

In all the sports games I've designed, I used what is now known as a *virtual reality* model. Games are played in a computer-simulated world that behaves within the real physical rules of our world which is measured in feet, inches, seconds, and minutes. Then, every so often, if the user desires, a graphical representation of what is going on in this simulated world is displayed.

One of the most common things to do in a game simulating the real world is to compare two distances. For example, is the distance between the batter running and first base greater than distance between the player who's fielded the ball and first base? If so, then the fielder should simply run to first rather than throw the ball, as throwing increases the chance of an error. Of course, there are other issues to contend with. For example, by the time the fielder catches the ball, he is usually either standing still or running away from first base, while the batter is already running full speed directly at first base. But we will ignore that for now.

The equation for the distance between the runner and first base (*drb*) can be measured between points (*rx, ry*) (the *x* and *y* coordinates for runner *r*) and point (*bx, by*) (the *x* and *y* coordinates for first base):

$$drb = \sqrt{(rx - bx)^2 + (ry - by)^2}$$

Likewise, the distance between the fielder (*fx, fy*) and the base (*dfb*) is

$$dfb = \sqrt{(fx - bx)^2 + (fy - by)^2}$$

Now compare the two distances: Is *drb* greater than *dfb?*

It turns out that

⇒Multiplication and division are two of the slower things that a processor does.

⇒Calculating square roots is monumentally slow by comparison.

⇒So, to make the program efficient, reduce multiplications and divisions as much as possible and remove square root calculations whenever you can.

If you remember your math (which is always a little helpful in reducing program size and increasing program speed), it is simple to change the algorithm for comparing the distance. Before you go on (if you want to test yourself), try to figure out a faster and shorter way to compare these distances.

A Simple, Faster, Smaller Solution   First, to make this algorithm faster, try to eliminate one or both square root calculations. If you examine some simple square roots such as those in Table 6-2, perhaps you can see the solutions.

TABLE 6-2

Number	Square Root
36	6
25	5
16	4
9	3

As the number decreases, so does the square root! So, in fact, you do not need to calculate square roots in the distance equation to find out whether one distance is greater than the other! For example, if one distance is 5 and the other is 3, then their respective "pre-square root" distances are 25 and 9, which have the same greater-than, less-than relationship.

This is another way to put it: The relationship of the numbers is the same as the relationship of the numbers squared. In this case, comparing the square of the distance gives the same information as comparing the distances. And not taking the square root in the distance equation leaves us with the square of the distance.

So now the algorithm for comparing the distances looks like this:

$$(drb)^2 = (rx - bx)^2 + (ry - by)^2 \qquad \text{square of distance from runner to base}$$

$$(dfb)^2 = (fx - bx)^2 + (fy - by)^2 \qquad \text{square of distance from fielder to base}$$

Is $(drb)^2 > (dfb)^2$? (comparing the squares of the distances) Not only is this faster, but also, by eliminating two square root calculations, we've made it smaller. In many cases these two results (faster *and* smaller) go hand in hand.

Are there ways to make this faster? Yes. However, with today's processors, it is a pretty close call as to whether the more complex steps required to eliminate some of the multiplications justify the increase in program size, as there may be only a small, if any, increase in speed.

Data versus Code: Take the Speed

⇒One of the great techniques (or tricks, if you must) for increasing computing speed is the use of tables instead of code.

- *Tables* are lists of data stored (usually sequentially) in RAM or ROM.
- *Code* is lists of computer instructions in RAM or ROM.

⇒*In most cases looking up data in a table is faster than calculating with code.*

Often, the use of tables comes at the expense of increased sized and limited flexibility, but if done well, the increase in speed is so significant as to be well worth it. Sometimes, the clever use of tables can even reduce the size of the code as well. Even further cleverness can improve flexibility by recalculating the contents of tables when the user "isn't looking."

An Example of Data versus Code   Continuing with examples from a virtual-reality style of baseball game, we assume that each runner has a running speed rating from 1 to 5, with 1 being slowest. When the batter hits the ball, we must give him a running velocity, to get him to run to first base according to his speed rating. We could calculate his velocity, or we could look it up in a data table.

To calculate velocity, we calculate how fast he's moving along both the x and y coordinate axes. Assume that in the baseball diamond, home plate is at $(0, 0)$ and first base, 90 feet away, is at $(63.6, 63.6)$. If the batter runs at a velocity of 10 feet per second, then we calculate his velocities as

$$rvx = 10 \times \frac{63.6}{90}$$

$$rvy = 10 \times \frac{63.6}{90}$$

This gets complicated quickly.

Instead, since he's running from home to first and he has a speed rating from 1 to 5, we can simply set up a little "lookup table" as in Table 6-3. Then all we have to do is to set up two blocks of memory in RAM (or ROM) and create the following instructions:

```
load Memory-location-#100 + rating into Register A
load Memory-location-#105 + rating into Register B
```

This looks amazingly similar to the example for drawing a pixel above. It's such a common technique that there are few, if any, algorithms that cannot be done in some fashion with tables. In this case we assume that the x velocities begin at location 100 and, since there are only five speed ratings, the y velocities begin at location 105.

TABLE 6-3

Rating	x Velocity (ft/s)	y Velocity (ft/s)
1	7	7
2	9	9
3	14	14
4	18	18
5	25	25

If You Didn't Read About How Computers Work, Read This About Data

Even if you skipped the above sections, one very important idea about the way computers work is *data sharing,* as I call it. Data sharing can be one of the most important design techniques for the life of a product from pre-design right through the production of sequels. Data sharing is the technique of creating databases of information that multiple programs can use to communicate with one another.

Again, I use a simple, real-world example. One unique feature from the original Earl Weaver Baseball is the ability of the user to edit and create his or her own stadiums. Instead of embedding the information about the stadiums in the program itself, we created a data file on the disk with all the information about each stadium. A separate program was supplied that could also use the "stadium file." This program did only a few things and was quite small, but it allowed the user to load the stadium file, look at each stadium, change the dimensions and attributes of the stadium, and save the edited stadium file back out to the disk.

Now this was possible only because we decided early on in the design process to do this, and so we designed the definitions of the stadiums to be a database of dimensions and attributes rather than to hard-code them. We did the same for the individual players (statistics, ratings, and names) and the teams (uniform colors, home stadium, name, etc.).

So we made it possible for two programs to share a few special databases. Where's the big payoff? Each time we made a new sequel for the product, regardless of the platform we made it for, we already had all the data for the players, teams, and stadiums ready to go. Another benefit was the fact that users began to edit these files to create other sets of players, teams, and stadiums which they traded, sold, and, in one case, licensed to Electronic Arts to sell to the public.

And, on top of all that, other baseball products began listing as a feature on the packaging that they were compatible with the Earl Weaver Baseball player databases. So we could continue to sell player databases to owners of our competitors' products. More importantly, while this is a subtle thing, it also helps establish in the mind of the users the value of the Earl Weaver brand even though they are purchasing a competitive product.

Other Uses of Data Sharing

Another common use of data sharing employed by experienced designers is the *mission disk*. Since the program knows how to interpret a mission file into a series of tasks, enemies, obstacles, terrains, vehicles, and equipment, the designer of such a program can sell disks with nothing but mission data on them. Most financially successful battle simulators and computer action games have this feature. Compared to writing a software program, creating this kind of data is almost trivial. So the cost of production of a mission disk is minimal. However, if you've hooked consumers on a $90 product and you can sell them a series of mission disks for even $10 per disk, you've increased your financial return enormously.

Similarly, the use of data sharing files to create what I call *attribute files* has proved to be a successful design technique. Often in role-playing games (RPGs), the character you create has a history of achievement, failure, injuries, knowledge, play style, physical capacity, and other attributes appropriate to the role-playing world. Each time the user saves or exits the game, this information about the character is saved into an attribute file. When the user starts up or continues a game, the program loads the attribute file data and continues with the user's character in its last known state.

As the user progresses through the game, he or she invests heavily in improving the character's attributes. At the end of such a game, the user has created a powerful alter ego and has nothing left to do with this character. Experienced designers have realized this fact, and they create new programs that can read the previous program's attribute file. This allows the user to start a new story or adventure with the character she or he spent so many hours perfecting.

Back to the Future of Data Sharing

The data-sharing technique allows multiple programs to communicate with one another, and it can be one of the best techniques for allowing multiple users of a program at the same time, or multiplayer gaming. Multiplayer gaming is one of the hot new game design topics of interest to designers, producers, and publishers. The only problem with inventing multiplayer gaming is that it has been around almost since the beginning of computer games (see the history section in Chap. 1).

In any case, when a little bit of information about each user is stored on a central computer, each user can see what all the other players are doing. For example, let's say the data-sharing file contains information about the coordinates (we continue to use x and y coordinates) of each user in the world, a facing direction (using compass points), a name, a creature type (from a list of creatures), a health attribute (e.g., a value from 0 to 10 with 10 being in great health and 0 being dead), and a current activity (from a list of activities). Then, after establishing the kind of creature the user is and the name desired, each user can move around in the world, pick a direction to look in, and do an activity. Every other user can, within a matter of moments, see where that user is and what that user is doing and how healthy (or near death) the user is.

Let's get specific: Say that picking a name of up to 20 alphanumeric characters and a creature type takes 21 bytes of data that are changed only rarely, and the position, facing direction, activity, and health of a player's character take up 7 bytes (1 byte for each attribute; each attribute can then be a value from 0 to 255). Further, say that each user's data need to be updated every 0.1 second. Well, we don't need to send 21 bytes of data for the name and creature type on each update; 7 bytes of attributes is sufficient. This means that 70 bytes of data per second has to be transmitted from each player (7 bytes, 10 times per second).

Going back up to the central computer (or server), we need to supply 7 bytes of data per character for every *other* character we can fit into our world. Further assume that we need to update the other characters' information only once per second on the player's computer. While it is true that each player needs to see the name and creature type for each other character, these data need to be sent only once, when each player starts up.

So, now to the determining factor: The number of players who can coexist at one time in this world is determined by the number of bytes per second that can be transmitted. At today's low-end equipment, of 14.4-kbaud modems, that's roughly equivalent to 1500 bytes per second. Thus 214 people can have characters directly interacting in the same world simply because they are sharing the same database.

What Computers Can Do That *Designers* Need to Know

Either you skipped the previous section, or you humored me and struggled through all the baseball metaphors and examples. In any case, now we get to the heart of the matter. As a designer, you must keep in mind all the things a computer can do. When I'm working with designers, we often go through this exercise of listing everything we can think of, in order to inspire our tired minds into taking advantage of the medium.

So, first make a simple list. A computer can

- Count
- Do arithmetic
- Remember what's been done
- Store data
- Look up data
- Manipulate data
- Make sound come out of a speaker
- Make graphics on a monitor
- Print on paper
- Choose random numbers
- Do logical comparisons
- Read a mouse or joystick
- Read a keyboard
- Send and receive data from a modem or over a network
- Look at its clock and tell the time and date
- Remember what it was doing and return to it after being interrupted to do something else

Refer to this list often as it is easy to forget some of the fundamental things computers can do when you get caught up in the details of design or production. Let's see how some of a computer's functions can be used to fill out a design.

Computers Can Count

Not only can the computer count as part of an algorithm, but also it can count the number of times something happens. For example, it can count how many times a user tries the same thing. If a user tries the same thing a few too many times, perhaps it is time to give the user some help (an under-used computer game feature, but one that is very simple to implement).

Here's another counting example that is too frequently ignored. Have your software count how many keystrokes per "command" users are making and how many times each command is used *during testing*. Again, this is fairly easy coding. Once you have this information, adjust your user interface to make the most commonly used commands require fewer keystrokes while switching the least frequently used commands to use a few additional keystrokes.

Remember that the computer can usually count anything that is going on from the user or the software. Then see if there are ways to incorporate these telling numbers into the design.

Computers Can Do Arithmetic

Unlike counting, I try to think of arithmetic not as a tool to monitor things in progress, but as a way to improve flexibility, speed up, and reduce the size of a program. In my experience, most newcomer designers and producers underappreciate the computer's ability to do arithmetic, and they focus almost completely on the computer's ability to do logic.

For example, if you are designing a game in which the user has to press a key or button at the right time in order to instruct an on-screen character to jump off a teeter-totter, you want the character on the other end of the teeter-totter to respond realistically. It would be easier to calculate the final movements of the teeter-totter based on the time of the first character's departure than to have a bunch of IF-THEN-ELSE statements to cover every possible moment when the user presses the key.

Computers Can Remember What's Been Done

Like counting, this feature of computer systems can be greatly underutilized in designing and testing products. If you're dealing with a computer, you have the advantage of large amounts of permanent storage (e.g., hard drives and floppy disks) to remember what's been done between uses of a product. Even if you're dealing with video game systems, there are usually some permanent storage technologies available for this use (e.g., on-board "flash RAM" that comes with the system or on the cartridge itself). In both cases, RAM can be used to remember what's been done in the current use of the product.

The most obvious use of this feature of computers is the SAVE-LOAD functions found in almost every type of product. Here's an example of a simple use that's rarely employed. If during the course of game play, the user keeps answering a yes/no question no instead of the default yes, you could switch the default answer to no and position the cursor or pointer on no to save the user some time and keystrokes.

A pet peeve of mine is that programs that bring up scrolling lists of things for you to choose from (as on the word processor I'm using) often do not remember the last item you used on the list, forcing you to scroll again. It would be truly simple to keep track of where you were the last time you used the list and to return you there. You could even postpone this automation by seeing if the user scrolls to the same spot the first two or three times using the list and then automatically start the user there. If there are lots of lists in the program, making it difficult to track them all, simply track the five most recently used lists. In any case, this is simple technology that many designers could use to eliminate a common frustration of users.

Here's another example. Have your program remember that the user keeps skipping an introductory sequence or has seen it a certain number of times, and skip the sequence automatically.

Yet another example is to keep track of which moves a user relies on to win a fighting game and then alter the computer opponent to anticipate those moves. In other words, the computer character looks as if it is learning about the user.

When creating Earl Weaver Baseball, I kept coming across bugs that were nearly impossible to reproduce and therefore almost impossible to fix. So I programmed an instant replay feature that remembered every keystroke and every random number that occurred during the sequence of a play. Then I could press a key ("I" for instant replay) that would play back exactly as everything happened. All of a sudden it was easy not only to fix bugs, but also to improve the algorithms and code. Having user-selectable instant replay was such a good feature that we included it as a key feature in the product for users. It was among the first products to ever provide this feature (especially completely under the user's control), and you can now find this feature on a wide range of sports, action, and simulator products.

Computers Can Store Data

This may seem such an obvious use that you don't think to examine it carefully. And most times you would probably be right. However, sometimes you can add to the user's experience or simplify the experience in certain types of products by providing a wide range of the types of data that can be stored.

From the nongame world, word processors have begun to allow you to store templates in addition to the actual files that you write.

During the development of Earl Weaver Baseball, I created the user-selectable instant replay feature as a debugging tool which eventually turned into a key feature of the product. In later versions, I realized that it might be fun for users to collect their favorite plays to share with friends, competitors, and the publisher of the product. So instead of allowing the instant replay data to vanish at the beginning of the next play, we gave the user the option of storing any just-completed play to disk. Through the life of that product, people occasionally sent me via E-mail the plays they wanted me to see. (Unfortunately, it was most often to point out problems they felt the game had; still, someone did send me a triple play just because it was neat.)

Computers Can Look Up Data

This feature is often left to programmers to deal with. However, designers and producers should be aware of how useful it is. Often data lookup is used for speeding up software through tables of numbers. Sometimes it is used for sorting through vast amounts of information, as in a database.

Knowing what kind of data will be available to you can be important. For example, if you can look up the settings of another similar product on the user's system, you might be able to automatically preconfigure your product when it is installed. Or you might be able to offer to clean up some disk space if the user is upgrading an earlier version of your product.

Computers Can Manipulate Data

Of course, manipulating data is, more or less, at the heart of what computers do. One of the things most often left out of designs, however, is the use of this ability to manipulate data to reduce the size of data. You can manipulate and thus reduce or compress data that are to be remembered, stored, or looked up. Even more importantly, you can use this technique to reduce the amount of data to be sent or received via modem.

To understand this kind of manipulation, you must understand how bits and bytes work. I won't go into much detail here, as many great books cover the subject. In today's PCs, data are measured in bytes, and each byte is made up of 8 bits. These bits have a value of only 0 or 1 which means there are a maximum of two values for each bit. This is why we refer to the kind of data in bits and bytes as *binary*. If you think of a bit as a digit, then you can look at each byte as something you can "decode." This is done just as you decode a decimal number; but instead of going from 0 to 1 like a bit, a decimal number digit goes from 0 to 9.

Binary numbers look like this: 00110010 (that's 8 bits, so it makes up 1 byte) which, except for the "leading" zeros looks just like a decimal number (except the digits are only 1s and 0s). One of the great manipulation abilities of computers is their capacity to decode a byte in many ways. One decoding method is known as *masking*, and it is also easy to do with decimal numbers. For designers, this is one technique to minimize the size of data. We can easily decode the number 12311997 as a date by subdividing the digits (in our heads) to 12 31 1997. The computer can do the same thing by manipulating the byte with "masks" to slice off sets of digits. In this way, groups of binary digits can be used to represent numbers that don't require the entire space of 1 byte (which, if you remember, goes from 0 to 255).

As an example, say you're making a game with 400 user-definable cows. Each cow can have one of four colors, can be 1 to 8 years old, can have one of three names (e.g., Bessie, Bossie, Booboo), and can be either yours or your neighbor's. At first glance, there are four pieces of information about each cow. The obvious thing to do is to assign 4 bytes of data per cow, 1 byte to store each piece of information. This is 1600 bytes. Using Tables 6-4 and 6-5 and the knowledge that each byte is made up of 8 bits, you can reduce the data for 400 cows to 400 bytes—a 75 percent savings! At these sizes, it may not seem significant but with larger databases, this can become significant in both disk storage and transfer time.

TABLE 6-4

Range of Values for
Partial Bytes

No. of Bits	No. of Values	Range of Values
1	2	0—1
2	4	0—3
3	8	0—7
4	16	0—15
5	32	0—31
6	64	0—63
7	128	0—127
8	256	0—255

TABLE 6-5

Compressing the
Cow Data

Cow Property	Values to Choose	Bits Required
Color	4	2
Age	8	3
Name	3	2
Owner	2	1
Total bits		8

By using the computer's ability to manipulate the data (i.e., to compress and decompress each byte into the four types of data required to define each cow), you can affect the way in which the data are used. If you have a limitation of 800 bytes of storage, by using this technique, you could have gone from limiting yourself to 200 cows (at 4 bytes per cow) to doubling your original capacity to 800 cows!

 ⇒On top of this, if you are designing a product that uses the data-sharing technique, this kind of data manipulation can really improve the ability to provide and share very large amounts of data.

Computers Can Make Sound Come out of a Speaker

This may seem like an obvious design use, but it is often unfortunately left to the last. In addition, it's used without much subtlety or cleverness. I categorize sound or audio into three subareas: sound effects, voice or speech, and music.

By leaving sound design to the end, designers often paint themselves into a corner technologically. They can run out of room in the system or on the disk, can run out of computing power, and can run into conflicts with the flow of the product.

It makes me crazy when I see a product in which a transition that could be smoothed over with the use of sound design elements (any of the three types) comes to an audio halt while the next visual or game play element is loaded.

Of all the multimedia elements, next to text, audio is about the smallest and most efficient. I believe there is little or no excuse for sound to stop during transitions. In my experience this is more often a design flaw than a programming problem. By the time it is brought to the attention of programmers and technology staff, it's usually too late to fix. This is the sort of thing that is relatively straightforward if done from the beginning of a product; but toward the end, forget it.

⇒Sound is also one of the easiest ways to reassure a user that input has been noticed. A simple but unobnoxious audio cue can go a long way to let a user know that a button click, a mouse movement limit, or a keyboard shortcut has been seen by the program.

One of the best uses I've seen of this was a product demo done for Activision where an on-screen character giggled whenever the user passed the cursor over its tummy (yes, it was a kids' game, but it made all the adults laugh, too).

Some Sound Ideas   Try to understand a little bit about how computer systems make sounds. For example, many computer and video game systems allow you to change the playback rate of a digitized sound. Changing the playback rate changes the pitch (faster playback rates make higher but shorter sounds). Likewise, many systems allow you to change the volume and left-right balance of sounds. You can use these features to greatly improve the quality of the sound design without creating additional sound components. However, as with covering transitions, if you don't plan this from the start, you don't stand much chance of being able to take advantage of it.

For example, you can take a single recorded birdcall and with some randomness change the pitch of the call each time it's heard. This has a remarkable effect: it sounds natural! To take it further, consider what I would do.

1. The birdcall is recorded at 11,000 bytes per second (bps). This means that played back at 11,000 bytes per second, it will sound just like the original birdcall.

2. We have four different birds (of the same or similar species) in a scene.

3. We can always get a random number between −500 and 500.

4. We assign the following average playback rates to each bird:

Bird 1   8,000 (a low voice)

Bird 2   11,000 (original voice)

Bird 3   14,000 (higher voice)

Bird 4   22,000 (voice twice as high as the original—this *is* how sound works)

5. Each time we play one of the bird's voices, we add their average sample rate to a new random number. This provides the following ranges of playback rate for each bird:

Bird 1   7,500—8,500

Bird 2   10,500—11,500

Bird 3   13,500—14,500

Bird 4   21,500—22,500

6. In addition, if volume goes from 1 to 10 with 10 being loudest and 1 being softest, using a random number from −1 to 1 gives the following ranges of playback volume for each bird:

Bird 1   1—3 (farthest away)

Bird 2   8—10 (closest)

Bird 3   4—6 (second to farthest)

Bird 4   5—7 (a little closer than bird 3)

7. Finally, if we use yet one more random number, the time between each bird's singing its chirp is from 2 to 7.5 seconds.

Any competent programmer should be able to take the above information and program it without much fuss (given that it's done early enough in the process of creating the entire program).

This effort will give a surprisingly natural sound, and all with one audio sample. Why? Because each bird is not repeating the exact same sound every time it sings. You may have to play with the random ranges, but the randomness provides a subtle change in the same sound each time it is played, and to our ears, that sounds far more natural than hearing the same sound over and over. Similarly, randomly changing the interval between chirps eliminates any discernible rhythm, which adds to the naturalness of the sound design.

I've found that sound effects and music created by using these kinds of techniques are rarely turned off by users (most programs nowadays allow users to turn off sounds if they want a quieter experience). So, sound isn't just a simple design element after all.

Computers Can Make Graphics on a Monitor

As with sound, graphics seen on the monitor seem like a simple design element to remember. However, while you create your design, consider visual elements that can qualitatively improve if you reflect on what a computer can do in regard to graphics.

Unlike the case of sound, a huge variety of technologies are used for creating graphics. You need to study carefully the attributes and short-coming of the platform you are designing for. Without going into much detail, Table 6-6 provides a list of things to look for with some sample ram-ifications.

As you can see, there are a lot of combinations of graphics technologies. On any one system, there are usually two, three, four, or more choices of these technologies. Designing your product with a system's strengths and weaknesses in mind can often endear you to the technical staff who have to program it.

A Graphic Example   When working on Return to Zork (see, it's not all about Earl Weaver Baseball), we were implementing a design that called for video footage to be composited over computer-generated backgrounds on a 256-color palettized video system. In addition to the great new tech-nology we were using to play back this footage at 10 to 15 frames per sec-ond, we had to figure out how to create and manage all the palettes. We had to consider these goals:

1. Select the best possible palette for each scene (there were almost 90 scenes).

2. Make sure that the interface elements always look the same. So they had to be created in colors that would always be available in each palette.

3. Create the best possible transitions from scene to scene without going to black in between, even if two scenes have different palettes.

4. Prioritize the palettes for skin tones whenever we expected charac-ters to appear in a scene.

5. Make the noninteractive "movie" sequence look as high-quality as possible even though it would consist of sometimes thousands of frames. (In other words, create a palette that would work for all the frames of a movie.)

This was a tall order, but with the technical and creative work from Activi-sion's Bill Volk, JP Asperin, and many others (including Sean Barger's team at Equilibrium), we found solutions to most of these problems dur-ing the design phases.

The solutions required a variety of techniques some of which were used during the creation of the art, some during the "engineering" of the

TABLE 6-6

Technologies to Look For	Technologies to Watch Out For	Ramifications
One-to-one mapping from RAM to screen		Faster than having to draw to screen via a special piece of hardware. Allows for direct manipulation of on-screen images.
"Blitter"		Allows for ultrafast copying of images from RAM to the screen including manipulation of the image during copying (such as flipping, color changes).
	Video RAM graphics card	Can only create images on screen by sending data through the processor. Cannot directly manipulate an on-screen image. Sometimes cannot "see" what is on screen from inside the computer program.
3D card or accelerator		Allows for ultrafast creation and manipulation of 3D shapes stored as sequences of vertices. Often includes lighting controls and texture mapping.
Sprites		Usually only found in video games (the Amiga computer had sprites, too), these are small animation rectangles which, because they can have transparent pixels, can move around, over, and under other image elements very, very fast. Sprites can often be manipulated without changing any data for the image (e.g., flipping horizontally or vertically, doubling in size, changing colors).
Planes		Usually found only in video games (the Amiga had planes, too), these behave like full-screen sprites. As they support transparent pixels, you can create layers of full-screen images that other planes and sprites can be seen in front or behind (like an old fashioned shooting gallery!).
Tile-based graphics		Imagine creating pictures on the floor out of small floor tiles that can be purchased in any of 10 simple geometric patterns. This is the premise of tile-based graphics. By creating a set of usually 128 or so basic shapes, you can stamp them on the screen in any order (reusing any shape as often as you like), in any orientation, with a choice of colors. This creates a very efficient way of creating pictures, as each tile is represented by a single byte in memory but covers somewhere between 64 pixels (for 8×8 tiles) and 256 pixels (for 16×16 tiles). This technique is sometimes emulated on computers to create very flexible, very efficient backdrops for games.
	Tile-based graphics	In early systems, you were limited to preset tile sets. Later, you could define one or two tile sets in memory. Lately, you have a lot of latitude, but still this can create a blocky-looking image in an effort to be space- and time-efficient.

(Continued)

TABLE 6-6 *(Continued)*

Technologies to Look For	Technologies to Watch Out For	Ramifications
Palette-based graphics		Usually coming in 16 or 256 color sets, each pixel on the screen is represented by an index into a palette. The palette is sometimes defined by the computer (0 = black, 1 = green, etc.), but more often it is defined by the designers (0 = black, 1 = dark gray, etc.) so as to have some logical layout and a range specific to a particular image. When you can specify your own palette, often you can create remarkable-quality images if you can design your production to use a small range of colors. For example, an image of mostly green, blue, black, and white typically will look better than an image with green, blue, black, white, red, yellow, and orange, because each color has fewer gradations to it. Sometimes this mode of graphics is emulated on higher-quality systems (see below) in order to conserve space and increase speed.
RGB-based graphics		Usually in 16-, 24-, or 32-bit versions, each pixel is represented by an actual color as defined by its red, green, and blue (RGB) components. RGB is used because of the type of color creation found in a cathode-ray tube (CRT), which is the same technology as a TV set and is known as *subtractive color* (as opposed to additive color which uses red, blue, and yellow as primary colors). In any case, the number of bits is usually evenly divided between the R, G, and B values. In 16-bit, you get 5 bits of each; in 24-bit there are 8 bits each; and in 32-bit there are 10 bits each. The extra bits sometimes have other uses and sometimes are left over and unused. This type of graphics gives you the greatest control over the quality of an image with the higher number of bits per color providing higher quality. The downside is that this requires an enormous amount of data to create imagery and a lot of time to manipulate them.
High-resolution	Low-resolution	The resolution usually refers to the number of pixels that can be displayed on the screen. Some systems have multiple resolutions. Typically, resolutions smaller than 500 wide × 300 high are considered low resolution. Low resolution usually means fatter pixels and higher speeds, as much less data and manipulation are required for imagery. For PCs, low resolution is 320 × 200, and high resolution is at least 640 × 480. This is 4 times as many pixels!
MPEG decoder		MPEG (Motion Picture Experts Group) compression is a technique for digitally encoding full-screen, full-motion video at 30 frames per second with CD-quality audio so that it can be played back on a computer system. If a system is equipped with an MPEG decoder, it can play back very high-quality full-motion video in low resolutions (newer decoders and the MPEG II standard allows high-resolution playback at even better quality). Often the decoder can adjust the size of the playback area and/or layer the playback images with other on-screen graphics (using the planes technology above).

art, some during the programming of the game engine, and some in the creation and/or creative use of special software tools for graphics.

First, we created the graphics at the highest resolution possible that we could afford. This included the way video that was recorded and digitized (with much technical and creative input from Dave Mangone and the team at Pacific Ocean Post) and which graphics were created using both 3D and 2D drawing, modeling, and rendering programs.

Second, we had to engineer the graphics. This is one of the unique aspects of computer software production. Someone has to convert the graphics from a "pure" high-resolution (in our case 640 $\times$ 480, 16.7 million colors) original down to a 320 $\times$ 200, 256-color usable image. (We used this resolution for the PC version and did the Macintosh version at 640$\times$480, with 256 colors.)

During the engineering, we had to pick color palettes for each image that would work within the framework of our goals. So, JP Asperin, the art director, and his team came up with a plan and several ideas of how to use the tools at hand to implement it. Bill Volk, the head of technology at Activision and, luckily for me, the technical director on the Return to Zork project, had many ideas of how to implement the things that weren't possible with the current tools. Sometimes, he'd simply program a new tool, and sometimes he'd contact the providers of the off-the-shelf tools and work with them to improve their products.

One of these products is Debabilizer from Equilibrium. For the last few years, of all the tools available to multimedia producers, this would have been voted, far and away, the most valuable. Not only will Debabilizer convert just about any graphics format to just about any other, but also it does a great job of creating optimal palettes. It can change palette style and size, create palettes for groups of images (hence a "movie" could have a palette created), and do many other analysis and conversion steps. On top of all that, it has a "batch" feature that allowed us to specify a sequence of steps needed to convert an image for our purposes and then execute those steps, automatically, on a bunch of images. This allowed us to do much of the engineering overnight, during lunch, or while our artists were doing something else.

While clever and creative use of Debabilizer allowed us to achieve many of our graphics design goals, it didn't quite do all of them just as we needed. For example, to reserve a set of colors for the interface elements, one of our first solutions was to add an extra portion to each image with all these interface elements stamped into a blank area. This was OK, but not efficient (especially for batch conversions), and it would become truly tedious should we need to change the colors of the interface elements.

The solution *we* wanted was to be able to convert the interface elements to a specific number of colors (for example, 32 of the 256). Then we wanted Debabilizer to automatically include these colors in each of the images we converted. However, we also didn't want any colors repeated in the palette, as each color was a valuable resource to us. So the image needed to be optimized for 224 colors unless some of those colors were in the reserved 32. In that case, the image was to be optimized for 224 colors plus the number of colors in the reserved space. This gives more unique colors and therefore a higher-quality image. However, the 32 colors for the interface elements had to remain in the same place in each pallet. So if a particular red appeared in both the interface colors and the optimal image colors, that red had to be stored in the same location in the palette as it normally appeared and had to be skipped in the series of reds that Debabilizer was building and storing for the rest of the image. Obviously, this got very complicated!

Bill and Joe worked closely with Sean Barger and his Debabilizer programming team to solve these problems for us. I believe that some of the solutions they came up with are now standard features of Debabilizer.

Another problem was doing transitions without resorting to black screens. Personally, I feel black transition screens should only be used on purpose as a visual design element. However, in many, many software products, black transition screens are relied on simply to provide a simple solution to technical problems with transitions and, in my opinion, because of a lack of design forethought.

Bill had already come up with a solution for this when working on The Manhole with Cyan (of Myst fame). The engine he came up with allowed for computer graphics versions of wipes, fades, and dissolves as most people know them from film and television. The dissolve was a particularly useful transition, as we could have it performed at varying speeds which allowed us much control of the rhythm of the experience. (This usually meant cranking up the dissolve speed to as fast as possible unless we were covering the loading of some data during the transition.)

The only problem with the dissolve as it was created for use in The Manhole and Leather Goddesses of Phobos (a graphic adventure based on the Infocom text adventure by Steve Meretzky) was that the software assumed that the palettes of the two images were either the same or, at least, virtually identical both in which colors were in the palette and the order in which they were stored in the palette.

For Return to Zork (RTZ) we only had the assurance that the colors of interface elements would be the same in the palette. There were usually 224 other colors that could be anything in any order! After much discussion, a solution was chosen: Sort each palette based on certain qualities of the colors which would allow the dissolve to be fairly effective in the use of Bill's algorithms. Again, this required help from Equilibrium.

We needed Debabilizer to be able to sort a portion of the palette (i.e., the portion not reserved for interface elements) based on certain attributes of colors as defined by our dissolve algorithm. We worked out a system for doing this and, considering the small palettes we were working with, created a much more pleasing and, if nothing else, purposeful style of transition.

If we planned to have any characters appear in a scene, we had to devise a system for creating palettes that would work with their faces and clothes. So we would use the tools in Debabilizer to create an optimal palette for two images of each scene: one with and one without the character. If there were more characters to appear, then we would use more images in the process.

We developed a lot of techniques and tools for meeting our goals. We combined a few to meet our last goal: Make the movies look as good as possible.

First, the game program engine was changed to allow the dissolve transition to work from a still image to the first image of a movie. Also, the dissolve was made to work from the last frame of a movie to the still frame that would appear after the movie. Originally, when the MADE engine (as it was called internally at Activision) incorporated the ability to play movies (in MADE's own format), there were no transitions other than "jump cuts" in and out of the movie.

Next, we realized that there were to be no interface elements available to users during the playing of a movie (they could click a mouse button or press a key to skip the movie, but they didn't need to see a cursor to do this). This meant we could free up the entire palette for Debabilizer to use for each image.

Debabilizer would already create an optimal palette for a group of frames, so we were ready to go. Of course, we felt there could be some major improvements. The biggest would be to allow the palette to change completely from frame to frame or, as a more challenging but more efficient solution, allow the palette to evolve from frame to frame. We did come up with ways to implement this, but I don't believe they made it into the product or any other of Activision's subsequent adventure games.

The only reason we could accomplish what we did to improve the graphics quality of RTZ was because we were thinking of these design issues very early. We kept an eye toward all the things a computer can do with its graphics capability.

Gonzo Graphics   As another, shorter example, when I was working with John Cutter from Starwave on The Muppet CD-ROM: Muppets Inside (see, here's another non—Earl Weaver Baseball example!), we wanted to create a truly Muppet-like opening. As this was an FMV playback product with the Muppets composited on 3D images, one thing we thought about was the fact that everyone seems to show video footage in little rectangles on the screen.

We knew that this was due, in part, to the limitations of double-speed CD-ROM drives on standard high-resolution PCs. These computers are only capable of changing about one-quarter of the screen during video-style playback. However, there wasn't any compelling reason that everyone chose to display his or her video in an index-card-shaped 320 wide × 240 high box (or smaller, but with similar dimensions).

Fortunately for us, the Muppets don't usually stick to convention, so we were free to think of other ways to use our one-quarter screen. This was our solution: We start the product by showing a video clip of the beginning of The Muppet Show with new voices singing words to introduce The Muppet CD-ROM. We show this video in a standard 320 × 240 window in the center of the screen. Then, a few seconds into the song, we simulate a computer crash, the video goes away, and the user's system appears to be dead. After a few seconds to let the panic set in (but not long enough to allow the user to press the Reset button), Kermit and Fozzie's voices can be heard fretting over the fact that their program has crashed. Kermit tells Fozzie to get out of there while he, Gonzo, and the rest of the crew attempt to sort out the problem. Then we see Fozzie's and Kermit's fingers pry open the screen from the middle as if it's a stuck curtain. Unfortunately, they can't get it all the way open, so our view of the Muppets working frantically in their Muppet Labs behind our screen is only about 160 pixels wide. Fozzie gets Rizzo to try to help him open the screen the rest of the way, Gonzo pulls the wrong cord, and…—I'm sure you get the picture.

It turns out that 160 pixels wide × 480 pixels tall is one-quarter of the full screen and is small enough for full-motion video playback. However, it is so unusual that it's very easy to buy into the fact that you're only seeing a part of the screen. Because of the production design of this element of the game, it makes you believe that there is more stuff back there and that you would be able to see it if only Gonzo and Rizzo could open the screen the rest of the way.

This was a case in which an understanding of the graphics technology not only provided a unique use of the technology but also helped to define some of the story elements and dialogue.

Computers Can Print on Paper

⇒Although you cannot expect a video game system to support printing, almost every computer system now has a printer attached to it. Yet, in my experience, for most products, printing comes after music and sound effects as a design element. This is especially true for games. Why this is, I don't know. I'll admit that I fall prey to the same tendency. However, there are things we can all try to think about when considering this underused peripheral for entertainment software design.

First, you can pretty much count on people having a printer hooked up to their computers. Second, the quality of those printers is generally pretty good these days, as most people have at least ink-jet-style printers if not color ink jets or laser printers. Finally, with the easy access to high-quality printers at photocopy stores, it is simple to create a file to be put on a floppy disk to be printed not at home, but at the photocopy store.

So everyone has access to reasonably good-quality printers. Now what?

Imagine This   Just to try to spark some ideas for future designs, here are a few simple examples.

In Earl Weaver Baseball (again!), we realized that people who play baseball simulators and fantasy leagues are used to holding some sort of baseball cards when managing their teams and making trades. So we did a bit of research and found out that at most stationery stores you can buy 3 × 5 index cards meant to be used with printers (in those days, this paper was actually "continuous feed" 3 × 5 cards that you could tear apart at the perforated edges after printing on a dot-matrix printer). As we already had an on-screen format for showing the statistics for each player, we gave users the option to print out "baseball cards" from EWB. They could print their teams, entire leagues, or just individual players. We included a few example pages of 3 × 5 continuous-feed paper so people would believe they could do this. On top of that, we included information from a paper company on how to mail-order this special paper in both white, and a wide variety of colors, so users could do creative things with the printed baseball player cards.

We found out that people liked to use their own names to create new player cards. We never expected that this would be so popular in general, and adding printing just increased the fun of that experience for many users. I've always believed that good design for interactive products will offer users the opportunity to do things that the designer never imagined. Brian Moriarity, a distinguished designer from the early days, refers to this as an emergent behavior.

The next design for EWB called for images that resembled the players printed (of course, there are additional legal ramifications for providing this feature).

My only other real experience with this was with The Muppet Treasure Island CD-ROM. Larry Kay, Mark Loparco, and Cheryl Weiner, the original designing and producing team, had quite a bit of experience among them and included the notion of printing out scenes from this adventure game. Users could print them out in color just to look at them or as line drawings so they could color them. While this wasn't necessarily brand new or unique, it did pose some interesting problems while at the same time creating an exciting feature. Because they were printing Muppet characters in the scenes, we had to be very conscious of the quality of the representation of the characters once printed. It took a few tries to get the quality right, but the production team was alerted early on that each printed image had to carry certain legal language for the copyright and trademark from Jim Henson Productions, so we never had any problems there.

Now, let me extrapolate both uses into a possible new feature. Since there are so many products based on famous characters and since users mostly have individual-sheet printers that can print on a variety of transparent label sizes, perhaps the industry could settle on some standard for computer game printed trading cards that could feature these famous characters and could be somehow unique to the person who printed them. Perhaps users could print only one card per person per product; maybe users could include their own scanned-in image(s) in the card. We even have ideas that would tie this idea to our Internet products.

A Virtual Printing Possibility   While I don't personally know of any products that do this, I could imagine a spy game that simulates some sort of operations room in which data are being fed to the user as if monitoring information from many outside sources. Typically in this environment, users see data appear on the screen (like E-mail from sources), hear audio over intercoms and phones, and see all kinds of dials indicating the status of various things. Why not use the player's printer to print out simulated faxes? This would add some dimensionality and further immerse (one of the buzzwords from the mid-1990s—don't forget to include it in your design proposal!) the player.

⇒So while even though so much thought has been given to the paperless office, maybe we should all give further thought to papering the game player's home.

Computers Can Choose Random Numbers

Computers can choose random numbers in a variety of ways. It's simple, it's easy, and it's often underutilized by designers. However, programmers have a close relationship with randomness (numbers as well as behavior) and, left to their own devices, will gladly handle this part of a design for you. While this is often not a problem at all, it does invoke the 3 A.M. Green Syndrome (see above), and it does displace a large amount of control that the designer should take responsibility for.

The use of random numbers as a design element and the specification for how the programmer should implement them are a subject that I covered in depth earlier. For now, let me say that random numbers are one of your best tools in creating a sense of naturalness. They can be used to great effect for repeated use of small sets of assets (see the Computers Can Make Sounds Come out of a Speaker section above) as well as to greatly enhance the quality of game play itself.

Now, this is one of my hard-and-fast design rules: ⇒ Be sure that the tools you intend to build your product with support programming with randomness. I cannot emphasize this enough. Even if you don't think there will be a need for the use of random numbers, there probably will. I cannot think of a product I've worked on in the past 15 years that hasn't needed this feature.

Computers Can Do Logical Comparisons

⇒Logical comparisons are one of the things that computers do at their most fundamental level. It is also one of the most misunderstood features by newcomers to the world of computer software design. Everyone seems to grasp the ideas of

If this, then do that; otherwise, do something else.

and

If $x > y$, do this; if $x = y$ do that; otherwise $(x < y)$, do something else.

Then they stop thinking about logical comparisons that computers can do. They are far from the end of the list or the limits of power and complexity of its use; once again, they leave this sort of knowledge and control to the programmer which, once again, puts them in danger of the 3 A.M. Green Syndrome's coming into play.

Logic is a branch of mathematics and is used quite extensively in the study of philosophy. (Personally, I believe this is one reason why many people have trouble communicating with anyone who has studied logic, such as mathematicians, scientists, philosophers, and computer programmers, because this group understands the language of logic and uses it in daily conversation.) This can be, quite admittedly, as intimidating as trying to speak a foreign language. As such, it is a powerful and complex language for the articulation of the exact consequences of how things compare to one another. Logic even has a notation all its own, and most computer languages support the use of shorthand versions of the logic symbols.

In the computer world, logic and arithmetic comparisons have been rolled into one subject in the minds of most people. As it more or less works to cover them together, I will do so at the risk of upsetting a few purists.

The first and foremost principle to consider is that the result of *any* logical comparison is either TRUE or FALSE. This is *not* the same as EQUAL or UNEQUAL, which people often confuse when first learning about this subject.

For the purposes of discussing the kind of logical comparisons that a computer can do, Table 6-7 is a list of the *operators* or instructions sup-

TABLE 6-7

Logical Operator	Example Computer Language Symbols
Equals	= , = =
Greater than	>
Greater than or equal to	> = , = >
Less than	<
Less than or equal to	< = , = >
Not equal, unequal	<>, ≠
AND	&, &&
OR	ǀ, ‖
NOT	~, !
TRUE	1 or 0
FALSE	0 or 1 (the opposite of TRUE)

ported by almost all computers and some of the computer-language versions of the symbols.

IF-THEN-ELSE   Now that you've seen a list of basic logical comparison operations, note that the most common reference to computer logic is missing from the list: IF-THEN-ELSE. That's because these three powerful words are the *syntax* of many languages (including a somewhat stilted version of the spoken language we use). The syntax allows us to insert the logical comparisons and the results in relatively easy-to-read instructions. Typically there are two uses of this construct: IF-THEN and IF-THEN-ELSE

```
IF (logical comparison is TRUE)
THEN (do this)
```

and

```
IF (logical comparison is TRUE)
THEN (do this)
ELSE (do something else)
```

Logical Examination   Let's take a quick look at what you can do with logic. First, you can simply compare two things with any of the operators listed above. Try to come up with examples for each. As you read through the list, you'll notice you "compare two things" with the last few operators. The operators NOT, TRUE, and FALSE only work on individual things.

The operator NOT is used to identify when something is FALSE. This may seem weird, but it serves a few purposes. First, it can make it for simpler instructions:

I'm going to the store if there are NOT eggs in the fridge.

---

as opposed to

If there are eggs in the refrigerator, then I'm going home; otherwise (or else), I'm going to the store.

Notice that the first instructions are more direct and to the point and leave it to us to make an assumption about what to do in the "else" case. The second set is clearer and makes no assumptions. To a computer programmer, the first is generally faster and takes less code while the second is more explicit at the cost of more code.

TRUE or FALSE   You cannot compare two things with the TRUE and FALSE operators listed above. This is a slightly more obscure use of computer logic but worth a quick look. A typical, but odd-looking use is

```
IF data in Memory-Location-#47 THEN go to the store.
      (condition)                (result)
```

This mechanism is opposite from the one used in the game show *Jeopardy:* The question must be in the form of an answer. More accurately, the condition (what follows the IF) must be in the form of a result (TRUE or FALSE). The way computers work, this instruction really is saying IF TRUE THEN GO TO THE STORE. But to a computer programmer, this is saying if the *value* in this memory location is the computer's representation of TRUE, then go to the store.

For example, many computer languages use zero for FALSE and any nonzero number to mean TRUE. So if you perform the same comparison many times (e.g., "how many eggs are in the fridge? 0 or 1, 2, 3, etc.), you store the result of that comparison in memory somewhere. Then you simply "test" to see if the value in that memory location is TRUE or FALSE (i.e., nonzero or zero).

As another example, in the course of a baseball play, many decisions are made by the players and umpires based on whether there are two outs already. If the program tests for this condition once per play and stores the result, then you can both speed up game play and reduce the size of your code by testing the memory location directly for TRUE or FALSE as opposed to constantly checking if #-of-outs = 2.

Follow the Logic   All the other logical operators in the list above compare two things and come up with a result that is TRUE or FALSE. This seems simple enough, and for most novice designers and first-time programmers, this is as much logic as they plan to use. However, complex logic made of multiple "nested" logical comparisons and operators can provide a high level of sophistication to your design. This, I suppose, seems like the bad news. The good news is that you use this kind of complex logic on a daily basis (at least I hope you do!). For example,

```
IF there are no eggs in the refrigerator AND I need eggs in the
house for breakfast tomorrow AND I have enough money with me to buy
eggs OR the store will take a check AND I have my checkbook OR the
store will take a credit card for such a small purchase AND the
store is still open when I leave work THEN go to the store to buy
eggs, ELSE get doughnuts for breakfast on the way to work tomorrow
```

It's a little hard to read this way. Readable formatting of this kind of conditional instruction(s) is often what separates the real programmers from the novices. With just a simple formatting change this becomes

```
IF there are no eggs in the refrigerator
        AND I need eggs in the house for breakfast tomorrow
        AND (I have enough money with me to buy eggs
            OR (the store will take a check
                AND I have my checkbook)
            OR  the store will take a credit card for such a
                small purchase)
        AND the store is still open when I leave work
THEN go to the store to buy eggs
ELSE get doughnuts for breakfast on the way to work tomorrow
```

Carefully reading through this example, you can get a good idea of how complex logic instructions can be. Notice the left parenthesis after the second AND statement. It's important to understand this part of the overall instruction as it contains nested logical conditions. What matters in this part of the instruction is whether any of the three conditions results in a TRUE value. However, in the second OR statement, both conditions need to be TRUE for that statement to result in a TRUE value. It's a bit complicated but absolutely worth working through.

Computers Can Read a Mouse or Joystick

Reading these two types of input devices is straightforward. Each in its way can give you information about which way it is pointing and whether a button is pressed. If you are designing a game for a specific, well-defined genre of product, consult a range of competitive products to see if you need to create an interface that works within an established framework.

Most mice and game controllers let you know when two or more buttons are pressed simultaneously. Imagine what would happen if in the next revision of your word processor you had to hold down both mouse buttons at the same time to highlight a block of text instead of holding down one button. (And this assumes you have two buttons on your mouse, which, of course, means you aren't using a Macintosh.) First, you wouldn't know that pressing both buttons is required, and you would be frustrated by using a familiar tool in a new way. Second, when you did find out, you wouldn't understand why they changed it and you would likely be unhappy with the product and its manufacturer. Finally, it would make you pause before purchasing other upgrades for fear that the manufacturer might have made weird changes yet again.

⇒If you do have the opportunity to design the use of the mouse or joystick, balance their standard uses with creative new ways to expand their use. Multiple buttons, the timing of holding and releasing, the speed of repeating clicks or presses, the distance of the mouse roll, the length of time a joystick is in a particular direction, drawing shapes with either device, alternating directions, and probably other things you can do with these devices are waiting to be fitted into products.

Computers Can Read a Keyboard

As with mice and joysticks, reading a keyboard is generally not too diffi-cult for a designer. Again, conform to any industry standards for the genre of game you are designing. Most keyboards allow you to read simultane-ously pressed keys if you're willing to find a programmer who can get you that information (simultaneous key presses are often required for action games and games with complicated interfaces). You can use the speed, tim-ing and repeated pressing of keys as different ways to use the keyboard.

Here is a list of keyboard issues that are worth keeping an eye out for:

ESC. Most keyboards have an escape key. If there's a standard use on the platform, use it. Otherwise, this is a good key to back the user out of the current game state.

Enter/Return. Different keyboards use different words for this key. Be aware of this when you give on-screen instructions (e.g., "Press the Return key…" doesn't work if there isn't a Return key on the PC key-board).

Tab/Shift-Tab. There are definitely standard uses of these keys that have moved from the world of databases into every other type of software products (i.e., the Tab key moves you from field to field and the Shift-Tab moves you backward from field to field). However, if you aren't allowing the user to move from "field to field," then you can probably do what you want.

F1—F12. Until recently, many keyboards only had up to F10. Again, in some contexts, some of these keys have standard meanings. Otherwise, they are a convenient way to provide shortcuts.

The number keys and number pad keys. Be careful about looking for numbers and using the number pad as a direction arrow or joystick substitute! Sometimes the NumLock setting can mess up users. (Users can specify that their computers start with Numlock on, which means that the numeric keypad cannot be used for its convenient cursor key layout for up, down, left, and right arrows.)

Use the alphabetical characters wisely. If layout is important, then pick keys that lay out well for right-handers and give left-handers an option to change this. Often games allow the user to change key layouts at will. Being left-handed, I'm appreciative of games that have an option to select an appropriate left-handed version of the interface. If alphabetical mnemonic relationships are important, focus on the most-used features that need key assignments. In this way, if you are forced to use an obscure key assignment, it is for a less-used instruction.

Shift, CTRL, ALT, Open Apple. While these keys can extend the number of assigned keystrokes you can have, you must be consistent in their use. These keys are called *modifiers,* and the type of modification each does should always be the same. The example we know best is the use of the Shift key to get to the capital or uppercase character on each key.

Computers Can Send and Receive Data from a Modem or over a Network

Modems are one of the computer devices that I consider both an input and an output device. For those of you who get confused:

▪ *Uploading* (or *sending*) data is the act of sending data from your computer upstream (like spawning salmon) or away from your computer to another computer.

▪ *Downloading* (or *receiving*) data is the act of bringing data down to your computer from another computer.

⇒In other words, my upload is your download. If you are one of "those" types, you could use a clever saying:

"I download, I own; I upload, I give it up."

(While this isn't entirely true, it can help keep the directions straight. To be accurate, the act of uploading does not actually remove data from your system after you've sent them upstream, so you will still probably own them on your system.)

Computers Can Look at the Clock and Tell the Time and Date

Here's a feature few newcomers think about: the clock. In every computer system, there is some sort of clock. In some systems, such as personal computers, the clock remembers the time and date. In simpler systems, the clock may simply keep on ticking (as a metronome does) as a timing resource for the processors and programmers.

In addition, many clocks are far more accurate than to mere minutes and seconds. You can often count on 0.01 second or more accuracy. This accuracy is a powerful tool. With this information you can get very precise data about (1) the response time of users, (2) how long they've been suffering through an activity, (3) how long the program has left to accomplish a task (so you can keep users informed), and (4) the day, week, or month in which something has happened. Also the clock is a useful system feature that you can integrate into your algorithms for random numbers and for scaling artificial intelligence.

Time for an Example In many chess games, the clock is used as a means of making the computer opponent (the artificial intelligence) behave with varying degrees of competence. Often chess AI is designed so that the computer "thinks" in discrete steps. At the end of each step, the computer formulates a next move. To make the computer smarter or dumber, chess programs change the interval for when the computer "thinks" its next discrete thought. For example, at the highest level, the computer may be allowed to think every 0.01 second while at the easiest level (for the human player), the computer may be told to think every second. That's 100 fewer discrete thoughts that the computer has every second.

No Time Like the Present One of the best uses of the computer clock I've been personally involved in is The Muppet CD-ROM: Muppets Inside. Designer and producer John Cutter and his team at Starwave came up with the notion of using the clock's calendar feature so that the introduction to the product would change. If you happen to play on your birthday or near Christmas or New Year's Eve and other holidays, there are special artwork and performances just for those intros.

During the design phase, the idea evolved further and the clock feature was used to keep track of how long it was since a player actually played the game. It was an almost trivial amount of computer programming: When the user quits the game, the time and date are read from the computer and stored on the hard drive with the user's other saved game information. The next time that user starts up the game, the software reads in the old time and date and compares it with the present. Depending on how long it has been since the user last played, an appropriate intro is selected in which Kermit and Fozzie discuss what's been going on in the user's absence. There are more than 20 different intros like this that welcome the user back from a few hours, days, or even weeks.

As this is the first thing players see when they start up the product, it has an *immediate* impact on players the second time and all subsequent times they start up the game. I cannot think of another CD-ROM or video game product that can say that.

Computers Can Remember What They Were Doing and Return to It

As with the clock, this is one of those things that few new designers think much about (if they even know about it). Unlike the clock, it's a little more difficult to grasp its significance. However, this is one of the fundamental computer features that has recently become an important buzzword: *multitasking.*

There are, in fact, several ways for a computer to multitask. The two most common are simultaneous processing (usually by multiple processors) and *time slicing* by a single processor. If you are working on a computer that can simultaneously process instructions, you are very lucky. However, this type of multitasking is limited to the number of processors installed in the system (the good news is that this is usually the fastest type of multiprocessing).

The time-slice style of multitasking allows you to have as many seemingly simultaneous programs running as time allows. As the name indicates, each program is allocated a slice of time in order to run (usually in 0.01 second).

How does this work? It works because of the very feature we're discussing: Computers have ways of remembering what they were doing and continuing that later.

Imagine working in a warehouse stacking small boxes. You sort the boxes according to information on the tops of the boxes, so many are spread around on the floor when your boss comes in and interrupts you. Your boss needs the way cleared so you can mop the floor immediately before the health inspectors come. You quickly gather up the boxes you're working on and push them on a nearby stack of boxes. You mop up the floor, the inspectors come and go, and then your boss asks you, "So when are you going to be done sorting those boxes?" You instantly pop the boxes off the stack and begin sorting them on the floor again.

I know it seems like a silly example, but the terminology I've used is quite similar to programmer-speak. Computers can interrupt their current task by "pushing" critical data onto an internal "stack" of other data. This information is typically the location of the next program instruction in memory and all the processor's register memory. Then the processor does the new task. When it's done with the new task, it "pops" the old information off the stack and goes along to the next instruction in the old task as if nothing happened.

This type of task interrupting is one of the more powerful features used in a computer, and sophisticated designers should at least be aware of it. Although it is not common for designers to determine when to use this feature, they should be aware that often this feature gets in the way of their best-laid plans.

A Matter of Priority   One feature in many computers that designers can use in relation to interrupting tasks is the priority level. Each program that can interrupt or be interrupted has a priority attribute set by the programmer. Higher-priority programs cannot be interrupted by lower-priority programs.

Typically, the highest-priority programs in your computer are the clock update and the mouse input (so that the mouse can be drawn smoothly on the screen).

So I find that the two most useful ways to take advantage of this feature are by switching priorities of programs based on the state of the game and using only certain subprograms when a specific event occurs by interrupting the flow of the main program.

As an example of switching priorities, say we're designing a navy simulation and the user's on a ship. The virtual crew members can think for themselves and, given the opportunity, express an opinion. The subprogram for each crew member runs in a 0.01-second time slice. These time slices are interrupting the main program which is simulating the water, weather, ship, and a war scenario. So, every 100 seconds, each crew member has "thought" for 1 second while the real world has continued for more than $1^1/_2$ minutes. As with the chess example above, at the end of each time slice, each crew member has formed an opinion about what to do. We often refer to this kind of programming as *background processing*.

Each crew member's interrupt priority is directly related to her or his rank. Depending on the rank of the highest-ranking crew member on the bridge, the program changes the state of the computer so all crew members with equal or higher rank (and therefore interrupt priority) are the only ones thinking. Now only those crew members will have a high enough interrupt priority to get a slice of time to think and therefore form an opinion as to what to do.

If an officer asks a lower-ranking crew member what he or she thinks, this crew member's interrupt priority can be temporarily raised to that of the officer so she or he can think for an allowable period and formulate an opinion. For example, the officer could ask a crew member for an opinion, and it might be up to the user to determine just when the crew member offers this opinion. The officer could push the crew member to decide more quickly ("I'm waiting") and could eventually lose patience. The user knows, however, that the longer the crew member takes to think, the better the opinion. So, the user has to balance the impatience of the officer with the desired quality of the crew member's response. Once the response has been given, the crew member no longer needs to "think," and everyone's priority is returned to normal.

Interrupt and Respond   Another use of the interrupt is to create a more instantaneous response to the user's input. In a simulated or virtual world, often the physics of the world is being updated very quickly, so things move in a relatively natural manner. If the user presses a key or button that initiates some move, such as the firing of a weapon or the swing of the baseball bat, the physical information about the motion of the object in question has to get to the program as quickly and accurately as possible.

Programmers have two choices. They can wait for the part of the program to run that checks for input, then react to that input (this is called *polling*). Or programmers can have the input device interrupt the main program. During this interruption, the information gathered from the input device can be used to create new physical information about the virtual object's new motion in the virtual world based on the exact time of the user's input. For many games this is an unnecessary technique, but it does demonstrate how you can improve the quality of the game play experience by allowing the main program to be interrupted by other programming tasks.

14

The Technical Design Document

Now that you've brushed up on how computers work a bit, this chapter will show you how, as the designer, you can apply some of this newfound knowledge in assisting in the creation of the technical design document.

The Technical Design

⇒This document, usually created by the technical director, the lead programmer, and/or the programming team, outlines all the tools, techniques, and engines they will use during the production of your design. While it isn't necessary to know everything about these technical aspects, it's a good idea to have a frank discussion about the possibilities and limitations that the technical design creates.

⇒Pay close attention to anything in this plan that limits the producer's ability to randomize events, adjust the rhythm and timing, adjust content, make last-minute changes, and provide acceptable transitions.

⇒If nothing else, learn how data are used in the program.

Data, Data, Data

I am a great believer that the data structures of a computer program are the very first thing that should be created when one begins work on a product of any reasonable size and scope. If this doesn't get done first, the programming team and the producers usually can expect many frustrations, delays, and unforeseen limitations. This is especially true whenever more than one or two programmers are expected to work on a product throughout its lifetime (including ports to other platforms and languages).

⇒First, the technical design should include a list of all things that define the world of the game that can be quantized into data files, data structures, program variables, and other data elements. Then each data element must be laid out in terms of its data size and relative position in the files and structures. You can think of this as the custom database that holds all the information of your game. Some products even license traditional database engines to speed up technical production and eliminate the need to write something that already exists.

⇒Every effort should be made to use the smallest possible data size with the greatest amount of flexibility. And always, always, always include some space in your data for expansion. You will undoubtedly use this expansion space before you ever release the first product. If you've planned really well, you might even end up with some expansion space left over for the sequel, so you can add features to the data without having to change the data layout!

When you lay out the data elements relative to one another, keep in mind the type and amount of use of certain elements. If certain elements are used more frequently than others or are required to be available at all times, group them together. Also, group data elements that are used together.

Ballpark Example

For example, when laying out the data for the editable ballparks in EWB, I subdivided the data into two sections within the file BALLPARK.DAT:

■ *Stadium names.* Each of the 32 stadium names is listed sequentially in groups of 16 letters (this translates to 1 byte per letter or 16 bytes per name).

■ *Stadium data.* Each of the 32 stadium descriptions is listed sequentially in 128-byte blocks of data. The data include the distance to each fence, the color of the fences, the type of grass, the wind conditions, the seating capacity, etc.

Why would I do this? Why not simply put the 16 letters of the stadium name with the stadium data? First, the stadium names are always used together and only when the user is interested in selecting a stadium from a list of stadium names. Second, it's a lot faster to read in all the names in one fell swoop as a block of 512 letters (32 parks × 16 letters each) than to read through a file that has names scattered through it every 144 bytes (16 name bytes + 128 data bytes). If the names were scattered throughout the file, the time to load the names and present them to the user would be significantly longer (i.e., the 32nd name would be more than 4000 bytes into the file). And, quite honestly, the code to read intermingled names and park data would be much more complicated. As it is, it is a very simple READ statement to load these names.

Lastly, the individual stadium's data are only used one at a time. So, to load up a park and draw it, the program simply multiplies the park number by 128 bytes, moves to that location in the data file, and loads in 128 bytes of information. Again, this is very simple and fast computer programming.

This data format for parks was one of the first data elements designed for EWB in 1985, and to this day it remains unchanged. We have even taken advantage of the few originally unused "expansion" bits and bytes to add features to the parks in later versions of EWB.

Masking Data

One of the great features of computers is their ability to easily subdivide or "mask" bytes of data into bits of data. Computers do this extraordinarily fast, and programmers can write code to do this with their eyes closed. However, often this feature is over- or underused in the design of data layouts for games. Striking a balance concerning how often this feature is used is crucial. And this is where the designer can be really helpful.

The way this technique works, in a nutshell, is that the computer can mask off any number of bits in a byte and look at the result as if it were an entire number by itself. While it doesn't work in exactly the same way, I'll demonstrate with the following decimal number:

44,729

If you mask off the three least significant digits, you get

44

If you mask off the two most significant digits *and* the least significant digit, you get

72

and if you mask off the four most significant digits, you get

9

In this way, you've only "stored" one number in memory, 44,729, but you can use it to represent three different types of data by masking off different sets of digits.

Now, here's the danger: If you plan your data layout and write your code to use this kind of masking and the third data element all of a sudden needs to be able to go from 0 to 14 instead of from 0 to 9, then you don't have enough digits to register all the values. Likewise, if the second data element doesn't need to be more than 0 to 9, then in providing it two digits' worth of space, you waste a valuable resource. If you were doing this with actual computer design, you would have a shortage or overage of bits instead of digits.

⇒Be sure to use this method of reducing your data size, but plan carefully.

A Speeding "Trickette"

Here's a little trick for using the masking technique that many people fail to consider. Sticking with digits instead of bits for now, we look at the above example and assume that one of these data values has to represent the speed limit on a road that's being described with data. Everyone's first instinct is to use either of the two-digit masks to represent a speed limit between 0 and 99. However, if you have to describe 100,000 roads, every extra digit required per road takes up 100,000 extra digits of data space! So what can you do? You could make a table or list of the 10 most common (or possibly only) speed limits used and "assign" them to the maximum number of values that one digit allows (in this case, 10). Or you could write an algorithm that will automatically create the real values you want. By using the table technique, the technical design could have a table like Table 6-8. Or you could have an algorithm or equation that looks like this:

$$\text{Speed limit} = 5 + (\text{value} \times 10)$$

Notice that the two "expansions" of the data value accomplish slightly different sets of speed limits. This is intended to show that in some cases,

TABLE 6-8

Data Value	Speed Limit
0	10
1	15
2	25
3	35
4	45
5	55
6	65
7	75
8	85
9	100

"looking up" data can be more flexible (sometimes at the cost of more space in your program because you have to store the data) while the algorithm can be extraordinarily efficient (especially if there is a simple relationship between the masked number and the real number and/or if there are many, many items to be expanded or if the expansion is a simple equation, as above).

Information Please

⇒One of the best uses of well-defined data layouts is the ability to store and share data among sessions, users, versions, and programs. Once defined, these data can be shipped over a modem or sold on a disk. They can be stored for later use or used to communicate individual player information in a multiplayer game. Data can be modified by producers, players, and computer programs to create new and interesting elements of game play. Data can be, in many senses, the very definition of a captured point in time for a computer game. Set data in the past, and you can load a saved game; set data in the future, and you can have a new mission or scenario disk; put data in the present, and you have the world coordinates for your avatar in a graphic MUD.

⇒In other words, whenever possible, define as much as possible about the state of the game and the game world in a data file that is as small as possible. Then use that file as one of your most powerful tools.

For example, if you want to create a multiplayer on-line "environment," one big concern is to minimize the size of the data file that defines the character and what it's doing. You could create a simple world where, for example, a list such as that in Table 6-9 might describe the data structure for your file.

Just for argument's sake, assume that each digit requires 1 byte. This means that you could update the on-line world of your character 20 times per second with only 440 bytes per second transmitted by your modem. It's no wonder that simple 3D worlds are so popular on-line. (In fact, when you do this with real bits and bytes, there are ways to make it even smaller!)

Naming Conventions

⇒As with the physical production design, I believe that there needs to be a naming convention section in every technical design document. My

TABLE 6-9

Data Name	Value Range	Data Size, Digits	Notes
Character type	1—99	2	1 of 99 preset characters that inhabit the world.
Name	1—10 letters	10	When logging on, check for uniqueness of name.
X location	0—999	3	The world is measured in feet and is 1000 square feet big. Characters can only move in 1-foot increments.
Y location	0—999	3	See location above.
Height off ground	0—99	2	Some characters can fly. No one can be more than 50 feet off the ground. Heights are recorded in $1/2$-foot increments.
Facing	0—7	1	Using major compass points, characters can turn in 45° increments to 1 of 8 directions.
Facial expression	0—9	1	Current facial expression. If user doesn't change expression after 30 seconds, reset to 0 (or neutral facial expression).
Total data		22 digits	

preference is to create a set of guidelines for naming things that the programmers will create as they program your game.

There should be guidelines for filenames (for both extensions and the kinds of names), folders or subdirectories, and data structures. In addition, to make the programmer's code more readable and more consistent, I believe there should be a naming convention for the internal workings of a computer language such as variables, functions, object classes, and so on.

For example, in the days before C++, I used these simple rules for C language programmers:

1. Functions—Always begin with a capitalized Verb, and capitalize each new word in the name.

2. Defined or constant values—Always use all-capitalized NOUNS or ADJECTIVES for values that never change throughout the program but should be referred to by name as opposed to numerical value.

3. Global variables—Always use a capitalized Noun (these are changeable data elements that are used throughout the program by any function).

4. Local variables—Always use a lowercase noun (these are changeable data elements that are only used by single functions or small groups of functions).

5. Keep the names as brief but clear as possible.

⇒By using these kinds of rules, all the programmers are forced to use similar types of names. Also, they don't spend lots of time trying to be overly clever about a name when they should be focusing on the actual task at hand. It does make it easy to read and follow their code, too.

As a simple example, say that you want a program to draw a red circle if the user clicks on the left side of the screen and a green circle if the user clicks on the right side. After detecting the mouse click, the actual code could look like this:

```
color = RED
if( MouseXPosition>MIDDLE_OF_SCREEN) then color = GREEN
DrawCircleInColor( color )
```

In this example, the colors RED and GREEN and the screen location for the middle of the screen are all defined or constant values throughout the program (possibly something like 2, 47, 320). The mouse's current x position (usually the position from left to right with extreme left being 0 and extreme right being the width of the screen in pixels minus 1) is a global variable that changes several times per second and something the entire program will want access to. The resultant color in which to draw the circle, however, is only necessary to notate for this part of the program code. So *color* is a local variable. Finally, the function DrawCircleInColor is a long but descriptive name that lets you know that this function has a very specific purpose.

On a technical note, notice also that this programming construct does not use an IF-THEN-ELSE format. I call this a *default-if-then* format. In other words, you set a default value for an upcoming action or actions and change it only if the condition in the IF statement is true. This is often a far more efficient way of programming regarding both size of code and speed of execution. This is especially true if you know the default value (in this example, RED) is used far more often.

Even in this example, if producers or designers saw it, they might realize that this wasn't at all what they had in mind. They may have envisioned the mouse click's having to be all the way left or all the way right to trigger the circle drawing. Clearly, the code above will always draw one of the circles, and it only checks to see on which side of middle the user clicked. You might prefer the code to read

```
color = BLACK
if( MouseXPosition<LEFT_EDGE_OF_SCREEN) then color = RED
if( MouseXPosition>RIGHT_EDGE_OF_SCREEN) then color = GREEN
if( color<>BLACK) thenDrawCircleInColor( color )
```

This may be more code, but it's what you want!

As this example demonstrates, once naming rules are established, it is possible for nonprogrammers to watch programmers change or debug code. This is an invaluable improvement to the testing and tweaking process, and, in my experience, most producers and designers never take advantage of it.

However, for those production teams who understand the value of a great naming system and do take advantage of it, ⇒ I have another rule:

Never use "dirty" words, temporary names, or attempts at humor in your names.

This may seem overbearing at first, but I've seen people become embarrassed and even very upset at a programmer's choice of names and use of language and humor in the middle of a source code file. Also, I've seen programmers themselves get completely lost due to the use of temporary names (such as Temp1, FOO, etc.). If your product is going to be a success, many people will end up reading the source code. Rarely is a programmer's source code as private a document as she or he thinks, and even more rarely does the programmer have time or energy to go back and "clean up" the source code files.

Implementation Schedule

Some technical directors include an implementation schedule in which they list the order in which they will create the elements of your product. If you are lucky enough to work with such a technical director, then I recommend that you discuss this list in some detail. I always recommend that the beginning, ending, and all transitions be programmed first. In this way, these elements cannot be skipped or put off until it's too late. I also try to get the following items added to the list or, if they are already there, moved up in priority:

■ Memory management, so that the program can preload any assets before they're needed and cache or keep any assets in memory that are often reused

- Static art and text display
- Error checking and messages (e.g., disk is full, printer's not on, no name entered for saved game)
- All the optional input devices work with the game code and operating system
- Saving and loading the user's preferences
- Saving and loading games
- The entire interface
- Replaying games (even if only as a debugging feature)
- A debugging system
- Any special data entry tools
- Demonstration programs of fundamental algorithms
- Navigation to every view or location in the product (with static placeholder art)
- Animation subsystems (Note how late this is—everything up to here is done pretty fast.)
- Audio and music subsystems (Tie this to the animation schedule as they're closely related.)

There are, of course, many other things to accomplish, but I like to see these things accomplished early and in an order similar to that above so that certain tools are in place before the project becomes big and unwieldy.

Cheat Keys

One last thing that must be implemented early in the process is the *cheat keys* (sometimes referred to as *shortcut* or *hot keys*). A list of these keystrokes should be created early and updated often. Insist on this feature so that you can jump to just about any place in your game, set it in just about any state, and trigger any event. This might mean that you have some keys to instantly navigate from place to place, some to instantly unlock puzzles, some to assign inventory, some to run up the score, some to trigger special sequences, some to run through an entire list of animations, and so on. Cheat keys are great for testing, and they make demonstrating the product to overly busy executives a much more pleasant experience.

Be sure the technical director plans to implement these shortcuts and allows for a huge variety of keystrokes. In a large game 36 different cheat keys may not get you very far (that is 26 alphabetical keys and the 0—9 keys). In addition, the keys may have another meaning to the game's interface. One way to solve this is to simply use the ALT and/or CTRL key to specify that you want the keystroke to be interpreted as a shortcut key. You can use ALT, CTRL, ALT-CTRL, ALT-Shift, and so on with each key on the keyboard to get a lot of shortcut keys.

There is another way, which I prefer, to create a password sequence that will put you into "cheat mode." For example, if you type ~123, the game could switch to cheat mode and allow you to type one more key. The advantage of the password method is that it allows you to leave the shortcut keys in the game without fear that a user will inadvertently press a modifier key (i.e., ALT, CTRL, and/or Shift) during game play and get a surprise. Also, the password method can be used in video game systems as well by holding down multiple buttons while the joystick is pointed in a specific direction, or by an unused sequence of button presses and joystick moves.

> *I know the password system scares some producers and executives, but we did leave in passwords to the shortcut keys in RTZ, and, to my knowledge, no one ever discovered them. The only precaution we took was to make different passwords for different versions of the game.*

A great but surprising use of cheat keys is as a help to customer service people. You must have a sufficiently obscure password if you intend to do this. If customers call in with certain kinds of bugs or if they are somehow stuck, the customer service representative can guide users through a series of keystrokes that will allow them to skip ahead (thus jumping over the bug or problem) or to further evaluate the situation.

Finally, be sure that there is some unique audio (preferred) or visual acknowledgment that the password and/or shortcut keys have been registered by the program, so that users have no doubt it's accepted their special input.

Technical Production Issues

The final section in the technical design document should be a list and discussion of all technical implementation issues that might cause the product not to be built on time or up to expectations. This could range from availability of tools and technology to a need for better support from an R&D group.

The producers and executives need to see a realistic assessment of the feasibility of building your product, and it's well worth the effort for the technical director to create an exhaustive list of potential problems with work-arounds and solutions thought out in advance.

What Designers Need to Know about Technology

I don't think designers necessarily need to know much about technology to create a great game design. I do think that the more they know, the better their chances of creating a design document that everyone can work from. The more the designer knows, the faster and smoother the production process goes. It is also true that the more the designer knows, the more the designer can push the production team to accomplish the really difficult tasks.

Knowing about the technology isn't the same as knowing how to program a computer. An understanding of the fundamental capabilities, the language of the technology, and the types of tradeoffs that need to be made in building a product helps to make a designer valuable to a production.

Of all the technical issues designers might want to be knowledgeable about, I think the most important are

- Game engines
- Code—what it is and what makes some code different from others
- Data—how data can be used instead of code
- Engineering art, sound, and music

Game Engines

Engines, also known as *game engines* or *software engines*, are computer programs that provide the underlying algorithms for the world being created on the computer. Engines can have subengines (which are rarely referred to as such) and can also be built out of other engines. Engines are so important because once an engine is built for one product, the engine can be used for countless other products.

The concept of creating an engine is a powerful, often misunderstood, part of the production process. Creating the engine of a game is often the most time-consuming and expensive part of the production. Companies that take the long view of the business invest in building engines that can be reused in other products. These engines reduce the time and money spent on creating follow-up products that use the same engine.

One of the trickiest things about engines lies in communicating what the engine is capable of doing in products that are not exactly the same. The technologist usually has an intuitive understanding of this, but unfortunately, hardly anyone else does. A lot of expensive, time-consuming reinventing of the wheel goes on in companies where creating and reusing engines are not part of the normal operating procedures.

So, what is an engine exactly? Using the word *world* to mean the world that the computer is creating, I define an engine thus:

> An *engine* is a program or subprogram that takes as its input some data representing the state of the world and some input from the user(s) and performs algorithms to create output in the form of behavioral instructions to the main program.

Notice that the engine takes data as input and creates data (the behavioral instructions) as output. An engine doesn't actually create any behaviors itself. This creates a *modular* part of the program that can be tested and fixed and even substituted without impacting the other portions of the program (such as reading input from the user or creating behaviors in the world).

You can think of an engine as a "data grinder." It is because of this grinding of the data that I focus so much on design efforts that create data structures to define the world and its behavior rather than too much program code.

Understanding what an engine does by my definition should make it clear how engines can be reused in many programs. For example, if you create an engine that reads text files and creates digitized speech, you could use that engine in just about every program that works with text.

Because I know the technical design so intimately, I list the subengines in EWB:

- *Physics engine.* It moves players and the ball inside the ballpark using velocities in inches per second, and gravity, taking into consideration the wind conditions, type of grass, and dimensions of the ballpark.

- *Stats engine.* It performs complex algorithms on the statistics to create the probability of the outcome of each play, subplay, and other statistics-related events.

- *Player AI engine.* Actually, each defensive position and baserunner have a subengine. It determines where each player should go, what direction he should face, and what action the player should take.

- *Offensive Earl AI engine.* Using Earl Weaver's philosophies along with the output from the statistics engine, this code creates offensive plays for the game to call, including pinch players.

- *Defensive Earl AI engine.* It creates defensive alignments and calls defensive plays and substitutions (including managing the bullpen).

- *Umpire AI engine.* It calls balls and strikes, outs and safes, foul balls, home runs, ground-rule doubles, and, of course, time-out.

- *User input engine.* It interprets the input for a given platform and assigns it to a standard input data stream for the game.

- *Graphics engine.* When turned on by the user, it looks at the state of the game (i.e., player positions, the player actions, and the ball's position) and the desired point of view and creates the images to draw.

This may seem like a lot of engines, but because all that the engines do is to pass data back and forth and all around, it's very easy to fix one engine without having the other parts of the program fall apart. It makes for a rich, complex game that's actually quite easy to test and change. For example, between EWB 1.5 and EWB II, not only did we switch from decimal numbering to Roman numerals, but also we removed the graphics engine to insert a 3D pick-your-own-camera-view engine and changed the Earl Weaver AI engines so they could accommodate "programmable" managers. The rest of the engines remained virtually unchanged.

Most successful companies in the business are quite disciplined about using engines. New companies that don't understand this have a hard time making economic sense out of the computer games world. If you spend $2 million on a product, you don't stand a good chance of making any money—not unless you leverage the work on the engines for that product into other products that cost only $250,000 to create. It takes a certain amount of technical savvy in upper management to believe in this type of production, but it is possible to make it work.

Sierra On Line and LucasArts are among the best practitioners of this technique. Early on (in the mid-1980s) their management teams decided to stick with their engines and to create product after product with the same engine. They made minor adjustments perhaps from product to product, but, in Sierra's case, they did not release a new product with a revamped engine for 2 to 4 years. In the meantime, they could create perhaps dozens of titles on the most recently used engine.

Also 7th Level has made a huge investment in tools and techniques for its games and animation engines. It obviously pays off in the number of high-quality products the company is able to produce in very little time. In the long run this is a powerful strategy.

How to Design an Engine

My recommendation for designing an engine is to start with the data that represent the word. First, quantify all the elements of the world, quantify all the inputs from the users, and quantify all the behaviors that you expect from the world. You are most of the way there in your work as designer. The engine takes the input from the world and the users and creates a list of instructions of behaviors. The engine is where the algorithms and logic of the world live. However, once you and the technical staff can agree on the data that define the world and the input and the quantification of the behaviors that are output, the definitions of these algorithms are a lot easier to create.

Data that describes the state of the world

Input from the users - Keystrokes, mouse clicks, etc.

The Engine of Your World - Algorithms and Logic that convert the state of the world and user input to behaviors

Data or "instructions" that describe the behaviors that should occur in the world.

Once you have the behavioral data, this information can be passed on to other portions of the program to demonstrate the behaviors to the player, to record the behaviors, and/or to change the state of the world based on these behaviors.

Designing for an Existing Engine

If you are going to design for an existing engine, get as much documentation as you can about the data structures that feed it and what it actually does. It is easy to fall into the trap of simply listening to a description of what others have done with an engine or, what is even more problematic, relying on other products' designs as the entire template for the engine. Most engines have more capacity than any one product takes advantage of. If you can see technical documentation, odds are good that you'll find uses for the engine that others haven't thought of.

If you know to look for these special or unique uses, you'll be able to expand the use of the engine from the last product created to yours. You'll also endear yourself to the technical personnel.

Upgrading an Engine

After you've studied and understand the inputs and outputs from an existing engine, you are likely to detect patterns in the way in which the engine behaves. These patterns often revolve on the predetermined limitations of the engine that were implemented either as a cost-saving device or as a shortcut by the programmers.

If you need a specific adjustment to the engine, often you can request this from the programming team. These small adjustments are often easy to make and expand the life of an engine by making it more flexible and powerful.

Code

I don't think that designers actually need to know much about the details of programming code. I've provided some information in this book, and studying that section (Chap. 13) will give you an idea of some of the fundamental principles and vocabulary that programmers use.

I *do* think that designers should have an idea about the *type* of programming language that is going to be used in creating their products. Table 6-10 lists the major types of programming languages and environments.

TABLE 6-10

Assembly language	Programming "to the metal" of the computer using actual code that the processor understands.	This is often slower to write but is the most flexible, powerful, and by far the fastest-executing code. Also, this code is the least "portable" to other platforms as it is written for a specific computer.
List-based languages	Many of the first languages such as Fortran and Basic fall into this category. You create lists of instructions with lots of "goto" statements that "jump" from section to section in the list of instructions.	Not too many game products are written in these languages any more. They are easy to learn, but because of the nature of list-based languages, they are often unruly to read and hard to debug.
Procedural or structured language	The best known of these is C. Instead of lists, specific tasks are programmed in subprograms referred to as *functions* or *procedures*. Each of these procedures has a name that can be "called" from other procedures.	These languages are easily structured so that they read almost like natural language by using procedure names that accurately describe what they do [e.g., "SwingTheBat()" could be the name of a procedure that is called from the procedure "TheBatterThinks()"]. This makes for easy-to-read and easier-to-debug programs.
Object-oriented languages	The latest craze is programming with languages such as C++. These languages flip the programming model on its head. Instead of writing procedures that manipulate data, draw graphics, and do other things, in these languages each thing or *object* knows how to take care of itself. So the programmer simply creates a bunch of objects that know how to behave. On top of that, object definitions or *classes* can be used to create other subobjects or children that possess the same basic behaviors as the parent with special behaviors of their own.	This is a very powerful language metaphor and worth reading about in a book dedicated to the subject. At this stage of the game, for all their power and robustness, these programs seem to be larger and slower. They can be easier to debug, however.

(Continued)

TABLE 6-10   *(Continued)*

Scripting language	A small set of programming instructions usually in a list-language-based format that give simple instructions to a software engine. Lingo is the scripting language for MacroMedia's Director multimedia engine. Many game companies have proprietary scripting language for their game engines.	These languages are often used by non-programmers or entry-level programmers to quickly create logic algorithms for game and multimedia engines. These languages usually lack much in the way of randomness and arithmetic and are completely dependent on the sophistication of the underlying engine. Depending on the scripting "environment," these languages can be very difficult to debug. However, the scripts are usually quite simple in comparison to other types of programming.

Programmers write their programs in one of two ways. One way is to use a *text processor* such as Brief, which is like a simplified word processor that is programmable so programmers can automatically format their code to look nice. The other way is through a visual environment such as Visual Basic that includes a specialized text processor already preprogrammed with "drag and drop" tools for creating interface elements and debugging tools.

In either case, programs are just a bunch of words in a computer file. These words or instructions have to be translated to something the computer can understand. There are two methods for translating a programmer's code to computer-understandable instructions: compiled code and interpreted code.

Compiled code takes the programmer's instructions and, using a compiler (or an assembler for assembling language), creates a file (called an *executable* program or application depending on which computer you're dealing with) that has computer-readable instructions in it. These instructions are in the native language of the actual computer. In the Windows world, these instructions are based on the Intel 80x86 processors (the Pentium is 80586), and in the Macintosh world the instructions are based on either Motorola 68000 (e.g., the 68030 processor) or PowerPC. In any case, these instructions are compiled to a computer-specific language.

Pros. Compiled code runs faster, is machine-specific so it can take advantage of special computer features, and is easier to debug.

The total size of the program is under the programmer's control, and this usually means you can optimize the program to be as small as possible.

Cons. Compiled code is slower in production because you have to compile it before you can run it. Programs are machine-specific so you have to recompile code for each target machine and hope that there are precautions taken for features that work on one platform and not another.

Interpreted code uses the programmer's instructions and feeds them to a language *interpreter* for the target platform. The interpreter takes each instruction and (when it gets to it) translates it to computer-understandable instructions. In this way a language that you write instructions for once could work on every platform that has your language's interpreter. Often interpreted languages "tokenize" the instructions you write so that the program files are quite compact in size.

Pros. Interpreted code runs as soon as you write it (i.e., no compiling is necessary, you just feed it into the interpreter), so it's very fast to create, run, and test algorithms. Cross-platform programs are easier to write. The code is smaller due to the tokenization, but often this is counterbalanced by the size of the interpreter. However, for downloading programs, this reduced size can be crucial to the experience.

Cons. Due to the nature of interpreters, interpreted code is slower than compiled code (usually a lot slower), so time-critical code is difficult, if not impossible, to write. As it's interpreted, some bugs may be almost impossible to find (if, e.g., the bug is in the interpreter and not in your code). Since it is cross-platform, you cannot take advantage of any special features of a specific system unless the interpreter supports them. As interpreters are general-purpose programs, they can be quite large, which reduces your ability to keep audiovisual assets in memory for transitions and such. Some interpreters are limited in their ability to do nonlogical algorithms such as random number generation and complex arithmetic.

When the technical design is being created, the designer has an opportunity to endorse the type of programming language and environment in which the product will be created. Keeping the pros and cons of each language and environment in mind should allow you to provide valuable input about which techniques will be used for your game.

How Data Can Be Used instead of Code

Throughout this book I've talked about using data to define a product's design. There are many advantages to using data as your main technical design tool; and, quite frankly, well-designed data structures can make planning and creating program code much easier and faster.

The biggest single advantage to designing the data structures is that everyone can see them, discuss them, and agree on them in short order. This part of the technical design does not have to be the exclusive domain of the technical team and is often the best mechanism for good communication between this team and the rest of the production staff.

I use the term *data structure* simply as a convenience because it is how programmers think of data. In designing the data that will define your world, you need to think in terms of organizing them as well as figuring out the ranges, values, and compression techniques. Organizing the data is often a matter of using database terminology or computer programming terminology. Either is fine as programmers understand both.

Using database terminology, you have

Records. A grouping of data used to describe one complete object. For example, the Department of Motor Vehicles (DMV) keeps a record of each driver. The data in each record is made from all of its individual entries that define us as individuals to the DMV (and everyone else who has access to their records). Each type of record you create will have its own name, for example, player record, weapons record, bad guy record, room record, furniture record, and scoring record.

Fields. The individual types of data within a record. To stick with the DMV example, the data for first name, last name, middle initial, date of birth, sex, height, weight, and so on are each fields within each person's record.

Data type. Each field contains a specific type of data. It's best to agree on types of data with your programming team as you may wish to have custom data types. Table 6-11 lists several example data types.

Index. The number of the record you are referring to. It is usually counted from 0. So if you have 10 records, they are counted from record 0 to record 9.

Computer terminology is almost the same. The main difference is that instead of referring to something as a record, you refer to it as a structure.

TABLE 6-11

String or text	A bunch of letters and numbers. Often the maximum number of characters is important to identify.
Number	A number stored in the computer's format (i.e., not as a string of characters). Again, a range of numbers should be specified so an appropriate number of bits or bytes can be assigned to the field.
Date	A special numerical field that computers code in their own way (be hopeful that they don't assume the 20th century!).
Boolean or logical	A single bit designating TRUE or FALSE in relation to the name of the field, for example, dead or alive, male or female, left-handed or right-handed.
Filename	Great for attaching images or sounds or other data to a record. This field has to have enough characters for the maximum filenames allowed on all the platforms you plan your game to work on (don't fall into the DOS trap of 12-letter maximums and no spaces unless you intend to support only DOS).
Single characters	A one-letter record that is often used for creating "types" of responses to the field name, for example, S, M, L, X for small, medium, large, and extra large or S, D, H for Sleepy, Dopey, or Happy.
Unique	A subtype specifying that a field must be unique. This is rarely used in programming data structures, but it can come in handy.

The subelements of a structure are usually referred to as *fields* with each field having a data type.

Regardless of which terminology you use, you should become familiar with one other term—*arrays*.

> An *array* is a group of records or structures of the same type that can be referred to by index.

Say that you want to create 200 records about individual stocks in a fictitious stock market. You would say in your design that you want an array of 200 stock records or a structure that is an array of 200 stocks. You would then go on to list the fields of the record or structure: name, ticker ID, outstanding shares, current price, today's high, etc.

By setting up arrays of records or structures, you can quickly refer to a specific record or structure by using its index (almost always, zero is the first record or structure index). So as you add stocks to your fictitious stock market, you assign to the new stock the index to the next available record. Then whenever the program needs to access the information for the new stock, it simply uses the index to find it. It's a very fast and very efficient way for the computer to work and communicate.

Using indexes into arrays of records is especially valuable in the on-line world where you may be able to get players to download something once, but don't want to burden them with subsequent downloads. An index into a set of records that they've already downloaded is at most 2 bytes of data to be transferred over the modem. But that 2 bytes can refer to hundreds or thousands of bytes in the records stored on the hard drives!

Lookup Tables

Of all the uses of data, the use of lookup tables is probably the best.

A lookup table is an array of data structures that provides precalculated information.

Since the data are precalculated, you save the user time by eliminating computer calculations, and you save programming space by eliminating the code in your program that calculates the data. Usually you have a program that you've used in creating the data (or a calculator and pencil) that allows you to enter the data before you ship your program.

Remember that an array is a list of data structures or records that are the same. To a computer this means that you do not have to store the index value in the lookup table. For a human to use a lookup table, the table usually needs to look something like Table 6-12. For a computer to look up a structure, the data table or lookup table would look more like Table 6-13. The computer doesn't need the field identifiers or the index. These pieces of information are inherent in the definition of the record or structure and in the use of arrays. The program can quickly find the size from the third record, which is s (remember, it's counting from 0, not 1) without having to store the index number anywhere.

TABLE 6-12

Index	Color	Size	Behavior
0	Green	s	Runs away
1	Blue	x	Shakes hands
2	Red	s	Looks blankly
3	Green	l	Jumps up and down

TABLE 6-13	Green	s	Runs away
	Blue	x	Shakes hands
	Red	s	Looks blankly
	Green	1	Jumps up and down

If you follow my advice in previous sections and quantify as many elements as possible in your design, you can translate those elements to lookup tables for the programmers. Lookup tables are very easy to program and extraordinarily easy to change. You can change the values in these tables while the program is running through the use of cheat keys, which is the fastest method of all.

Lookup tables can be stored as disk files, downloaded over the Internet, and changed in real time. These tables can be modified in so many ways that they can and should be one of the central features of the technical design of your product. It may take some thinking and planning, but it is well worth it.

Although indexed lookup tables are the most efficient, there is another type of lookup table which is what I call the *cross-reference table*. In a cross-reference table, you include a field in your data structure or record that is unique and is called the *identifier*. Then the program scans the records until it finds the record that has the unique identifier.

In fact, indexed lookup tables are simply cross-referenced lookup tables in which the unique identifier is the array index. The array index is implied by the record's position in the array and therefore doesn't need to be written down anywhere.

For example, using the cross-referenced lookup table technique, your program "scans" the same table as above, looking for the behavior "shakes hands." (If you plan to use your table this way, you must ensure that each behavior appears only once.) Once the program has scanned the table, the program knows the color and size because of the data in the fields of the record. Also the program will know the index of the record because computers track the index of the record as they scan through lookup tables!

One word of caution: If you are using either kind of lookup table, be sure you have a *default* record in case the index is out of range or the cross-reference identifier doesn't exist. For example, in the indexed lookup table, if you only have 10 records and the engine tells you to look up record 22, the program needs to know there are only 10 and needs to pick a record from the table as its response. This is called the default record. Similarly, if in scanning the table there is no exact match, there needs to be a default record. This is a good time to review Ned's first rule of AI. In these cases, don't do anything stupid. It's better to do nothing at all.

Engineering Art, Sound, and Music

I use the term *engineering* for multimedia elements to mean the process by which an original piece of art, animation, video, sound effect, or musical composition gets translated to a format that the computer can display or play back. Each type of multimedia is engineered in its own way, and these techniques, while often the domain of programmers, are useful to know. Once any asset is engineered, it is considered digitized or in a digital format.

The engineering techniques for the different types of multimedia assets are listed in Table 6-14.

The more you know about the specific techniques the production team will use, the better you can assist them in creating the best use of the assets in your product. Many designers choose not to get involved with the engineering side of things, which is completely understandable. I suggest, though, that even a rudimentary understanding in advance of production will allow the designer to work more closely with the technical director in establishing tricks and techniques for improving the presentation of the product.

TABLE 6-14

Art	Scanning	Art on paper is scanned into a computer via a scanner. There are a variety of quality settings that scanners support.
	Digitizing	Images on film or video can be "captured" by a computer.
	Palettizing	Taking a digital image from any source and selecting a limited set of colors for the image to be drawn with. If the set of colors is too small or the image has too many unique colors, some colors are created by *dithering*, or mixing dots of different colors to give the illusion of a new color.
	Scaling	Changing the size of an image. Scaling down (making smaller) usually works better as you are eliminating data from the image. Scaling up requires the computer to make up or manufacture data to fill in the image.
	Rotating	Sometimes images need to be tilted or rotated. Many art programs can do this.
	Flipping	Flipping creates a mirror image either left to right or top to bottom.
	Transparency	Selecting a color on the image and specifying that it is to be considered transparent. Using this technique, computers can layer images on top of one another. However, using transparency means one less color is available in the palette for the image.
	Compression	The technique of reducing the size of an art image file by using complex mathematical algorithms. There are many compression formats, and each format has its own pros and cons.
FMV	Digitizing	Capturing a sequence of video or film frames. After digitizing, all the other art engineering terms apply (including transparency).
	Delta compression	After the first frame of an FMV, only the parts of the screen that have changed in each subsequent frame are stored (delta is the mathematical expression for the difference between two things). A combination of using standard image compression techniques and saving only the recording of the delta frames creates much smaller FMV files.
Animation	Component animation	Individual frames of animation are processed just as other art and FMV. However, if animations can be broken down into component parts (e.g., arms and legs, faces, mouths, leaves, etc.), then only those moving or changing parts are stored. This allows reuse of the components in a variety of sequences.
	Registration	As animations often can be placed in various places and can move in various ways across a variety of backgrounds, the registrations or exposure sheets notate the relative placement of animation frames or cels, their durations, and their orientations (using flipping and rotation).
Delta compression		See FMV Delta compression above.

(Continued)

TABLE 6-14 *(Continued)*

Sound effects	Digitization	Capturing a sound effect digitally either from a live microphone or from a "line" to a CD player, record player, tape player, etc.
	EQ	Equalizing sound effects puts all the sound effects on a level playing field and creates special effects. You can ensure that volumes are all the same, that certain effects (e.g., echo, trailing off) are incorporated into the sounds.
	Playback rate	Sound effects are usually digitized at 44 kilohertz (KHz) which is music-CD quality. Sometimes you need to reduce the playback rate in order to save space or because the system cannot support 44-KHz audio. Typical rates are 22, 11, 5.5 KHz, and so on.
	Looping	Engineers have to work hard to make sound effects loop seamlessly. It's often best to design the sound effects so they don't have to do this. Otherwise, there is a lot of work to eliminate pops and annoying repetitious sounds.
Music	Digitized	If music is to be digitized, then all the techniques for sound effects apply. I strongly suggest never reducing the playback rate to below 22 KHz. Also, if you are going to use digitized music, use acoustic instruments.
	MIDI	Recording music in the MIDI language or format for playback through a synthesizer. There are standard MIDI synthesizer engines that support General MIDI which has standard instrument assignments.

PART 7

Interactive Storytelling

Importance of Interactive Storytelling

⇒I believe the future of interactive entertainment lies in our ability to come up with ways to tell interactive stories. The better the story experience, the easier it will be to attract new consumers. Also, as the experience improves, our ability to tell stories that inspire, motivate, break our hearts, and teach us lessons will improve. At this point in the development of the art, we are just scratching the surface of interactive entertainment as a storytelling medium.

⇒There will always be a place in the computer and video game world for straightforward action games and other games of solitaire to distract, amuse, and escape with. The audience for these kinds of games is well established. If we want the interactive games and entertainment audience to grow, our best chance is to create new ways to make stories players can interact with.

Whose Story Is It?

One problem I found with writers who express an interest in writing for interactive products is the question, "Whose story is it anyway?" Is the story the writer's or the players'? As you read, I think you'll see why this happens.

When talking to writers about working on a project, we usually discuss only two types of writing: fill-in-the-blank writing and interactive writing. For a fill-in-the-blank writing job, the producer supplies the writer with an exact list of dialogue lines, on-screen text, and possibly a back story to clean up. With this list, the writer knows exactly what to write and generally feels pretty much in control of the back story and the writing that has to be done.

⇒In interactive writing, the writer is given a premise, a loosely defined story, and an approximate amount of dialogue to write. The writer is expected to figure out how the dialogue, on-screen text, and back story all fit together. So, in an interactive writing job, the writer actually has to do some of the game design.

In both kinds of writing, the story is essentially established before the user sees the product. Because the story is preestablished, I don't think either of these kinds of writing actually creates the type of storytelling that is truly interactive. The fact that I feel this way (and usually say so to the writer) sparks a conversation as to what I think an interactive story ought to be.

⇒I think an *interactive story* is

A story that unfolds around the player(s) who is (are) interacting with characters and a world. As the player interacts, the elements are created for a unique experience that communicates the tone, sequence of events, consequences, drama, and message of the story.

When I explain this definition to many writers, their first response is, "Then it's not the story I've written." In fact, they're correct in the strict sense of the definition. In the interactive story medium, though, I envision a way for writers to "write" the elements of a story without actually writing the exact dialogue, sequence of events, and descriptions for each scene. We've got a ways to go before there is a story engine that can allow writers to write an interactive story that fits my definition, but I'm confident that it *will* happen.

Branching Stories: Where Everyone Starts

⇒When writers, designers, executives, or, for that matter, anyone begins thinking about interactive stories, they always begin with the same idea: Create a story that branches and has more than one ending. It's not a bad idea. As a matter of fact, some products have enjoyed a certain degree of success with this model. But the branching story has some severe limitations as a real solution for interactive story design.

⇒Branching stories work as follows:

Step 1. The user interacts with the world and learns about a part of the story through linear elements.

Step 2. The user reaches a *node* in the story. A node is sometimes called a *decision point.*

Step 3. The user chooses some action from a set of two or more actions.

Step 4. Based on the user's choice, the story continues down a new path or branch.

Step 5. The entire process repeats itself (go back to step 1).

Graphically, a branching story is designed as follows:

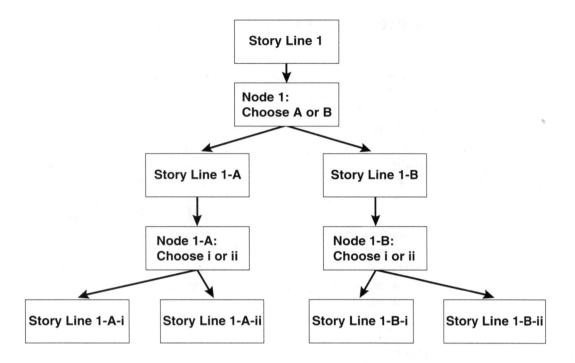

As you can see, for a story of any complexity, you can end up with a lot more than four possible endings. And this model assumes that you have only two choices at each node. If you had three choices at each node, there would be 12 endings for only two levels of nodes!

So one problem with branching stories is the amount of material and writing you have to do to produce all the content for each branch of each node. Another problem is that players can usually sense that they are playing a game with a branching story line. What do they do? They systematically try all the nodes. There's nothing really wrong with this except it sort of takes them out of their "suspension of disbelief" for a second while they keep track of the logic of the branching.

Finally, I'm not so sure that users like a variety of endings. There are many opinions on this subject, but my feeling is that people do like a good story, a good story has a specific point of view or message to deliver, and the ending is a crucial part of that effort.

Improvements to the Branching Story

Some obvious improvements can be made to the branching story. In the collapsing branching story design, some of the branches "fold back" or collapse into the main trunk of the story so that there are few, if any, optional endings. The collapsing branching story is the most popular solution, and it looks like this:

⇒No matter how you work your way through this story, you arrive at the same ending.

⇒Another solution to the volume of material and huge number of user options is the dead-end branch. As the name implies, going down a dead-end branch stops players in their tracks as they attempt to get through a story. When players reach one of these dead ends, there are several possibilities. The two most popular dead-end branch options are to (1) kill players or (2) send them back to a "safe" part of the branching story. It's a matter of opinion as to whether killing the player is good or bad, but in any case, the dead-end branch is a very popular technique.

Branching Stories: Try It Once, Then Try Something Else

Designers, writers, and producers have tried for years to make branching stories or narratives work better with varying levels of success. I don't think there's a future in it, and I'd like to see attempts to go beyond the branching narrative fill the retail shelves. Someone will solve it, but only if that someone abandons the basic branching structure.

The Sideways Hourglass Model

One attempt at an interactive story model that I've explored is the sideways hourglass. Imagine a story line that is a series of inciting incidents and plot twists. An *inciting incident* is an event that launches a major or minor story line plot. A *plot twist* is an event that causes a surprise turn in the expected plot line.

⇒In the sideways hourglass model, you create a world that the player can explore and interact with in relative freedom. While the user is interacting, you simply "drop" inciting incidents into the world to start plot

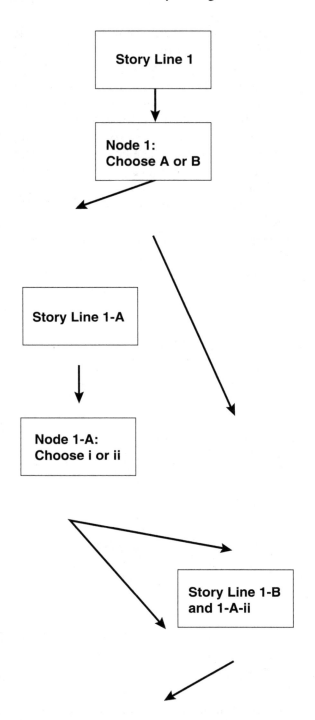

lines and "drop" plot twists into the world to turn the story. For example, after the user explores your world for a few minutes, you could blow up a building near where the player is standing in the world. This explosion can be the inciting incident in a story about arsonists or terrorists. But because the location of the explosion was determined by the user's location in the world, the principal characters in the story may be different. Later in the same story, as the user gets close to identifying a likely suspect, the suspect is killed, creating a plot twist. The character who died may very well have been "selected" by the computer based on the user's honing in on the character as a suspect.

⇒By inserting the inciting incidents and plot twists into a world that the user can freely interact with, you create a series of "funnel" points at which the story is forced to behave in a certain way in order to advance the general story that you want to tell.

The sideways hourglass model looks like this:

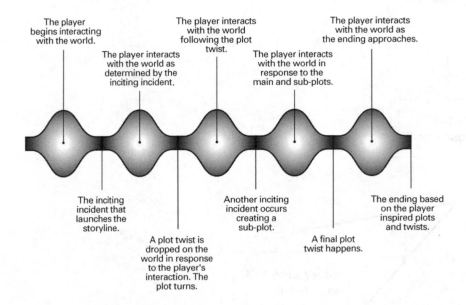

The player begins interacting with the world.

The player interacts with the world as determined by the inciting incident.

The player interacts with the world following the plot twist.

The player interacts with the world in response to the main and sub-plots.

The player interacts with the world as the ending approaches.

The inciting incident that launches the storyline.

A plot twist is dropped on the world in response to the player's interaction. The plot turns.

Another inciting incident occurs creating a sub-plot.

A final plot twist happens.

The ending based on the player inspired plots and twists.

The sideways hourglass model requires a lot of sophisticated programming, but it can be done. The player can wander freely "inside" the story until a major event has to take place, and then the world and the characters in it must respond to the new state of the world.

Story Puzzles: Locked Doors and Consequences

⇒At the core of almost all interactive stories are puzzles. It does not matter if the story is in an adventure game, an RPG, an action game, or a MUD (multiuser dungeon or domain). If there is a task to achieve, there always seems to be a puzzle to solve to achieve it. It may be a simplification to refer to achieving a task as a puzzle, but it is the best overall description of what players do in story-based products.

With few exceptions, every puzzle in every game to date can be categorized as a locked-door puzzle. In a classic locked-door puzzle, the player is told to get a treasure on the other side of a locked door. The player has to find a key or otherwise get through the door to get the treasure.

Getting past a villain with certain fighting moves, playing cards with a good guy to get crucial information, finding a key on the ground, constructing a bomb to scare or kill a monster, finding a ladder to climb into a tower, finding out the entire rhyme to yell to get Rapunzel to let down her hair, finding the big stick to break open the treasure chest—these are all examples of locked-door puzzles.

There's a definite pattern here. In locked-door puzzles, there is only one way, or possibly two ways, to find the "key" and get past the "door" of the puzzle. You are rarely given the kind of choices we face in the real world, and therefore the player rarely faces any serious consequences. You find the key, you get past the door. You'll deal with whatever is on the other side when you get there.

⇒I believe the gaming world is ready for a different kind of puzzle. Some games, I'm sure, have even attempted this. The alternative to the locked-door puzzle is the *consequential puzzle*. In the consequential puzzle, players are told that there is a locked door and are given a wide variety of tools, keys, and other techniques to get past the locked door. If players choose to burn down the door, the entire building might go up in smoke; and that may be a good thing, or the players might have to pay the consequences for their rash action throughout the rest of the game. Players might choose to pay someone all their money for the key and end up penniless; then there might be no money left to purchase food or anything else. Players might decide to break down the door and, seeing the boss monster on the other side, realize that they cannot step back through the door and close the monster out!

⇒The point of the consequential puzzle is that, instead of finding the one specific key, players have to live with the consequences of their choices of the type of solution. These consequences then have a ripple effect on the entire sequence of events in the story. This ripple effect includes changing future puzzles, behaviors of characters, the behavior of the environment, and so on.

⇒Using consequential puzzles with the sideways hourglass is one possibility for creating stories based on the players' interactions rather than a small set of predetermined branches with locked-door puzzles.

Problem Stories

There are certain well-known stories that I believe pose special problems for interactive storytelling. When I teach, I always present these stories to my class. Then we brainstorm for solutions.

⇒I used to believe that the interactive medium would be mature when we could produce an interactive version of Romeo and Juliet. After all, Romeo and Juliet has been interpreted in every other entertainment medium I can think of from painting to musical theater. After espousing that goal for many years, I've concluded that it's probably not possible. Because of the kind of tragedy that the Romeo and Juliet story is, it's virtually impossible to imagine players killing themselves in order to play out the final moments in the story. One of my students suggested, however, that it would be possible to produce a Romeo and Juliet as long as the user didn't play Romeo or Juliet. So there is still hope.

Another, similar story is the Boy Who Cried Wolf. Again, in order to reach the moral of the story, the boy (presumably the player) has to do the "wrong thing" right three times in a row. In other words, the player has to cry wolf three times even though the player has been warned not to cry wolf. Once again, the only solution seemed to be having the player be anyone else other than the protagonist (in most of my classes, the wolf was the most popular alternative character to play).

A third problem is the knife-in-the-ceiling story. In this scenario, players are in a multiuser environment where we, the producers, are trying to tell a story. At some point, we introduce a knife in the kitchen. All the players who wander into the kitchen do about the same thing: They take the knife and put it in their pocket. After a while, most players have removed the knife from the kitchen—everyone, that is, except one player who throws the knife into the ceiling, where it sticks.

Seeing the knife in the ceiling, the production staff gets very excited that there is a unique disposition of the knife by one player. They want to evolve the story about the knife in the ceiling and how it is used to murder someone in an upcoming part of the story. The only problem is, How do we deal with the other 10,000 people who have taken their knives home?

⇒So far, there haven't been too many good solutions to the knife-in-the-ceiling problem. But when it's solved, there will be some interesting interactive, multiplayer stories on the Internet.

The Future, Part 1: The Story as Part of the Environment

⇒By integrating the sideways hourglass, consequential puzzles, and several of the key principles of game design, I believe that we can design stories as part of a world's environment. By using randomness and statistics to determine the rhythm of the inciting incidents and plot twists, we can create a natural-feeling story. And by incorporating artificial intelligence, we can make the environment adapt a story based on the players' interactions with the world following the incidents and twists.

The Future, Part 2: RPGs Meet Stories

After creating a design in which the story has become part of the environment, we need to incorporate the players' characters as characters in the story. I believe this will be best achieved by using RPG techniques. As the players advance their characters through the world and the story, their characters are gaining and losing qualities and attributes. Incorporating the changing qualities and attributes of the players' characters will even further engage players in the stories.

My Challenge to You: Designing Algorithmic Stories

⇒All these ideas about the future of interactive storytelling seem to lead to the idea of the algorithmic story. In an algorithmic story, the writer creates the attributes, behaviors, and tone of a character but not really any exact dialogue or behaviors. You could think of this as an interactive soap opera in which the arc of the story goes on and on and the behaviors of the world and interesting, unpredictable characters are what engage the viewer and players.

As the players move through the world, experiencing inciting incidents and plot twists created by a story engine, the writer's characters respond and create their own dialogue and behaviors based on the writer's "definition" of the characters.

⇒To me, the algorithmic creation of a writer's characters with a genuine story unfolding around a player's interactions is the future of all interactive entertainment design. It is my hope for the future of the business that *you* will design it.

INDEX

About the Author

Eddie Dombrower is Vice President of the Interactive Division of The Jim Henson Company, home of the Muppets and a world-leading center of interactive design. Eddie was the creator of the bestselling "Earl Weaver Baseball" and Executive Producer of "Return to Zork," and has been Team Leader at Mattel Electronics (home of Intellivision) and Product Designer for Atari. In addition, during his 17-year career in interactivity, Mr. Dombrower has designed and produced highly successful interactive CD-ROMs and computer games for such renowned companies as Electronic Arts and Activition.